# Finding Meaning,
# Facing Fears

# Finding Meaning, Facing Fears

## Living Fully Twixt Midlife and Retirement

*Second Edition*

Jerrold Lee Shapiro, Ph.D

 cognella® | PRESS

cognella® | PRESS

**To the future:**
*William Myer Vandeford*
*Lydia Jean Vandeford*
*Evelyn Kate Vandeford*


**And in memory of five friends who left us way too soon:**
*Gordon W. Bowie*
*Mary S. Bowie*
*Michael J. Harris*
*Don Odermann*
*Dr. Paul B. Pedersen*

You all brought richness to my life.

# Contents

## Part III  Planning for Retirement

## Part IV  Realities and Opportunities

# Acknowledgments

No project like this is ever the sole work of one individual. Many have inspired, supported, and helped me craft this book. For the first edition, my wife, Dr. Susan Bernadett-Shapiro read all drafts and made significant recommendations for changes and clarification. She has greatly supported me and influenced the past 40-plus years of my thinking, feeling, and being. My son Gabriel listened to my ideas and offered "straight-from-the-heart advice." Dr. Michael Diamond read early drafts and made recommendations that led to a far better book. Our 50-year personal and professional relationship has been very influential in my life and work.

The project would have been impossible without the interviewing skills and hard work of my five research assistants: Beth (Anstandig) Killough, Michelle (Del Real) Rivera, Kate Viret, Edna Wallace, and Gregg Williams. As alumni, they are now serving the mental health needs of our community. For the second edition, Heather Valentine, another alumna of the Counseling Psychology program at Santa Clara University, provided encouragement and help recruiting some of the interviewees through her social media network.

I also had the ongoing professional support of an internal research grant from Santa Clara University (my professional academic home since 1982) and personal support from my colleagues in the Counseling Psychology Department.

I owe a great deal to mentors who have helped me "grow into my professional paws." It was my very great fortune to have the opportunity to meet and talk with Dr. Viktor Frankl on three occasions from 1960 until shortly before his passing in 1997. Those conversations were transformational, and his influence permeates this book and my life work as a psychotherapist and professor. My doctoral advisor, Dr. Richard Steffy at the University of Waterloo, remains a model for me as a professor and a professional.

Dr. Larry Peltz, my close friend of over 45 years has always been a great sounding board, a source of support, and source of uncommon wisdom. His ability to hear what is beneath the surface were inspirational during the lengthy process of both first and second editions.

Several other "Hawaii-era" friends were most encouraging, especially during the days when this project was considered too far ahead of the curve of "publishing realities." In particular, Drs. Elaine Hatfield and Richard Rapson from the University of Hawaii strongly inspired me to pursue my dream to write the book I wanted to write. Ronnie and Harvey Hartenstein also encouraged the second edition, especially with the addition of the financial chapter.

This is my fourth book with my editor, Kassie Graves. Her belief in my work and unwavering support has been remarkable. Amy Smith, my project editor at Cognella Academic Publishing has been instrumental in bringing this book and a recent text with Dr. Terry Patterson, *Real-World Couple Counseling and Therapy*, to fruition with amazing speed.

I particularly want to express my gratitude to the many interviewees for their willingness to participate, offer their time, and, most of all, their honesty—sharing intimate details of their lives, relationships and aspirations. Finally, I extend great thanks to my graduate students in counseling psychology since 1969, who have always pushed and inspired me. Without them, this project would have been impossible.

# Author's Introduction to the Second Edition

The full title of the first edition was *Finding Meaning, Facing Fears in the Autumn of Your Years.* It seemed apropos to describe the third quarter of life that way. Autumn was described as a time of bright colors, full harvest moons; a time to reap and savor what we have sown for the first half of our lives. It is an ideal time to reexamine our lives, set out in new directions, or recapture pleasures we had to set aside while building our adult lives.

Yet despite the intent and seeming appropriateness of that subtitle, many loved the book but described feeling disquieted by thinking of themselves in their "autumn years." As one listener called in to a radio interview I was giving said, "I am 66 years old, but I like to think of myself as more like 46. When I see the word "autumn" I think of my 90-year-old parents, not myself."

It would be easy to dismiss such concerns as psychological repression and denial of aging, but he was not alone. The 46-year-old moderator of the program added, "Thanks for that comment (Bob). I am in the age group and I think autumn is the *next* stage of life."

The new title *Living Fully Twixt Midlife and Retirement* is an attempt to respond to those concerns about aging without losing the significance of this important life transition. It also reflects to some extent a decade of change in Western culture about the time of life prior to retirement for two generations: the baby boomers and Generation Xers.

The first edition focused entirely on the baby boomers who were at the time between 45 and 65. The current book incorporates new research into Generation X, many of whom have now reached their 40s and 50s.

# COVID-19, General Uncovering of Institutional Racism, Climate Disasters, Political Unrest, and the Disastrous Year 2020

It is impossible to convey a real sense of what life is like during the years 45 to 65 without considering the disruption and risk of the COVID-19 pandemic and its sequelae in 2020. As Dr. Jay Lebow wrote, "The world is experiencing enormous stress with COVID-19, and the broad impact on individual and family life clearly is pervasive."[1]

This (hopefully only) hundred-year event has caused major changes to the interviewees' lives. Any sense of what life is like during and after the crisis is resolved is necessarily incomplete and likely to remain so for many years. As De'Andre asked when he got the online survey in July 2020, "Should I fill it out like things were before March or as it is now after 4 months of seclusion and two of being unemployed?"

Thankfully, he did both. Most of the interviewees described life before (and hopefully after) the crisis as well as their current experiences of being unexpectedly out of work or having remote employment, being too distant from others, or too close, and many described financial, physical, and social distress.

---

1  Lebow, J. (2020). The challenges of COVID-19 for divorcing and post-divorce families. *Family Process*, 59(3), 967–973 (p. 967). https://doi.org/10.1111/famp.12574

# The Human Pressure Cooker Called "Shelter in Place"

As population density increases, experiences of anxiety and depression are known to increase as well. These conditions have typically been the province of those in lower socioeconomic areas. With the risk of severe illness and potential death looming, shelter-in-place requirements, and the corresponding shutdown of most recreational activities, these conditions of close living have been visited on most of the population.

When couples and families are forced into uncharacteristic full-time living together, there is a blurring of boundaries between work (for those who still have jobs) and home, with attendant increases in reports of anxiety, depression, episodes of bipolar illness, and spells of atypical anger. Turn up the heat in any small group setting and there tends to be a movement toward greater intimacy, equality, and connection, or the opposite: more conflict, frustration, anger, feelings of entrapment, and an underscoring of differences. This is being reported all across the world and reflected in the responses of the interviewees. Bruce reported,

> Basically, we had grown far apart. We were heading for a separation or divorce after the kids left anyway. But now everything has got worse and there is no way to separate; financially or physically. Even if we could afford it, there is no place to go to get away. So here we are stuck living apart together, sharing a kitchen but not meals, sleeping in separate bedrooms with a DMZ [demilitarized zone] in the hallway.

Tatiana reported that her wife of only 7 months had become physically aggressive and abusive during the seclusion they were enduring. "I never knew she had that side of her" she continued, "Nora is like a caged lioness, almost panicking to get out and I'm in the way."

Weng Su wrote,

> Ben has always been a workaholic, but now he is working from home and it's harder for me and the kids. He always seems upset by the noise, the mess around the

house and especially our high school junior who is not doing schoolwork as much as video games with friends. He just didn't see those things before, because he was always at the office and I got to clean up and make a nice dinner before he got home.

By contrast, consider the words of 60-year-old Liliana,

We have been very lucky our whole lives: good marriage, daughter who has done well and enjoying a lot of the same things. Since we are both working from home, we get to take breaks together, and even after thirty-five years, he is still attracted to me and has never lost the romance. I am embarrassed to say this with so many people suffering, but for us the seclusion has been positive.

These experiences are but samples of a wide range of reactions of couples who have been forced together more intensively by the pandemic. There is an anticipated increase in number of break-ups and divorces when people have the opportunity, something already reported in China.

These people have only experienced secondary effects. Of course, others have felt the virus more personally and devastatingly. As Claire said,

My own parents died a while ago, but Andy's were healthy until this COVID virus hit. They both came down with it in their assisted living place in Vancouver, so Andy went there to help. He couldn't even be in the hospital when they passed. There was nothing he could do except clean out their place alone. Now, he's in quarantine before he can get back to America and be with us. He had a (we think) positive test in B.C., but three negative ones since. Still, no word when he will be allowed back in the country.

There are widely reported increases in work stress, frustrations with home schooling, guilt over too much screen time for children, and a loss of contact with colleagues. In Dr. Lebow's description, this provides "a hothouse of interaction during a time in which there are limited possibilities for escape into the outside world." This experience seems to reify the lyrics of Dan Hicks' tune of several years ago, "How Can I Miss You When You Won't Go Away?"

# Health, Financial, and Social Issues for This Age Group

## Health

On the health front, boomers at the older end of this age group are aging into the "danger area" for COVID-19 infection. Anyone who is in their 60s or older and especially those with other vulnerabilities are considered prime risk by health officials. The question arises if anyone in this age group doesn't have some vulnerability.

As Robi reported, "I am in good health, in reasonably good shape for sixty-three. I exercise regularly, but I do have hypertension and so my doc said that I have to be especially cautious, because if I get infected, it could be much more serious."

Eliana is 55 and has been a physical therapist and personal trainer for many years. She looks and acts very fit, yet 3 years ago she was treated for breast cancer. She is also at high risk.

Many authors have used the term "existential crisis" to describe the general feelings of vulnerability of those in all post-midlife age groups. As Ken Dychtwald and Bob Morison relate in their (2020) book, *What Retirees Want: A Holistic View of Life's Third Age*, "It's almost as though the entire world has had a collective near-death experience—with everyone realizing that a part of their life has died, and they themselves, or their loved ones, may be at higher risk than they were a few short months ago."[2]

## Finances

Financial dilemmas have reportedly hit people in this age group particularly hard. Most were already struggling to build up their retirement savings. The loss of jobs, shelter-in-place requirements,

---

2   Dychtwald, K., & Morison, R. (2020). *What retirees want: A holistic view of life's third age*. Wiley.

and economic downturn has forced many to reassess. Maddie summed up a lot of others' experiences when she wrote,

> I was planning to retire at age sixty-four. My husband who is four years older planned to retire the same year. According to the financial advisor at his work, we would have almost enough to live our lives in retirement if we downsized our home and our spending. We were both on board. Then I was furloughed about two months ago and he had his salary and benefits cut. We kind of lost our plan. Now we are dipping into our savings just to pay expenses and it looks like in the best scenario, if I get my job back, I will have to work until I am sixty-eight and he until he is seventy-three.

Maddie and her husband Jake will likely have to make the choice to delay their plans for retiring, and it is unclear if they will be able to have the kind of life in the years after work that they envisioned.

Ali's situation was far more dire. The 60-year-old speech therapist with Type I diabetes was working in a nursing home when the coronavirus hit the United States. His position was considered essential, but suddenly he was working in a very dangerous environment. To compound matters his long-time live-in partner had been working in an upscale restaurant in a local mall. His position permanently vanished when the mall closed and the restaurant owner declared bankruptcy. Ali believed that his income was the only thing that paid the rent and food, and yet he was terrified of the daily risk of an outbreak at work.

Most dire are the thousands who, having lost jobs, have also lost their health care at a precipitous time. Bobbi said, "The worst thing was that when I got laid off, I also lost my healthcare. They told me I could pay the COBRA for a year, but there's a 67 percent increase in cost and no salary to pay it. ... Plus this is no time to have no healthcare during a pandemic."

These were not isolated examples.

Our interviewees listed as a greatest concern "running out of money." Although most mentioned the financial factor, it was noticeably more pronounced for those in their 40s and early 50s—members of Generation X.

## Social

Another much stated concern was the impact of isolation on mental health and on connections to others. For some, it was too much togetherness and sometimes enhanced stress; for others it was painful loneliness:

> "I can see my grandchildren on video, but I can't hug them."
>
> "You know, I love my husband and my children, but I am used to getting away for a good part of the day, not 24/7 with them."
>
> "I had to leave the office and work from home. It's a great commute, but the kids are needy and want daddy all day. You know, they see me, especially my four-year-old, and for her, it's time for play with daddy, even if I'm on a conference call with customers."
>
> "The loneliness is screaming at me constantly. I am all alone in my apartment and the world and no longer have any social outlets."
>
> "I was just getting back into dating after my divorce, and now, anything but an online video date could be fatal."
>
> "My kids are back from college, my mom and mother-in-law have moved in, both with dogs, and we just have a small three bedroom house. The college kids are sleeping on the living room couches and I just feel trapped."

The anticipation of many was that when work-life ended, there would be an enhanced freedom and opportunity to do "what I want when I want." For some that meant play time, volunteering in their communities, time with friends and family, or a new career or avocation. Those between 45 and 65 were working hard now with the dream of what Dychtwald and Morison call "time affluence." As the virus and its economic impact has grown, many now believe that those dreams seem unattainable, except for a few of the wealthiest Americans.

From August 6 to 10, 2020, the American Psychological Association's annual convention, normally attended in person by tens of thousands, was a virtual event, and the dominant theme throughout the 4 days of events was the impact of COVID-19. The most glaring conclusions drawn were concerns about reported increases in depression and anxiety, and of family violence, related to the forced physical closeness. Corroborating these findings was an emergency room nurse in a major city hospital who related, "We feel that we have a handle on safety measures for COVID, but there is a huge increase in patients who are violent or victims of violence." By the end of 2020, she reported that upsurge was accompanied with a severe shortage of staff and hospital beds for the escalation in numbers of new COVID-19 patients.

All these difficulties are, of course, occurring in an environment in which all remediating counseling and therapy has to be delivered online via video or telehealth. From a psychotherapy perspective, one of the dominant antidotes to both anxiety and depression is a sense of agency—feeling in control of one's life. A pandemic, like most tragedies and disasters, removes the illusion of control. Such an event also diminishes a sense of personal denial of our human frailty, and we are faced much more poignantly with our vulnerability and mortality.

## Increased Awareness of Systemic Racism

In the summer of 2020, the pandemic crises merged with the long history of racial injustice in the United States. Asian Americans have been targeted, in part because of xenophobic remarks made from the Trump Administration blaming China for the pandemic. Sparked by the murder of George Floyd by a Minneapolis policeman, demonstrations broke out in many U.S. cities and worldwide. The Black Lives Matter movement and the hopes for a more just society concurrently magnified awareness of the discrepancies faced by many minorities and anyone in lower socioeconomic strata of our culture. The vast discrepancies in health outcomes from the pandemic were also exposed in national media. The people most at risk were those people of color in lower socioeconomic strata of society. They were far more likely to be unable to maintain social distance, often were essential workers with greater exposure to the public, were most likely to have little or no savings to tide them over financially, and far more likely to suffer more severe consequences of the virus and economic misery.

## Political Divisiveness

When there is a crisis that doesn't seem to respond to normal solutions, there is a natural tendency for people to look for bold new ideas. Sometimes, those whose views are on the fringe of mainstream beliefs, often called "3–4 standard deviations" (sigma) from the norm, can be a beacon of new edgy ideas, but are also often quite dangerous to society as a whole. As this is being written, the divide between Left and Right is increasingly dominated by more extreme activists. One unfortunate characteristic of extreme Left or Right viewpoints is that they are inevitably built on reviling the other. There is some group (the other) that is seen as destroying society and must be stopped. This kind of destructive, often paranoid thinking cannot be a long-term successful force in successful democratic politics. When one cultural sub-group is built on hatred and paranoia of another perspective or way of life, it is not only dangerous to the minority groups singled out, but powerfully self-destructive as well.

Misinformation and mendacity often feed conspiracy theories and general mistrust of others. On September 10, 2020, reports widely circulated that Bob Woodward's[3] new book, *Rage* and an accompanying audio recording indicated that President Trump knew of the dangers of COVID-19 and yet lied to the American populace about its severity for months, while the infection rate and death toll mounted. In December, 2020, *Washington Post* columnist Marc Thiessen wrote, while the surge in virus cases and the death toll were hitting daily record highs, "President Trump says he is focusing '125 percent of my energy' on changing the results of the 2020 election,"[4] primarily with unfounded "quixotic" claims that he had been reelected.

Similar divergent thoughts were very much represented by the interviewees. For minority interviewees, the increasing division in our politics were repeatedly described as reasons for grave concern.

---

3   Woodward, B. (2020). *Rage*. Simon and Schuster.
4   Thiessen, M. (2020). Trump risks a GOP disaster in Georgia. *Washington Post*, December 1, 2020.
https://www.washingtonpost.com/opinions/2020/12/01/trump-risks-gop-disaster-georgia/

# It's Not *All* Doom and Gloom

With this "perfect storm" of crises, there is potential for a multitude of negative feelings and an ongoing sense of hopelessness. There is, of course, opportunity in every crisis, and the hope is that to the extent we can survive, we will emerge stronger. This was reflected in many of the interviewees.

A large majority of the people who responded to the crisis described feeling much more aware of themselves and less concerned about others' judgments as they reached the post-midlife period of life. Another large group were well represented by Sam's statement, "I know what this means financially is that I will probably have to work into my seventies, instead of sixty-five, but that has made me more interested in working smarter and doing more of what I want to do."

Similarly, Mari wrote, "I am fifty-seven. Before COVID-19 I was planning to keep doing my job until I was sixty-two or so and then pack it in. Now that I see a future of a decade or more of work life, I decided to find a way to open my own place and work for me. I was running an Airbnb for a few years as a sidelight, now my partner and I are going to buy a B&B and run that. It's been something I always wanted to try. Now I can."

Finally, Stanley said, "I didn't sell in my 401(k) in 2008–2009 and I didn't sell in March (of 2020). I work and am heavily invested in high tech and the 401 is soaring. I will start taking some chips off the table now and should have enough to live on, when I retire in four years."

Many of the interviewees reported great hope for more equality and diversity in the country. One even said, "Having an [overtly racist government] has actually been good in pointing out how corrupt and how systemic the racism is. Maybe tomorrow will actually fulfill the constitutional promises for all Americans."

Several described themselves as optimists and reported hope for a new day with fair values and a moral government.

# What the Pandemic and Related Crises Mean for This Book

The final group of surveys/interviews of individuals in Generation X and boomers for this study and book occurred during the COVID-19 crisis in America. With the United States experiencing the greatest number of infections and deaths of any country in the world, both primary and secondary effects of the virus were present in people's minds. A number of survey questions specifically asked about differences in attitudes, beliefs, and experiences both before and during the crisis. Because this is a longitudinal study, it seemed likely that interviewees were able to distinguish the normal life experiences from the pandemic-related ones.

The massive collection of crises of 2020 has certainly raised awareness about significant problems in the ability of the environment to support life, the need for changes in health care, new attention to the financial planning, and vulnerability to events beyond our control and one's sense of mortality.

The older group described facing some sense of ageism in health care and expressed fear of triage decisions based on likelihood of longevity. Minorities of all kinds became far more vigilant to signs of danger of becoming targeted.

As sobering as this new, or renewed, awareness may be, it does offer an opportunity to look more deeply and with greater nuance at what this life-transition stage has to offer. In the following chapters, we will explore a host of issues that are being faced by all of us as we transition toward later life.

# Part 1

## Life Transitions and Development During the Post-Midlife Years

# chapter one

# Introduction to the New Life Transition

*We live in the post-modern world, where anything is possible*
*And almost nothing is certain.*
*This awareness endows us with the capacity for self-transcendence.*

—Vaclav Havel

Like many of my contemporaries, I had a big 50th birthday celebration. Among the characteristically humorous greeting cards was one from my long-time friend and primary care physician. "Congratulations on your 50th" proclaimed the outside of the card. On the inside in near-calligraphic script was the personal message, "Your gifts include an invitation for membership in AARP and an appointment with my office for your first colonoscopy." As expected, the shock of receiving my first copy of *Modern Maturity*, now rebranded *The AARP Magazine*, was attenuated somewhat by the actuality of the second "gift."

I was not alone in my discovery.

According to health and Census statistics, we have been blessed with a capacity for longevity that was only dreamt about in prior generations. Although it is lower than many other "first-world" countries, according to Census statistics the average American woman who reaches 50 has a life expectancy of 85; 92 if she avoids cancer or heart disease. A man who reaches age 65 can now expect to reach 81.

What does this mean to us? How can we understand the new opportunities, possibilities, challenges, and dilemmas that emerge as a result of a longer and hopefully healthier life? Do people age differently and, if so, what leads to those differences? Can you rely on the classic, traditional descriptions of what is likely to occur in your life after middle age, or are there new stages of development that have evolved because of your expected longer life span? What is really important when we are between the ages of 45 and 65 in America today? How are individuals in this age group similar? How are they different? What roles do culture, family, finances, and spirituality play in our lives? What has been the impact of the tumultuous year 2020? Why is it important to you?

In 1995, in *New Passages*, the late Gail Sheehy[1] described a life transition she called "middlessence" that led into a life stage of second adulthood from 45 to 85. Similarly, author and *Wall Street Journal* columnist Sue Shellenbarger[2] in *The Breaking Po!nt*, charts some exciting possibilities for women as they enter this period of relatively uncharted territory.

Many authors and social scientists have been paying great attention to the boomer generation as they pass through midlife and enter a new phase of life. In 2007, a news headline read, "3 Million Americans Turning 60 this year!" Author Bill Geist[3] noted that someone turned 50 every 7 seconds.

## Some 2020 Statistics

According to a Census study by Bloomberg,[4] 50% of the U.S. population (roughly 165 million) is older than 38. The expected total

1   Sheehy, G. (1995). *New Passages: Mapping your life across time.* Random House.
2   Shellenbarger, S. (2005). *The Breaking Po!nt: How female midlife crisis is transforming today's women.* Henry Holt.
3   Geist, W. (1997). *Big 50-oh.* William Morrow.
4   https://www.bloomberg.com/news/articles/2019-06-20/half-of-americans-are-now-over-the-age-of-38-census-data-show

U.S. population in 2024 is 338 million (although this number may be mitigated somewhat by reduced birth rates, the COVID-19 pandemic, and recent restrictions of immigration).

The latest Census statistics[5] indicate that there are a total of 20.8 million (10.5 million female) between the ages 45 and 49; 21.9 million (11.6 female) between 50 and 54; 22 million (11.3 female) between 55 and 59, and 20.3 million (10.6 female) between 60 and 65.

According to Deutsche Bank,[6] roughly 10,000 Americans turn 65 each day, the standard age for retirement and Medicare. The two largest components of the overall population totals are baby boomers (b. 1946–1964) and, even more, Millennials (b. 1981–1997). The X generation (1965–1980) is smaller both in number and in the span of years in the cohort.

Because of the size (40% of the American population) and inclinations, the baby boomer generation has left unique marks on our culture. They have also been well analyzed as they have aged. Considerable research described them in their 20s and 30s. In the last decade of the 20th century and first decade of the 21st century, major studies have described the boomers in midlife. The broadest and most significant has been reported by the MacArthur Foundation in MIDMAC and the landmark MIDUS study.[7] The national study, spearheaded by Orville Brim, Carol Ryff, and Ronald Kessler, provided the data for most of the subsequent commentaries and analysis.

Millennials have also received much attention and study. By comparison, to date far less attention has been paid to Generation X; indeed, this generation has been described as "the neglected middle child."

Although we do know something about the midlife transition of the older group in our 45 to 65 age range, given the expected extra longevity, it is time for us to explore what comes after midlife. This is truly new turf!

---

5   This may be impacted by the 2020 Census.

6   https://news.yahoo.com/americans-retiring-increasing-pace-145837368.html

7   Brim, O.G., Ryff, C.D., & Kessler, R.C. (2004). *How healthy are we? A national study of well-being at midlife*. University of Chicago Press.

What are the normal needs, desires, and stresses of these 80-plus million Americans?

Prior to the boomer generation, most people went from midlife directly to old age. For reasons of health, social mores, personal expectation, and roles, the average individuals in previous generations got old in their 60s, began a decline, and passed away soon thereafter. Today, that decline is more characteristic of people in their 80s. Indeed, many popular publications have proclaimed that "60 is the new 40." But are you really 40? As we shall examine in this book, it is more apropos to consider 60 as the "new 60," and we need to recalibrate our understanding of what's normal for people in these "stretch years" in the new millennium.

I have worked with clients in this age group for many years as a therapist and consultant. Their stories, successes, and dilemmas, as well as my personal experience, have led to daily questions and in-depth study about the unique challenges of women and men as they traverse a path that has only recently come to light for the majority of people in developed countries.

During the first decade of this century my team and I at Santa Clara University in California began a series of lengthy personal interviews with a representative group of men and women aged 45 to 65, the first half of Sheehy's "second adulthood" grouping. The assumption was that as women and men left their midlife transition and moved into this new stage of life, there would be some very predictable general trends, as well as individual differences. To be careful about our conclusions, we also engaged in a two subsequent nationwide internet-based surveys (2008, 2020). These data were then combined with the existing literature and personal material from my own 50-year clinical psychology practice with adults and those of my colleagues.

This book presents the results of these findings and makes recommendations for anyone already in and those entering this new phase of life: the *stretch* between midlife and old age.

## Who Is in This Generation?

A few of our generational icons include, in no particular order, Barack and Michelle Obama, Tom Hanks, Tom Cruise, Denzel Washington, Jon Stewart, Stephen Colbert, Dave Chapelle, Bill

Gates, Dr. Dre, J-Lo, J.K. Rowling, George Clooney, Larry Bird, John McEnroe, Ron Howard (little Opie!), Whoopi Goldberg, Eddie Murphy, Michael Jordan, the late Robin Williams, and a few who only need one name: Oprah, Madonna, Demi, and Magic.

Jane Fonda, Grace Slick, Paul McCartney, Paul Simon, Joe Biden, Elizabeth Warren, Bernie Sanders, Donald Trump, Bill and Hillary Clinton, Steve Wozniak, Goldie Hawn, Judy Woodruff, Susan Sarandon, Barbra Streisand, Mick Jagger, Samuel L. Jackson, Meryl Streep, Billy Crystal, and Kareem are well past this stage and at 70-plus are officially in the group we now call "young old age."

Lin Manuel Miranda, a Gen Xer, won't reach 45 for 5 years, Tom Brady for 3 years, and David Ortiz will get there in 2021.

Perhaps the cultural icon that is most surprisingly in this demographic is Kermit the Frog, who is in his mid-60s.

# A New Stage of Development

In the early 1900s life expectancy at birth for men was 48 years; for women 51. In 2020, Census figures indicate that men today can expect to live to be 76 and women 81. Indeed, since 1980 our overall life expectancy has risen 16%.

What do these 30 years of extra time mean in terms of our lives? Are we doomed to more of the same or to suffer a lengthier decline into medical procedures, infirmity, dementia, and death?

# The Joke About Longevity

The good news is that you are likely to live longer than your ancestors. The bad news is that those years will be tacked onto the *end* of your life. Were I to rearrange the plan, I'd prefer adding an extra decade in the 30s.

Indeed, as social scientists begin to unravel what happens to people during their life trajectories, it turns out that the "joke" is just that. Life for most, it turns out, is not just a longer, slower slide into oblivion. We have discovered already that the years don't just get appended onto the senior years of life. Indeed, the two new stages of development that have so far emerged are an extended adolescence in the 20s, in which marriage and many career commitments are postponed as is a post-midlife period prior to true old age. What is significant is that both longevity and cultural shifts have created the first generations to have both the opportunity and necessity of dealing with these new life stages.

One way to think about the years 45 to 65 is to liken it to baseball's seventh inning stretch rather than football's 2-minute warning. These years may be a time to pause, reflect on what has passed, and stretch our capacity for what lies ahead. This book explores these years (45–65), for the more than 80 million Americans who are currently in the age group and those who will follow shortly.

## Why Is This Important to You?

Your expected extra longevity brings with it a host of benefits and serious challenges. On the plus side are a plethora of opportunities to grow psychologically and spiritually, to recapture those skills and avocations that were set aside to be responsible adults: earning a living, raising families, growing the community, and expanding the cultural possibilities. On the minus side are some realities that prior generations never had to face and a lack of models from history.

What could possibly be more precious than time to be alive, enjoying family, friends, community, and personal passions? You will have a chance to live in a world more aware of and hopefully freer of arbitrary gender, racial, religious, or class distinctions. You will be able to experiment more with fantasies, new careers, opportunities, and time to try something that is not of the basic life program that you chose before you were 30. You will have a greater opportunity to give back to the world the benefit of your experience and to think about and implement your personal legacy. In psychologist Erik Erickson's terms, you will be able to have a lengthier time for generativity and mentorship.

### Dollars and Sense
There is also an ironic darker side to extra years of life. Financial experts have been shouting from all media, warning that despite the anticipated greatest one generational transfer of wealth expected to occur in the first third of the 21st century, many are likely to outlive their finances.

Indeed, that wealth transfer has so far impacted primarily the 5% at the top of the wealth ladder. In fact, as people live longer, they use up significantly greater amounts of their accumulated "estates." There is also a growing phenomenon among many of the older individualistically—oriented baby boomers that it is better to spend their money than to leave it to heirs. The bottom line: The majority of us will have to support ourselves for an additional 15 to 20 years.

Most will have to work longer to earn the money to live up to their current lifestyle. It seems clear now that there will not be corporate or government underwriting of the costs of longer life. Unlike our parents' or grandparents' generation, only a minority of workers will enjoy the kind of defined benefit pensions that make living without earned income fairly easy. The United States is the only industrialized nation to not offer guaranteed medical care to all citizens. The ever-increasing costs of good medical care and the fact that employers are the source of medical plans will force many who can to stay on the job. Medicare, available at present for those 65 and above, is increasing in out-of-pocket costs annually. Full Social Security benefits, which will click in for the older members of this generation at age 67 or 68, were never intended to provide full support for elders, and with increasing costs of living, will cover less of their basic needs.

As many financial planners will tell us, the low rate of American saving and the compounded rates of inflation make it clear that retirement age will inevitably drift upward.

Living longer also means that we will have to be more aware of caring for our bodies. Eating healthier, exercising, and focusing on the physical side will potentially increase capacity to best traverse this developmental stage.

Finally, there has also been a change in forms of relationships in this generation. This is the first generation in which divorce (parental or personal) is more likely to have touched the majority. Complex family obligations with blended, step, single, and same-sex households will make some of the future connections less based on culturally expected duty and responsibility as much as on the capacity and desire to assist elder family members.

With all these potential plusses and minuses, it is important that you do not waste this opportunity if you want to do this stage right. *Finding Meaning, Facing Fears* will help you explore the major questions and to underscore the answers that we already know. Some of the themes we will explore in depth are

- rebalancing and "re-hirement" (post-career vocation) as options to traditional (albeit shorter) retirement;
- the sources of personal answers—an extensive menu of new options suited to discovering anew and exploring and understanding inner resources;
- methods for uncovering and following these inner yearnings with warnings about predictable trap doors;
- differences and similarities for women and men; and,
- most important, how to use this life stage to plan and prepare for the subsequent ones (such as retirement).

It is indeed a time for you to "stretch" in your capacities, to face, conquer, or dismiss old demons and to meet new challenges with greater resources than were available to your ancestors. It is also a period in which you may embrace less rigid gender-specific roles. The period is marked both by more similarities than differences between male and female needs and expressions and a need for greater acceptance of both sexually related and interpersonal differences.

This updated second edition of the book is arranged in four sections and 16 chapters. A chapter on financial concerns with a 2020 perspective is an addition in this version.

*Finding Meaning, Facing Fears* blends together interview data, personal reflections, clinical work, and the extant literature to create a complete picture of this new stage of life. Replete with vignettes of real people from all walks of life, it is intended for the lay public, and although it covers topics in depth, it minimizes the use of professional jargon. Throughout the book, queries, exercises for the reader, and recommendations for self-help and reliable professional assistance are offered.

A unique focus throughout is on an ongoing, essential tension between two basic psychological forces: need for security (and the stagnation of the status quo) and a need for freedom (facing the fears of the unknown). In each chapter, readers have the opportunity to understand how the internal and inevitable tension between these two instincts drive a search for personal meaning and a mechanism to make choices in both macro (lifestyle) and micro (moment-by-moment) instances.

# chapter two

# How Old Are You? It Depends!

*All the world's a stage,*
*And all the men and women merely players,*
*They have their exits and entrances,*
*And one man in his time plays many parts,*
*His acts being seven ages.*

—Shakespeare

When you were young, your chronological age was very important to you. You may well have been "this many," holding up your fingers, or "3 *and a half*." Perhaps you stretched the truth a little to claim you were 5 when there was still a month or two until your birthday. Between the ages of 45 and 65, we rarely report that we are "62 and a half," nor are we at any rush to claim that we are 50 when we are 2 months shy of that birthday!

As a developing child, your age and your capacity to accomplish certain goals went hand in hand. You were expected to crawl, stand, and say a few words by age 1, say a few sentences by age 2, be reliably toilet trained between the ages of 3 and 4, and read sentences in the first grade. Throughout your first few decades, you were compared to your peers to determine if you were "normal," "advanced," or "trailing."

Great success at an early age may have engendered terms like "child prodigy," but who is judged on potential for future success at age 55? Indeed, is our age at all relevant when we are adults? The basic notion among many human development experts is that the changes that occur in childhood and adolescence are quite predictable and very meaningful in charting future success and competence. Failures to master certain stages within a predicted time window are often related to problems in later life.

## Stages of Development

It's easy to ignore developmental guideposts once we reach adulthood. In fact, most writings about life stages are focused on the first 20 years of life.

For example, infants and younger children need a secure attachment with their primary caregivers or they may face significant difficulties in their capacity for successful relationships throughout their lives. The impact of early developmental stage problems is important enough that we are wise to also consider adult stages of development and their influence on successful adjustments as we hit midlife and beyond.

In *As You Like It*, William Shakespeare[1] characterized seven stages of man (life) with a symmetry from "the infant, mewling and puking in the nurse's arms" to "second childishness and mere oblivion, sans teeth, sans eyes, sans taste, sans everything." Reflecting the realities of his times, he was not particularly sanguine about the effects of aging. Indeed, most individuals in their 40s at the turn of the 17th century were facing the deterioration of old age.

Shakespeare was neither the first nor the only significant writer to try to depict life's unfolding stages. The Talmud—the great Jewish religious work of commentaries on the Torah—delineates in Ecclesiastes, seven stages: from the "infant king" to the "decrepit old man." Solon, the Athenian lawmaker and philosopher (circa

---

1   Shakespeare, W. (1623/2019). *As you like it*. (Act 2, Scene 7). Simon and Schuster. (Folger Library Ed.).

6th century BC), identified 12 stages: prebirth, birth, infancy, early childhood, middle childhood, late childhood, adolescence, early adulthood, midlife, mature adulthood, late adulthood, and dying and death.

At approximately the same time as Solon, in another part of the world, Confucius explored the stages from a cultural viewpoint that revered age and wisdom. He included the stages of birth, young adulthood, age of independence (30), age of mental maturity (40), age of spiritual maturity (50), age of acceptance (60), age of uni-fication (70) and funeral service. Confucius's conceptualization uniquely took into account and paid homage to the rare few who lived into their 50s and beyond.

In modern times, specialists in human growth and development have also pondered the typical life path. Early in the 20th century, Sigmund Freud startled post-Victorian society with his five psycho-sexual stages (oral, anal, phallic, latency, genital) of development from birth to puberty. Erik Erikson expanded on Freudian and Con-fucian notions with his eight stages of man, actually adding three stages of adult life. His inclusion of adulthood was extended further with Daniel Levinson's four stages of life—each lasting approxi-mately 25 years—and in the popular realm, in *Passages*[2] and *New Passages,*[3] the late Gail Sheehy included additional descriptions of later life phases, a welcome equal focus on women's lives and more contemporary labels for the stages. In 2020, Dr. Ken Dychtwald and Robert Morrison described four ages of life: the first from birth to 30 (a time for biological development, learning and survival); the second from 30 to 60 years of age (focusing on creating a family, parenting, and productive work); the third from 60 to around 80, which allows for further development of the "interior life of the intellect" and experimentation; and the fourth of 80-plus years of age as old age.

---

2   Sheehy, G. (2006). *Passages: Predictable crises of adult life.* Ballantine.

3   Sheehy, G. (1995). *New Passages: Mapping your life across time.* Random House.

# Nature and Nurture

Developmental stage-centered models indicate how the lives of human beings will progress in a fairly stable, predictable pattern with successive tests we all must face and the more complex tools we possess as we mature. Success at each stage is predicated by relative triumphs over prior challenges. The stability of the progression of stages across cultures and centuries confirms the power of a hereditary process—or "nature."

When it comes to us as individuals, however, what nature gives us at birth is only part of the story. In addition to the predictable stages is a unique, dynamic growth process, often referred to as "nurture." We all manage the stage-related challenges in our own way, and each of us can muster some level of success at *every* stage. Our environment modifies nature. Many developmental experts have focused on how this process unfolds.

Jean Piaget, the great Swiss developmental theorist, focusing primarily on children's cognitive and psychological development, envisioned a series of progressive interlocking steps, each with a phase of taking in (assimilation) and adjusting to (accommodation) life's challenges. As we will explore later, how we—as 45- to 65-year-old adults—assimilate new material and adapt determines our capacity to meet our age-related challenges.

# Why Is This Important?

Doubtlessly, you have asked yourself questions about how well you were keeping up with your peers, such as

- What is normal development for people my age? Am I normal?
- Am I above average?
- Am I living up to my potential?

As mentioned at the beginning of the chapter, in many areas of life we are judged against a peer-based standard. However, characteristics such as physical and emotional maturity are important for determining our success as well.

# Physical and Emotional Maturity

Among the most striking aspects of the junior high and early high school years are obvious differences in physical and emotional maturity. Girls mature earlier than boys, and youth with adult characteristics are in the same classes as peers who still look like they did in elementary school. A common joke at boys' Little League and soccer games is that some of the competitors are already shaving.

Is it a problem if you are in your junior year of high school and still haven't hit puberty? Aside from the size discrepancy with peers and the social implications, do we consider such physical issues as a reason for special attention, consultation, or remediation?

When Lila was 9 years old, she was still wetting the bed occasionally at night. Her parents consulted with various physicians and worked out a system that worked well at home. They made sure that she didn't drink after dinner, used the bathroom as late as possible and made her responsible for stripping a wet bed and using the washer and dryer. Within their family, the situation was only a minor inconvenience. However, outside of the home it was a social dilemma for Lila. She wasn't willing to join her friends for the normal sleepovers. She was afraid to go camping or on overnight school trips. She felt increasingly like a social outcast. The social lag prompted her parents to seek more vigorous treatment for her. Within 6 months, her bedwetting had abated and she began to flourish socially. An added bonus was that her schoolwork improved.

Lila and her family were rewarded by looking at norms and seeking help, but the standard may not be as useful in other situations. In fact, peer-related comparisons can be quite deleterious to personal growth and self-esteem.

# Other Developmental Lags

Les still feels like a "late bloomer." He found his career in his 40s after several false starts. He married for the first and only time at age 39. At 56, he is the father of three, including an 8-year-old. He and his wife have only recently begun a savings plan for the children's college and their own retirement. For all intents and purposes, Les is doing well in his life. He is gainfully and pleasurably employed. He has a good family life and a modest home in a good community. He has friends and extended family who care about him. Although he is older than the other parents at the kids' soccer games, he enjoys them a great deal.

Yet, neither Les nor his peers are easily able to stop competing with one another. In fact, he is quick to note that by comparison to a few of his boyhood friends, he is far behind. They have higher positions, more money, children already being launched, and nicer possessions. Their children go to private schools and have advantages. They take lavish vacations.

Do we compare Les to more successful friends and examine primarily his lesser capacity to move through the life stages with his age group, or are we to see him for his notable, albeit less timely, successes? Would it serve him to look at his personal life path rather than at the broader cultural norm? The answer is complex, because both are important.

## Are Developmental Stages More Important for Children Than Adults?

For children, the stages are many and marked. One such measure is visibly displayed in many homes by the height lines marked on a doorframe like tide markings on a seawall. Each grade in school brings tests and an annual report on academic and social growth. We look seriously at developmental lags. We grade children according to their capacity to manage age-related challenges. We even have terms such as "developmentally delayed" for children who achieve at a slower pace. This may be quite trying for the child and their parents.

Manny, now 60, described himself as a "lifelong klutz." His inability to learn to run, jump, dance, and play games on his elementary school playground caused no small amount of ridicule and questions about his motivation. It also impacted his self-esteem to the point that even after he was physically more coordinated, he lacked the belief that he could succeed in "normal" activities. Although he first went to college at age 18, he didn't graduate until he was 26, and he has stayed in the company that first hired him. Even today, although he appears fit and is an avid hiker, he avoids any competitive activities such as joining his wife for bridge, golf, and tennis.

The question today for Manny is whether the childhood experiences colored his self-perceptions or whether he has remained somewhat behind his peers and continues to avoid reexperiencing the childhood feelings of shame and ridicule. Manny attributes these difficulties to inherited slower brain development, and he carefully tutored his two sons through school when he saw them similarly noncompetitive with their peers.

That childhood stages are significant is beyond question for physical, social, and psychological aspects of life experiences. The question then is whether there are similarly important stages in adult development.

## How Should We Compare Ourselves After Midlife?

If it is no small challenge to accurately depict childhood development, it is far more complex to identify the stages of adult development.

Measuring the social and emotional successes of a developing child or adolescent involve a comparison to their age-related group and well-established norms. To understand what is a normal or healthy standard for people in the 45 to 65 age range we have to understand two aspects of their lives:

- the common travails of people between midlife and retire-ment and
- their individual histories

What is most interesting is that these stretch years have only begun to be charted. Despite observations that go back to the beginning of recorded time, there has been only modest interest in this age period before now, in part because the numbers of individuals who had an extended experience after age 45 was relatively small. Everyone beyond midlife was lumped together as "elderly" or, more recently, "seniors."

How should we compare ourselves to our peers? Finding "normal" age-related development during the post midlife years is far more complex than it was to compare relative skills in grade school. How should we capture in a unique manner our own stage of develop-ment after midlife? Are there other guideposts besides the elapsed years since birth?

# So, What Is Your Real Age?

To best understand our true personal age during the autumn years, we can look through six lenses:

1. Chronological age (how many birthdays)
2. Body age (level of health/deterioration)
3. Psychological age (how well we have mastered earlier developmental challenges)
4. Social age (the maturity of our relationships with others and our community)
5. Functional age (relative capacity for psychological responsibility)
6. Reference age (the age we identify with inside)

# Chronological Age (Number of Birthdays)

What similarities are there among 60-year-olds? What are the norms for 45-year-olds? How well do you compare to others who are also 55?

To some extent, all of us have connections to our age group because of shared events. Within our age group of 45 to 65, there are some obvious differences. Those boomers in the older half of the group are old enough to recall the assassinations of John F. Kennedy, Bobby Kennedy, and Martin Luther King, Jr., as well as Woodstock, Vietnam, the "summer of love" and other events of the turbulent 1960s. We were coming of age during the women's movement and the sexual revolution. By comparison, those generation Xers who are currently in the 45- to 54-year range were either young children during or born after some of these marker events. In interviews, they specifically referenced evens such as 9/11, the Iraq War, the 2008 recession, the elections of Barack Obama and Donald Trump, the iPod, the now ubiquitous internet and smartphones, and the 2020 "summer of discontent."

Similarly, our music and popular cultural preferences fit into somewhat related categories. Were you starting college or in diapers when the Beatles appeared on the Sunday night *Ed Sullivan Show*? Did they play "My Guy," "I Love Rock 'n Roll," or "Girls

Just Want to Have Fun" at your senior prom? Were you in Vietnam during the war? Some younger boomers came of age during the end of the Cold War, the Three-Mile Island meltdown, the Iran hostage crisis and gas lines.

Can you recite the names of the entire Brady Bunch (including the housekeeper)? That'd place you in the middle half of the group. Do you recall what it was to be an Oscar Meyer wiener? Are your memories of fads more oriented around hula hoops, white go-go boots, mood rings, and Rubik's cubes or iPods, laptops, and video games? How do you do with the crossword puzzle that appears in the monthly *AARP magazine*? Do you *receive* the *AARP magazine* yet? You will when you turn 50.

## Body Age (Health Level)

Have you gone to a high school or college reunion? There is an inescapable perception when we attend such events. Some of us age faster than others. Both genetics and lifestyle play a huge role in how we age. At her 40th college reunion, Rebecca saw her classmates for the first time since she graduated and moved across the country. Some she recognized immediately "because they just hadn't changed at all." Others seemed to have aged typically and were very much in tune with her self-perception. A few "had gotten really old. They looked like my parents," and one fellow, whom she dated briefly during her junior year, seemed physically as if he could be a junior today. She opined after the event, "I guess I'm okay because I seemed to be somewhere in the middle. We were all sixty-two-ish, but some of us appeared thirty-five-ish and others seemed closer to seventy-five."

How do we reconcile those differences? Rob, at 71, could easily pass for being in his 50s, while Dennis, who is 67, seems like many who are in their late 70s.

What accounts for such differences? In addition to our genetic inheritance, many health factors deeply influence our appearance and our self-perception of our age. Our body age seems very connected to the amount of long-term stress in our lives. Dennis has had four marriages and three divorces, at least 15 different positions in his career, and several uprooting relocations. Two of his children have been convicted of crimes, and he suffers from a host of hypertension-related problems. He is also still a "pack-a-day" smoker.

Rob, by contrast, has been married to his second wife for almost 30 years. He has worked in the same organization, gradually ascending the ladder of success, and now is in phased retirement. Their children are launched and successful. His health has been excellent, and aside from some aches and pains, he manages to play tennis and swim and "can still shoot hoops with my grandson."

In addition to stress, a number of health-related factors are well known to affect aging. Physical factors in aging include high total cholesterol or a poor total high-density lipoprotein (HDL) ratio, high blood pressure, diabetes, body fat, asthma, lung disease or pneumonia, heart problems, digestive problems, need for long-term medications, cancer, surgeries or hospitalizations of any kind, and poor dental health. In addition, there are hereditary factors. Parental and close family members' longevity is related to our own slower aging. By contrast, coronary (heart) or chronic illnesses in the family are related to faster aging.

Lifestyle patterns such as smoking and other addictions, poor diet and eating habits, poverty, depression, anxiety, and lower levels of education are correlated with poorer health and faster aging. Long-term satisfactory relationships, active engagement in life events, job satisfaction, and reasonable or better financial status augur well for lower body age. Responsibility for pets or companions also seems to slow the aging process. Although engaging in hobbies and sports often slows the aging process, risk taking and extreme athletic activity may shorten life expectancy.

## Psychological Age (Mastery of Earlier Developmental Challenges)

Our current successes are built on earlier progressive achievements. When we remain stuck in prior stages with unresolved conflicts, we have less emotional and psychological energy for current life issues and events.

Lamar is a good example of this. He grew up in a troubled home in Baltimore. He was the youngest of three children born in a 23-month period. When he was only 2 years old, his father left the family without notice. Lamar's mother was an alcoholic who actually gave him and his sisters away to relatives and friends at various points while they were growing up. When he was 15, he was sent across the country to Oakland, California, to live with a distant relative. Although his adjustment was difficult, he was finally in a stable home with caring adults. The cousins with whom he lived supported him and sent him to school to get an AA degree and a position as a computer technician. To this day he refers to them as his "true" mom and dad.

Lamar's life was stabilized only after many significant losses. He was abandoned by both of his biological parents. He lost contact for a time with his sisters and several prior caretakers. Although he has been able to overcome these traumas in many ways, he remains very untrusting in close relationships. He describes himself as "a little crazy jealous" and "way overprotective" of his three daughters.

The effects of his early experiences have not been fully overcome by the later security. Indeed, his positive experiences have only increased his fear of losing a loved one. As a young man he was too quick to get close to women he dated, and then he became aloof to protect himself from their (imagined) inevitable rejection. Although he can now see how he precipitated most breakups by his neediness, he still has difficulty keeping it in abeyance. He adds, "I know my wife loves me, but I still feel like at any moment I might screw up and she'll just take off with the girls and I'll be left alone again."

Because he has not fully mastered the psychological challenges of a secure early attachment, he will likely face a difficult transition when his daughters begin leaving home for higher education. In fact, he strongly favors having them stay at home and commute to a local college.

Cassie suffered from quite opposite childhood experiences. The only child of "helicopter" parents, she had an excess of security and very little chance to experiment with freedom. Her mother was always the volunteer room mom in grade school and her father switched jobs so they could live close to her high school. He picked her up from school every day and drove her to extracurricular events. Both her parents were frequent chaperones at school fieldtrips. Cassie related, "We were that family that was always early going to church and late leaving. We were home as a family every night and only had family vacations. In fact, the only time I can remember being away from my parents was when I was with my mother's twin sister and my cousins or my grandparents, who lived behind us."

Cassie's life crisis began when she was 18 years old. A stellar student, she won a scholarship to a prestigious university several hundred miles from home. After just 2 weeks at school, she became homesick. Her parents were on the next plane out and actually brought her back home. Since then—for almost 30 years—she has bounced from school to school and job to job. She married a man who was the son of the family pastor in what she describes as "basically an arranged marriage." They never had children and live just three blocks from both sets of parents. Reportedly, her mother is still her best friend. They have lunch together most days and she reports being very close to her father.

Cassie had no shortage of love or attention during her formative years. What she lacked were opportunities to be independent. At each point when she could face a step in the direction of freedom, she and her parents managed to reinstate the secure status quo. Cassie has been unable to develop many of the more adult aspects of life. She remains a child to her parents and to some extent to her husband, claiming that they are not that interested in sex or in being apart from their families of origin.

Awareness of our personal history and patterns is a solid step toward being conscious of our personal current needs, desires, and fears and helps free us to make current and future choices. If, for example, our personal challenge is for security, because of certain fears of rejection or abandonment, we will likely have a strong automatic pull toward the safety side of issues. In that case, our challenge will be to extend ourselves, to try novel activities, and to push ourselves to face fears of unknown possibilities.

Perhaps Cassie could have been helped by an understanding that she feared independence, primarily because she had little experience of it. Knowing that could have led her to take some relatively safe small steps to be on her own and in doing so learn to expand her life experiences. She is aware enough today to know that she faces a life crisis when her parents are no longer able to be central in her life. Similarly, by awareness of the losses he suffered as a child and how they caused him automatically to grip too tightly to loved ones, Lamar may be able to let go at times and allow love to return to him voluntarily.

## Social Age (Cohort Comparisons)

As we age, we become less egocentric and more aware of how we fit with others in our lives. We expect children and adolescents to think of themselves first. We expect young adults to be competitive as they build their positions in life. We expect new parents to put their children and family life before their own desires and needs. What do we expect during the stretch years?

The answer depends in part on our underdeveloped side. If we have focused until now on caretaking and the needs of others, this is the time we need to be aware of personal desires. By contrast, if we have focused until now on our own needs and desires, the growth edge in our lives during this period lies in concentrating on others.

Leroy is the primary caretaker of his young grandchildren. As he approaches 60, his social world is populated by others who are coping with young children—primarily people in their 30s. Similarly, Melanie moved into her mother's retirement community to provide care as her mother progressively slipped into dementia. Melanie's social network is primarily others who live in the community—in short, people 20 or more years her senior.

In a sense, Leroy and Melanie, who are approximately the same chronological age, are almost 40 years apart in social age. They are both single, but Leroy's social group consists primarily of young parents in their 30s. His closest friend is a divorced woman with two children who is 18 years younger than he is. Melanie's social group is primarily seniors. In fact, she was beginning to date a retired man she met in an adjacent apartment.

Are we defined by the company we keep? Sometimes—as different parts of ourselves emerge in differing social environments. A somewhat humorous example of this phenomenon is what occurs during high school back-to-school nights. While on the campus for the evening, almost everyone seems to act somewhat like an adolescent—students, teachers, and parents.

Who is in your social network? Are you engaging in activities that are characteristic of that social group? Do you feel the age of those around you?

For today's boomers and Gen Xers, there are some vital benefits to having social networks. Our social network provides us with support in many realms of life. It acts as a buffer against the impact of major life events. It decreases our risk of disability or decline in activities of daily living and enhances both our mental and physical health. If we suffer an injury or illness, the social network enhances our likelihood of getting back on our feet quickly and gives us a greater sense of personal control over our lives. Finally, having a group of close friends has been shown to actually increase longevity.

It is important for people of this age to have enjoyable and meaningful social relationships. A happy marriage, supportive family relationships, and close friends are particularly positive for emotional health. There are also some potential downsides. Being close to others increases the risk of meaningful losses, and certainly if the relationships are overly conflictual or filled with arguments and interpersonal problems, they can have a negative impact.

Most of the interviewees made a point of describing participating in family and community activities as a major source of personal satisfaction. Being involved plays an important role in improving self-esteem and giving meaning to life. This is true for people of all ages, but especially those leaving midlife.

The salience of social contact has been exacerbated by the impact of the COVID-19 crisis and resultant sheltering-in-place. While working from home or furloughed from work, we have lost many of the easy, in-person social contacts a work environment often provides. Our online networks, social media, virtual gatherings, online cocktail hours, and video-conferencing calls to friends and family have emerged as social lifelines.

## Relationship Age (Relationship Maturity)

One aspect of age is how well we master relationship challenges. Are you still single when most of your peers are in long-term relationships? Have you ever been able to stay in a long-term committed relationship? This may not be very important for a 25-year-old but may be quite significant for someone in the post-midlife years. Have all your relationships ended within a certain prescribed period or in a predictable pattern? Was there a sudden unexpected loss of a relationship? How have you dealt with that?

Lani described her "relationship situation" like this: "It didn't matter at all that I was single through my twenties, but when I hit the big three-oh, I wanted to find that one guy and have a family. So, when I met Keoki, I was primed and after just a few months I had our whole life planned out."

Lani was in her relational age group when she was single in her 20s, married in her 30s, and then divorced in her 40s. At 52, she described herself as "a very independent woman, but I need to have a partner. It's no good to be a third or a fifth wheel with couples or to just be around my single friends, who are down on men. I need another relationship just to feel like I am back on track." Lani was feeling out of the range of her generation and wanted to belong in the age group again.

Are we loners or socially connected? The crucial issue is whether we have chosen what works for us. If you are comfortable with your relationship status at any age, it is probably relevant for you, but if you feel disquiet while out of line with your peers, there may be a misalignment.

Tanya felt very much out of her group when her husband of 20 years passed away suddenly. "In the wink of an eye, I was a widow instead of a wife." At 55, she didn't have many others who shared her life experience. In fact, she lost not only her husband but also her social network of couples. By her description, she now was in a group of women who were 20 years older than she was, and she wasn't ready.

External events can exacerbate the discrepancy and a sense of being out of step with peers. In the pandemic-related social isolation forced on so many in 2020, single people seeking a new relationship and those in enforced long-distance relationships have reported higher rates of loneliness and depression.

# Functional Age (Psychological Responsibility)

Our current age of psychological functioning is related to all the prior ones and to how well we can deal with life events in an age-appropriate manner.

Julianne found firsthand the frustration of trying to deal with life's crises with skills that work primarily for much younger persons. Even in her mid-50s, she rides an emotional roller coaster as she deals with shifting alliances among her friends. Recently one of her best friends reportedly exposed some confidences and said some nasty things to a third party about a social event that Julianne hosted at her home. Her reaction was threefold: First she felt deeply hurt by what seemed to her a betrayal; second, she gossiped bitterly about the other woman; and finally, she cut off all communication with her.

Each of her reactions is understandable and may be somewhat functional, yet it is as if Julianne had not learned from earlier slights the mature skills needed to handle such a situation. Yes, the situation was hurtful and she may have done well to limit contact and confidences with this other woman, but the total embargo on communication had implications in their mutual social circle that harmed Julianne more. The upshot was that she was invited to fewer events because the other woman was expected to be there.

Cleo reacted to a disappointment at work in a different way. Having been passed over for a promotion that was given to a much less qualified person, she resolved to work even harder, throwing herself into the work to impress the boss who had slighted her. She worked longer hours and was always there when the boss arrived at the office and after he left. In this way, she hoped she could impress him with her dedication and motivation and get the next promotion. Were she in her 20s, that approach might have been successful, but she was close to 60 and the toll of all the extra work was exhausting her and creating problems at home, as she was less available to be with her husband.

Both Cleo and Julianne were responding to predicaments in their lives with skills that had become anachronistic by the time they reached their stretch years.

Age-relevant functioning can go the other way as well. James was using skills that would better fit someone in his 70s than a person who just reached his 60th birthday. He said, "I've become one of those old curmudgeons out guarding my tomatoes and waving my cane at any kid who walks by close to my lawn." He focused much of his day on his diminishing energy and vigor and on a host of symptoms such as poor sleep, decreased memory, and slower healing. He confessed, "I am getting old before my time and increasingly impatient at myself. I think I'd rather become the gentle old guy with the great stories like my granddad."

James is dealing with his aging by using skills that he predicts will be appropriate in the future but are premature today. By being an "old man" at 60, he avoids facing what it is like to be 60 and function age appropriately. Like Cleo and Julianne, his use of skills from other developmental stages causes him to miss out on stretch years problem solving.

Our functional age is the measure of the extent that we are ready to deal with the issues that this age throws at us. This means having completed enough prior challenges to allow us to bring our psychological maturity and energy to bear on current issues.

# Reference Age (the Age We Identify With Emotionally)

One of the most enjoyable questions we asked our interviewees was their age of identification: the age they thought of themselves as. This query is unique in age research. Most interesting was that common answers were generally approximately 25 years younger than their chronological age. Most of them laughed at the question and then almost universally identified a particular emotional age. This emotional age often refers to the pop culture with which we identify. I may be 65, but the "good" music of my teens and the emotions that accompany music, films and events that speak to me from my past influences how old I see myself today. Most individuals I interviewed were quick to warm to a discussion of this age.

"Don't get me wrong," said Chad, "I know I am sixty-four—'Will you still need me, will you still feed me,'—but when I think of myself, I am much closer to thirty-five. I still think I have the energy and wherewithal to mount those challenges like way back when ... If I don't pass a mirror, I still think I have a full head of hair and am a 'catch' to those young women. It's like a part of me thinks I can start a whole new career push in a new field and have plenty of time to do it."

Amir added, "It's like a part of me is still ready and able to lace 'em up and play basketball against the undergrads instead of the over-fifty league. When I see the other seniors, I think for a moment that I am the age of their kids, not actually older than them."

I experienced this quite directly in my clinical practice a few years back. I had a new couple referred to me. Although they were clearly seniors, their marriage was only in its 3rd year. Their concerns were primarily about their communication, the upset of their adult children at their marriage so late in life, and financial styles that were clashing as the honeymoon period of their new relationship was wearing off. They were both quite charming and willing to work on their issues to make the relationship a success. The first session went well and I was quite happy with my ability to work with seniors with an unusual problem for folks I thought of as "elderly." It came as quite a surprise to me when I reviewed their intake forms after the session and discovered that they were both younger than I was, her by 10 years. My personal reference age as a younger professional was showing!

Recognizing our reference age can provide us with guidelines for nostalgic pleasures. Recently, Conrad and Jane went to a concert series that featured bands popular in the 1960s and 1970s. They saw Bob Dylan, the late Leonard Cohen, and the Rolling Stones. Conrad recalled, "It didn't matter that their voices were shot and we were mostly hearing their music with a nostalgic ear. Jane and I both felt like we were back in our dating days, and we got to live those days again." She added, "It was like we were transformed into our long-haired, sexy, rock-and-roll days. It was great; there was even the telltale aroma of dope in the air as it passed through the audience. I didn't take a hit this time—too much worry about the germs—but I didn't need it to feel high all night ... I really liked Connie as a thirty-year-old and I felt very sexy ... No more details."

Those younger (generation Xer) interviewees had a much smaller gap between their chronological and reference ages than the "ever youthful" boomers. As Annie said, "I am forty-six and I think of myself as somewhere in my early forties."

A few of the replies were more nuanced. Doreen replied, "I am fifty-one and I think of myself as emotionally as maybe thirty-one, but after a long week of work on Friday night, I think I'm closer to sixty-one."

# When Are the Different Age Measures Significant?

Sometimes the various ages are well aligned. Rosa is a good example. Postmenopausal at 58, she is experiencing some characteristic aches and pains. She has some insomnia, had a brief bout of anxiety and depression earlier, but is now relatively comfortable emotionally. She has been married to the same man since she was 24 and describes their relationship as "comfortable." They have three children who are all launched and gainfully employed. They plan to pay off their mortgage in 2 years and have been relatively good at saving for retirement. Her eldest daughter is now pregnant with Rosa's third grandchild. She is currently employed as a manager and looking forward to a retirement in the next decade. When asked about her reference age, she laughed and immediately said, "Thirtyish," but quickly indicated, "unless I look in the mirror, then I am pretty much fifty-eight."

What does it mean when our body age and our reference age are ill aligned? What are the implications when I think of myself as a 30-year-old, my body feels like a 65-year-old, my relationships are characteristic of an 80-year-old's, and my level of responsibility is that of a 23-year-old? What does it mean when my relational progress is stuck in fantasies about the high school sweetheart who got away? What is the psychological trap when I am living like a 75-year-old when I am 50?

Are there implications of being similar to the others in our age group? Is it important to "act our age" any longer, or are there advantages to being different? The best growth will occur when the lenses are coordinated, and any that are off represent areas of potential growth. Unfinished business may occur in any combination of the different age measures.

Well-understood discrepancies among the six ages are often the areas of greatest potential growth. When I know, for example, that my developmental lag is in a particular area of life, I can pay greater attention to that aspect and catch up.

## Exercise: My Life Timeline

On the line in the figure or on a piece of paper with the timeline copied on it, draw a horizontal line indicating the arc of your life, with the left end indicating your birth and the right end your death. Place an X on your current age, then put in relevant age markers such as when you got your driver's license, graduated from high school, married, had a child, got a new job, and so on, and indicate anticipated coming events.

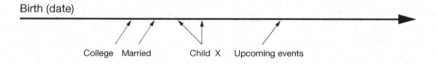

IMG 2.1

Using a different colored pencil or pen for each, indicate on the timeline your chronological age (X), your estimates of body age (B), psychological age (P), social age (S), functional age (F), and reference age (R).

- What do you notice?
- Make a list of key memories.
- What does your current age mean to you?
- Which of your recent or upcoming birthdays marks a milestone?
- What issues from your childhood still impact you today?
- To develop your understanding, review keepsakes, photos, family histories, and personal memories.
- What strengths are symbolized by these keepsakes?
- What is unfinished in your life?
- What reparative methods can you take to realign, catch up, and move forward by maximizing your personal strengths and minimizing weaknesses?
- How can these be integrated into a more comprehensive appreciation of the unique challenges that life has thrown at you?

For your reference, here is a model timeline provided by one of the interviewees in the research project.

**An Example Time Line**

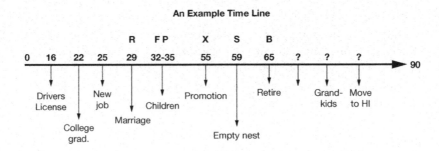

IMG 2.2

# chapter three

# Finding Meaning

## Existential Questions

*I've done everything right.*
*Why aren't I happy?*

What is my life all about? What is my raison d'être? How may I understand the meaning of my existence? What mark will I leave on this earth? Since the beginning of recorded time, these questions have been paramount in the speculations of poets, philosophers, theologians, novelists, historians, and social scientists of every stripe. During midlife and soon thereafter is the time in our lives when these questions take on a personal urgency.

The answers are complex, involving both our hearts and our minds. As we try to understand the meaning of life, we also have to come to grips with natural phenomena in our lives.

- "The more things stay the same ..." Regardless of what you have typically enjoyed earlier in life, in the third quarter of our lives we may become aware of new desires, new preferences, and less interest in what gratified us previously.
- Life throws us curves. It is easy to be seduced by the pursuit of what we believe is *supposed to be* and lose sight of, or be surprised by, *what is*. Life is

unpredictable. The discrepancy between hope and reality is uniquely powerful during the years following midlife.

- I did everything correctly, why aren't I happier? What happened?

There is an important difference between *doing things right* and *doing the right thing*. The latter reflects our core values. It is essential to recognize that the right thing is a moving target. It changes as we age and as circumstances shift. Reconciling the differences between trying to do what is right in our hearts and what looks good to, or is expected by, others is no small endeavor.

Facing these issues hinges on an awareness of things that bring greater meaning to our lives, such as coming to grips with mortality, exploring our spiritual side, rediscovering old relationships, or creating new ones. These topics are so far reaching that I've dedicated entire chapters of this book to each.

In this chapter, the focus is on the psychological side of the quest for meaning. It involves two internal, apparently opposing forces that create a vibrant tension throughout our lives: our needs for freedom and those for security. Each time we address this tension there is an opportunity for personal growth.

## Freedom and Security

Two prophets of the boomer generation underscored these needs. In his classic song, "Me and Bobby McGee," Kris Kristofferson, focusing on the pain of abandonment, speculated that freedom represented little more than nothing left to lose.[1] In another song from the same era, "Help Me Make It Through the Night," he pleads with a potential partner to help him stave off the loneliness and provide even temporary respite from feelings of isolation.

Robert Frost offered an apparently opposite perspective, in his homage to the freedom of choice in his famous poem:

> Two roads diverged in a wood, and I,
> I took the one less traveled by,
> And that has made all the difference.

---

1   The song "Me and Bobby McGee" was made popular in a rendition by the late Janis Joplin.

Is this a true dichotomy? Must we either pursue Frost's freedom of choice (and regret options lost) or should we shy away, fearing that it comes at the expense of security "with nothing left to lose." Perhaps rather than straightforward contradictions, these two forces offer us a tenuous connection that offers an engine for psychological growth. The tension between needs for freedom and security begins in earliest childhood, well before midlife or beyond. It is particularly consequential at this time, because we need to become increasingly aware of the choices the struggle generates. Personal meaning may be discovered, not from adherence to one or another side of this psychological coin, but from awareness of the tension and conflict between opposite sides of ourselves.

For children and adolescents, each stage unfolds naturally as they develop increasing maturity and skills over time. Early examples of the dual pressures of security and freedom may be readily observed even in toddlerhood (which Erik Erikson described as the stage of autonomy versus shame and doubt). The child holds tight to mother for a while and then ventures forth to some unseen limit, only to run back to mother, in British psychiatrist, John Bowlby's terms "as if pulled by an invisible elastic band."[2] Then, temporarily sated with security, the child ventures off again, perhaps two steps further into the unknown.

The toddler's testing of freedom and security is a model for all transition points in life but comes to full fruition during these post-midlife years. As many existential philosophers and therapists have opined, it is through this constant struggle that we come to discover or create our life's meaning.

Having found our primary careers, begun our families, and struggled with worldly events, it is normal for us to turn inward (again) during the era that includes our 50th and 60th birthdays. Many of those interviewed revealed that their personal questioning of life's meaning escalated between their late 40s to mid-60s. This questioning becomes far more poignant when fears of illness or death are increasingly present in our lives. The existence of a pandemic like COVID-19, and the way we respond, necessarily exacerbate our awareness of the limits on human life and add pressure to our decisions about how we want to spend our time.

---

2 Issroff, J. (Ed.). (2005). *Donald Winnicott and John Bowlby: Personal and professional perspectives*. Routledge, p. 17.

The introspection is often reflected in a renewed spiritual quest as well. In addition to rethinking the nature of relationships and careers in our lives, we have to consider how much we want to keep doing what we have always done as adults and how much we want to spend the latter half of our life in alternative pursuits. Is this the time to take an inner journey on Frost's road less traveled? And if you do, will it make all the difference?

To engage in such a quest, it may be important to begin with a review of your natural tendency toward freedom or security before considering what alterations might lead to fruitful discoveries. What is your characteristic approach? Do you tend toward security before freedom or vice versa? Does excessive caution hold you back from important adventures? Are you prone to trying out new things without fully considering the ramifications?

Perhaps you have fulfilled the "good kid" role well into adulthood, trying to do what was expected and to do it as well as you could. Is now the time to consider using your skills to pursue goals that you set personally? By contrast, if your lifelong tendency has been to focus on exploration and freedom, might it be a time to examine both your long-term fear of being tied down and the value of security itself?

It is important to keep in mind that an overall balance between these two needs is likely only over extended periods of life. At any moment in time, one side of the equation may take primacy. Sometimes, the better choice may be the reassuring, comfortable, and soothing road *more* traveled. At other times, the familiar can seem more like a highway to entropy: full of shrinking possibilities and leading nowhere. It is not the existence of security and freedom in our lives that leads us to greater understanding of the unknowns; it is our ability to embrace the tension between them and to face the anxiety that will occur when we break out of our normal patterns.

## Facing Fears: The Waimea Rock Challenge

Several years ago, when I was practicing in Honolulu, I had two clients who were approaching their 50th birthdays with some angst. They both decided spontaneously to test themselves on "the Rock."

On the North Shore of Oahu, at Waimea Bay, there is a large rock that juts out into the ocean. It is a place where individuals (primarily teenaged boys) "test their masculinity" by jumping off the top of the cliff into the ocean swirling below. Anita, my 49-year-old client, drove out to Waimea Bay, climbed up on the rock, checked to see that the tide was in, held her nose, and with a running start leapt off and into the Pacific. She returned to therapy the next week exhilarated and delighted with herself. She described the event as "life-changing."

Less than 10 days later, Carlos made the same pilgrimage. He climbed up on the rock, looked down at the ocean, stood at the precipice, went back from the edge, and sat down to consider before again going to the edge. He did this three times and then climbed back down and went home. In his next therapy session, he was surprised that he did not feel like a failure. Indeed, he claimed to be experiencing the event with some elation. He opined, "You know, I knew I could do it, but that wasn't me. I need to deal with my demons in other ways."

How could this be so, that both of these individuals could respond to the challenge in such different ways and both feel good about it? The answer is emblematic of the challenge of this age. The important aspect of a dilemma is *facing the fear*, not necessarily being counter phobic[3] about it.

For Anita, who was overly concerned about "dotting the i's and crossing the t's," her action in the face of danger was a marker of positive change. Of course, it was fortuitous that her impulsivity had such a safe outcome. Carlos's history was characteristically marked by incautious risk taking. His ability to recognize danger and to heed his own warnings provided him growth, too.

They each faced this particular fear and made a decision about how to deal with it. Facing the fears and the tension is the key to decision making. By exploring both security and freedom needs, we have all of the internal data, rather than just one side of the equation.

# Real Fears and Fears of Fears

Consider the difference between two different kinds of anxiety: existential (real) anxiety and neurotic anxiety. The former is the healthy fear of the unknown that is a cornerstone of life and emotional growth. The latter represents anxiety that keeps us from facing those fears. Both Carlos and Anita looked at their very real

---

3   To psychotherapists a phobia is defined as an irrational fear. A counter-phobic reaction is an irrational response to the anxiety by doing exactly what one most fears.

fears of mortality and decided how to respond, based on their personalities and their previously preferred method of doing things. The fact that they responded in opposite ways shows that there is no universal right way to explore a fear.

Had they avoided the challenge because they worried about traffic, developed a psychosomatic head ache or stomach ache, or didn't get to Waimea because they couldn't decide on which bathing suit to wear, they would have been giving in to the neurotic (fear of) fear instead and missed out on the true test.

This is the essence of the post midlife transition. Any changes in routine or life path evoke anxiety. Shifts in relationships, work, and health; losses; and retirement concerns are but a sample of the issues that often create anxiety. Negotiating these transformations leads us along the path to growth and meaning. Anita's way was to embrace the unknown and charge ahead into the jaws of her anxiety. Carlos's way was to bring himself to the situation and carefully evaluate the possibilities, make an informed decision, and take a very different action. In fact, Carlos's greatest personal fear was that he would either be frozen by indecision or conversely succumb to impulse—both approaches that were all too familiar to him. For Carlos, the best path was a reasoned moderate action.

The years between 45 and 65 are replete with both the opportunities and needs to reassess, realign, and rebalance. Each time we enter a period of change we have to acknowledge, tackle, and embrace our fears of the unknown. The true victory is *in the struggle*, rather than in a particular resolution. Losses are the inevitable outcome for individuals who rigidly hold on to the presumed safety of the status quo. Inadvertently, they are taking the larger risk: stagnation.

How can this be? If you continue to do what has been successful, why in the world would those methods fail to work when you are in your 50s? I wish I had a better answer to that question. The fact is that if you continue to do what has worked previously and the situation is gradually shifting, at some point the results of your actions will no longer bring you the expected benefit.

Joan, a 54-year-old nurse, had been accruing increasing responsibilities as a manager in her hospital. During her midlife transition, she separated from her husband of many years to "find out who I was, when I wasn't Mrs. Johnny." When she came into therapy, she was considering reconciling with her husband and had just been offered a major position as head nurse in a new health facility. She related her feelings of pride in being recognized and offered the new position, but she also was finding it difficult to say yes. When we began discussing what she most enjoyed about nursing on a day-to-day basis, she quickly replied, "I love OB [obstetrics] nursing and being with the new parents." I inquired whether the new job offered those possibilities and she quickly responded, "No, the new job was mostly hospital committees, HR, troubleshooting, scheduling—all that admin stuff that I am very good at, but don't really enjoy that much." She added, "I just don't know if I can turn down such a good financial offer."

As we discussed her financial needs, she said two things that brought her choices into sharper focus. The first was that, although it would be nice, she didn't need the extra money and it was the higher status that was compelling. The second was that when she left her husband, she discovered quickly that she didn't leave her unhappiness, because it was in her, not between them.

Most important was that Joan make conscious choices, based on an evaluation of internal as well as external needs. From this perspective, the meaning that derives from facing the conflict is the more salient goal, and deciding to continue working at what she loved doing rather than automatically choosing the highest rung of a career ladder set by others was a major choice for growth in her life.

Joan is continuing to explore her options. Among her questions are how much she should do what is expected of her (doing things right) and how much she should pursue doing what fits best with her values and fosters her personal growth (doing the right thing). In the course of making a career decision, she is actively exploring specifically what will bring greater meaning to her life, including her spiritual pursuits, coming to grips with mortality, the meaning of her personal existence, and what she most wants in her marriage.

Naturally, she will experience some anxiety at doing the less expected as she explores the untaken roads in her life. Yet it is likely that the anxiety she experiences during this endeavor will be healthy anxiety, part of being more fully alive.

Were Joan to follow her characteristic paths, she would shut down those nagging questions and automatically take the promotion. Predictably, the initial reaction would be relief. Opting for the status quo would help her feel safer and generate far fewer questions from others. However, by avoiding those internal questions and not considering alternatives she risks a sense of personal stagnation and would have to deal with neurotic anxiety: the fear of fear.

When the environment changes, new perspectives and behaviors are required to avoid a down spiral that results from holding on too tightly to the familiar.

What if my daily driving commute to work has always taken about 25 minutes? Over the years, housing developments have gone up around the route and two major companies have moved their offices further down the road. Those shifts in population and work locations have now made my 25-minute commute at least 45 minutes in duration. I could adjust to the extra time in my car, or I could take an alternate route, but instead, if I keep going down the same path expecting that the 25-minute commute will return, I will become increasingly frustrated.

What keeps me from noticing the new demands? In a word: *fear.* If I change what I am doing, I make the outcome less known. What if I take a new route and my new "shortcut" to work takes 60 minutes? That worry about unknown consequences might keep me from experimenting.

Frequently it seems that knowing bad news is easier than not knowing. How else can we explain the common response of relief when someone who gets bad news from a physician after several tests? Knowing somehow trumps the fear of the unknown.

Those fears of fears, famously articulated by President Franklin Delano Roosevelt during the dark days of WWII, are far more difficult to face because they regenerate constantly and preclude our freely exploring aspects of our lives. Unlike the very real fears of *actual* dangers, they operate unconsciously to keep us from *considering* the actual dangers. Neurotic anxiety cuts off the process of evaluating whether our novel thoughts, explorations, and actions truly are as risky as they seem. They obviate our quest for personal meaning and opportunities for courage.

At age 62, Douglas is a self-described "neurotic wreck." He calls himself "the poster boy for delaying gratification. I couldn't face the idea of going out in the world after I got my medical degree, so I went back and got a Ph.D. in molecular biology and when I was offered a job at [a major university hospital], I decided I'd be better prepared if I also got my law degree." Opting to stay in school was not the only area of his life in which he avoided the fears of being an adult: "I was twenty-seven when I had my first real date. She already had two kids and was financially broke. So after about a month, I moved her and the kids into my place and we got married." He describes his 25-year marriage to Dora as "comfortable. She's no challenge to me intellectually, but she's very nice and the kids like me. It's just not what you'd call passionate. We have sex about once a month, whenever she initiates, but I don't think it's that good for her and it's just ok for me."

Although Douglas reportedly has a genius-level IQ, a very well-trained academic mind, and has achieved success, he constantly complains that his life is bland, but that any potential changes are far too threatening. One example he gives is that his wife surprised him for his 50th birthday with a cruise to the Greek Islands to view the ancient ruins, something he always said he wanted to do. Unfortunately, he rarely left his cabin on the ship and was worried about any number of harms that could befall them at the architectural sites. "I think she finally gave up trying to make me have a good time after that trip," he recalled.

Similarly, he is a great fan of baseball and relishes watching his hometown Chicago Cubs, following the box scores and keeping Cubs' memorabilia. Yet he admits that he hasn't been to a game at Wrigley Field in almost 2 decades. He recalls that his father took him to the last game he actually attended.

"I worry about the crowds, parking, or taking the train and walking a few blocks in that neighborhood. I'd start worrying if I had the right tickets and how I'd get back to Evanston (less than ten miles from the park) after the game. The last time my cousin was in town, she bought tickets and offered to pick me up and take me to the game. I was relieved when I woke up the morning of the game with a bad sore throat, and couldn't go ... you'd probably say that I made myself sick to avoid the whole thing ... maybe what I worry most about is risking pleasure."

It is clear that if Douglas is to begin to make any progress in his life, he will have to face uncertainty by actually getting out of the safety bubble in which he lives and deal directly with some of his unknowns. It is maladaptive for him to have to develop an illness to avoid doing something he is likely to enjoy. He may well decide that going to a Cubs' game is not worth the potential downsides, but he does have to face the decision more directly and consciously. This is a step on his path to find meaning and to have a less anxiety-deterred third quarter of life.

# Finding Meaning

Acknowledging, facing, and coming to grips with underdeveloped parts of ourselves is one major pathway to greater self-understanding and meaning. These stretch years are the ideal time to reexamine our lives, often spurred on by a marker such as a 50th or 60th birthday, the last child graduating or leaving home, or the birth of a grandchild.

How do we square what we are doing with what we want to be doing? What is working? What isn't? What happens if we simply continue on the same path? Are there alternative pursuits that will serve us better? What relationship, career, community, or spiritual quests are now desirable? What aspects of the familiar must we bring along on the new journey?

## We'll ~~Cross~~ Blow Up That Bridge When We Get to It

It is common for boomers and Xers at this age to report a growing sense that something is missing as we follow the familiar trajectory of our lives.

Two weeks after being offered a long-desired promotion to chairman of the science department, J.D., a 52-year-old high school physics teacher, reported,

> I don't know. Things just don't have the same pop any more. I used to think what I was doing was really important, and maybe they are to the students, but I am ready to leave high school and do something that suits me. I think it's time for me to be the student or just to get away from it all.

While appreciating the honor and recognition the new position offered, J.D. was seriously considering retraining for a new career. Similarly, Mei Lee, a 58-year-old pediatrician, reported,

> I have a good profession that I love. I have a great husband and three kids who are doing well and are a great pleasure to me. My parents now live near us. My health is good. I have friends at work and at home. I feel almost embarrassed to admit that I have this longing for something more; something that will excite me, something that will answer my questions about, is this all there is?

Mei Lee's career and early life decisions turned out to be good ones, but it does make sense that some choices she made as a teenager may not be as suitable for her as she approaches 60.

How may J.D., Mei Lee, and others face their doubts? How are they to derive personal meaning by acknowledging these new stirrings and their struggles to face their fears of the unknown? *Now that I'm all grown up, what do I really want to be?*

Even the question can provoke anxiety. Perhaps you have avoided pondering such things, because breaking out of your comfortable pattern will expose you to disquieting or threatening unknowns. Might you even reevaluate decisions that were appropriate for earlier times and decide post hoc that you made an error? Often the anxiety emerges without any conscious awareness or obvious events. Could long-buried experiences as a child or adolescent still have a partial hold on you today? If they do, did you adapt to the stress unconsciously to protect yourself psychologically from the anxiety? If these unconscious protective responses developed long ago, maintain your safety, and keep your life working, do you want to mess with them even a little? Do you risk crossing new bridges if it means destroying your way back home?

The good news is that awareness of what drives certain predilections is unlikely to force us to change or face unknown fears. Instead, the self-exploration offers both understanding and options. Being aware of an array of possibilities creates a more conscious enterprise, not necessarily the need to make radical shifts. When we understand all of our needs and evolving desires, we may opt for more of the same, small shifts or major breaks with past behavior.

## There May Be Fewer Trophies

One potential loss to consider is the loss of kudos that come from following the line and succeeding along pathways that are set by those who offer those rewards.

J.D. may decide to leave the cocoon of his high school science department, but he is not about to give up his lifelong passion for teaching and science. He may well move those jewels to a novel setting, one that better suits him as a person over 50.

Mei Lee's exploration of what more there could be in her life did not lead to any dramatic familial or career changes. Although she was enjoying all the parts of her life, her days were too full. She was missing time to be alone, to ponder the unknowns, to explore lesser known parts of herself. Although her high school decision to pursue medicine turned out to be good one, it necessitated her leaving behind a host of other possibilities, talents, and creative urges that were now reemerging. Recapturing personal time and exploring those other capacities were important in her redefinition of her life as she approached 60.

## Who Am I Now?

As we rethink some of the decisions we made actively or passively when we were in our teens or 20s, we may have an opportunity to retune them in ways better suited to our more mature lives today.

Perhaps the most integral component of personal meaning is self-definition. If you spent much of your life doing what was expected as a child, adolescent, young adult, and parent of children, your responsibilities were clear. Do well enough in school (as defined by family and subculture), find a long-term relationship, make a living and a life, raise a family, and during the "power years" find advancement and build whatever future is possible.

If we have done what was expected for decades, a burgeoning question may begin to emerge during the midlife years and beyond: "Who am I?" If the question is submerged—or remains unanswered at midlife—its volume increases during the ensuing years. Willie was about to retire after 30 years of military service. He was in his early 50s when he came into therapy, ostensibly to deal with what to do after retirement. He described himself as "a good father to my children and the troops, a Scoutmaster, a good husband for my 29-year marriage and a success in my job. ... So what's the problem? All those things are what I was supposed to do. I have never really thought about what I want to do. Really, who do I want to be?"

He was questioning whether the sum of his roles in life, father, husband, and soldier, were sufficient to define him, or whether there was something more. Was some meaning in life eluding him, perhaps being obscured behind the very roles that represented his success to date? When I asked him what it would mean to him if his life were to end this way, he replied, "On the one hand, I'd say that I was a good man and served my country and my family pretty well; on the other, I wonder if there's something else I need to do before I head off to St. Peter. ... I don't know what that could be, but I really want to find out."

If this is the time for him to begin to make personal choices, it requires a recognition of who he is and what he really wants in this next phase of life. In fact, Willie is like many men his age who have dedicated their lives to the male prime directive (to protect and provide) and is less familiar with the word "want" than the word "need."

After several sessions and some hard, internal work Willie began to talk about two of his personal desires: "trying my hand in painting and getting a dog. I never had a dog because my deployments meant that my wife would have another responsibility and I gave up my painting when I washed out of an art class in high school." When asked what happened, he replied tellingly, "Well the teacher wanted us to do the assignments a certain way and I was into painting what I wanted—you know, free-form."

At that time (age 15), he told himself that painting wasn't for him and he looked elsewhere for success, finding it in sports and in the military. After mulling it over for some time, he did try to recapture some aspects of his boyhood that were cut short. As he described it later, "Getting the dog was great; I like the long walks with her and the affection and just the daily care. Plus, my wife is in love with her also ... seems she always wanted one too, but never wanted to add to the burdens around the house either." He continued laughing, "The [adult education] art class was another story. To be blunt, I am especially untalented. I think my old teacher was kind when he told me the problem was that I wouldn't follow the rules."

Something of note did come out of his art class. Discovering that "I sucked at painting, made me wonder what else I really wanted to try. So now I am on a quest. I know that it won't involve painting or drawing, but I am surprising myself with how open I am to failing at new things." For the first time in his adult life, Willie pursued something for which there were no easy accolades, promotions, or encouragement, no anticipated rewards. He is actively pursuing interests to discover more of who he is. As an added bonus, he has been meeting like-minded friends in his classes.

Cecile pursued a different path. A lifelong homemaker, mother, and community volunteer, she discovered a surprising drop in energy when her children left home. At first, she explored treatment for depression, but later began to understand that the nest was truly empty and she had time to care for herself. She began by attending classes, seminars, and a few retreats through her church. She began reading more philosophical and spiritual books. For Cecile, the quest required that she stop doing so much and focus more on her inner life and personal desires. During her first therapy session the following exchange occurred.

> Cecile: "I know this may seem crazy, but I am wondering whether the only reason for me to have been so busy with home, kids, and neighbors over the years was to avoid looking at myself."
>
> Therapist: "Of course, that is possible, but what if you did the right things for then and you have been so successful that you finished and ended the job? Maybe it's time for you to focus on what is right for now."
>
> Cecile: "That's a nice way to put it! I seem to have these yearnings to know better how I fit into the universe. Do you know what I mean? Could we talk about why are we here anyway? What does my life mean now that I've 'been so successful'?"

Cecile needed to become more aware of what was going on inside her and what meaning she could make of her life. She was able to do so in psychotherapy, exploring first what aspects of self she cut off to be a mother and homemaker. When she described coming to North America when as a shy teen, she felt so isolated and undesirable that she set out to do what was expected so well that neither she, nor it, could ever be questioned.

When the therapist inquired about her negative traits, she produced a litany of frailties. When he responded by asking, "So, what if those are all true? What does it mean if you are really that inadequate?" She expressed fear of being abandoned and how she always did things so people would love her. She described a decade-long attempt to "make my husband happy, just so he'd stay with me."

Over time and through her hard emotional work, Cecile was able to live more within her own skin. She was able to begin a process of discovering who she was, "warts and all," and became more and more comfortable with ambiguity, both her place and meaning in the universe and with the risk of not always being responsible for others' moods at the expense of her own. Of course, Cecile's personal work is always in process, but as she discovers more and more of herself, she is increasingly comfortable with what she calls her "naked search."

## Why Now?

Although questions of personal identity accompany us throughout life, many of us put such queries aside either in our late teens or early adult years to make our way in the world. During midlife, discomfort with the status quo causes those contemplations to reemerge. After midlife, they become a powerful quest for many. It becomes progressively more important to question, if not discern, who we are in the larger scheme of things, to wonder what we really want from our lives, to make a statement involving our being on this earth. It is a time to rethink and reflect on what we are doing and square that with what we want to be doing.

Although it may have served us well to pursue certain relationships and career moves assiduously until now, it is important to consider whether continuing to pursue these into the future will bring continuing benefits, or whether minor alterations or major shifts may be of value.

Engaging in activities that may generate acknowledgment by one's peers or the powers that be may be of value, but the intrinsic value of doing what is right far outweighs the next trophy on the mantel. Similarly, the kick from retail therapy or purchases are time-limited and generally offer little lasting satisfaction. It would be a rare person on their deathbed who decries not spending more time at the office or having acquired another possession. Indeed, once we downsize or after we die, most of our accumulated awards and possessions will not be cherished by the next generation and are destined for yard sales or the landfill. As one of my long-time colleagues relates, "I told my son to dump the award certificates and degrees, but to keep the frames."

## So How/Where Do You Find Meaning?

Is personal meaning something to be discerned or decoded by understanding some absolute truths? Or is there no universal truth, but only meaning we give to our experience—a personal truth we encode? Most religious-spiritual paths begin with the former assumption. The alternative is to focus on our personal experience of what is, rather than what ought to be. Exploring the real versus the anticipated allows for enhanced awareness and self-knowledge.

There are, of course, as many answers to the big questions in life as there are seekers. Any practice that involves contemplation and introspection opens potentially fruitful paths. Perhaps a teacher, spiritual leader, psychotherapist, or elder can walk with us part of the way or at least prime the pump of the search.

The importance of self-knowledge and awareness is hardly new. Ancient Greek aphorisms advocated the search as crucial to a full life. The inscription over the front court of the Temple of Apollo at Delphi, and of the Oracle was, "Know Thyself." Similarly, Socrates is credited with saying, "The unexamined life is not worth living." Beginning in the early 20th century, Freud, and most psychotherapists who followed, offer self-examination and awareness as pathways to fuller living.

## Awareness

Regardless of our personal process, our search for meaning will involve at least two components: (a) an increased focus on all our senses, particularly those that are less commonly addressed and (b) slowing down and spending time exploring our natural, semi-automatic thoughts, tendencies, and reactions and questioning whether we are behaving congruently.

When we are on automatic, we don't acknowledge all of the feelings and sensations available. For much of our lives, focusing on all of our feelings would inhibit necessary activity. Some of our action-based successes to date have been served by suppressing some other sensations and perceptions. Who hasn't rushed through a quick breakfast, barely tasting the food, to get to the daily chores or challenges or put everything else aside to meet an important project deadline?

During the stretch years it becomes more important to sit sometimes and smell the coffee, rather than use it solely as a morning brain and colon activator! This is the era of life to become increasingly aware of those previously suppressed feelings. What are you feeling from moment to moment? These data may now be better suppressed less and savored more. What does it mean to you to have certain physical sensations or feelings? What is your body, or your unconscious mind, trying to tell you?

Marie (age 64) said that there was a nagging sensation that something was amiss in her life. She ignored it to do what she "needed to do." Focusing her energy into her work, she had been a successful real estate broker and life partner. It wasn't until the advent of her 63rd year did the "little bell become so loud I couldn't ignore it." With support from her friends and life partner, she decided to take a "six-month sabbatical to listen to my inner voice."

What emerged from her awareness and pondering was a decision to risk greater intimacy in her primary relationship and to become more authentic with her customers when she was showing properties. She concluded, "I may have lost a few sales by being more into my potential buyers and sellers, but the ones who did work with me had a much better experience and were so grateful. I also have been far more open with Lily and she has reciprocated in ways that I have never experienced before. I even decided to officially 'come out' to my brother and sister. They knew, of course, but now we could all talk about my life and theirs in a real way ... You know, I feel more alive than ever and I think I am far from done in my getting to know myself."

Marie's greater sense of her emerging self is significant; she was confronting the aspects of herself that she had kept out of awareness and took some calculated risks with Lily and her siblings.

Action is not always linked to increased awareness. Marie seemed to discover some parts of herself that she wanted to change, but other people may seek new awareness for its own sake. At 58, Lori described herself as one of those people who has always sought inspiration and answers to life's big questions in literature. When she reached her mid-50s, she began rereading books that she enjoyed years before. "To my surprise, there were so many new meanings in those books. I did understand them as a young woman, but now the wisdom of the authors comes through in a truly deeper way." She paused and added, "Or maybe I am just reading new depth into the books. Either way, I just feel more inspired and so much more open to learning about myself and the world."

Exploring awareness involves a shift in our method of self-questioning. Rather than ask ourselves "Why?" "How?" or "What if?" the most salient question for sake of awareness is "What is?". The shift in focus to the here-and-now moments of experience provides very different sets of data. We become increasingly involved with *being* rather than with problem solving. Among the driving forces of such awareness is an acknowledgment of mortality and the implications of the end of life as we can know it, regardless of belief in a hereafter.

## Here and Now

Being more aware makes each experience richer, vibrant, and more poignant. Trying to overcome the here and now to get to some predetermined success often results in unintended or reverse consequences.

Like many men in this age group, Liam reported that his sexual desire and potency were now question marks. The more he willed himself to stay erect, the less he was present for the sexual experience with his long-term partner. Over time, their sexual activity had decreased in both frequency and importance, and when they were sexual, he was increasingly thinking about it so much that he was consequently enjoying it less. A classic Type A personality, Liam had been advised by his doctor and his boss to try meditation for stress reduction and as an adjunct to medication for his high blood pressure. As he practiced meditation, he discovered that he was becoming aware of many unanticipated sensations in his body. Bringing his newfound skill to the sexual area of his life, he was able to experience far more gratifying experiences in which he "just focused on my body as it was and didn't worry about what kind of erection I was having." Although their sexual frequency remained lower than in prior years, Liam reported that it was better than ever before.

It doesn't require intense physical activity to increase one's awareness. Yuki said that she had always loved music as background to her active life. As she focused more on becoming aware of her senses, she said, "I am really into the music and lyrics. The other day I was listening to the sound so closely, I thought I could hear the finger-light movements as the violinist moved up and down the neck. It was exhilarating—almost like I was there in the room with him. It made me both feel soothed and energized at the same time!"

## What We Resist—Persists

Avoidance may be one pathway to better self-knowledge. Are you so security conscious that you customarily avoid novel activities? This may be the time to explore what activities you avoid and what fear is underlying that avoidance. This is not an invitation to be counter phobic, to engage in these activities although or because they are scary. Rather, it is an opportunity to identify and reconsider what types of activities or thoughts you characteristically sidestep. There may be some kernels of meaning in examining what about those activities may be problematic.

They may be small things that you have good reasons to avoid or larger ones that limit the amount of desirable freedom. Cliff grew up in a "meat and potatoes" home. "Every meal consisted of over-cooked beef, pork or chicken, well-done potatoes and frozen green beans or peas and carrots." When he left home, he "experimented" with a few other kinds of food: take out Chinese food, pizza and pasta (with marinara sauce), and some fried seafood. As an adult he replicated this simple "all American Midwest" diet. Whenever his friends went out to more exotic foods cuisines, he demurred. His minimal experimentations with spicier cuisines had left him feeling unsatisfied or suffering with digestive problems.

It was useful for Cliff to examine the impact on his life of the social limitations. He decided that he was willing to stick to his culinary preferences rather than risk the unknown cuisines or leaving his comfort zone. He didn't need to explore in this way, but in examining the hanging on to his traditional stance about food, he discovered a pattern of limiting his opportunities at work and in other realms. He began to try thought experiments that were somewhat out of the box on the job—nothing dramatic, but opportunities to grow in new directions.

By contrast, Barbara was "always on the go." Physically fit and relatively healthy for a woman of 55, she adored walks, hikes, cycling, tennis, and most other physical activities. Her children joked that she'd be the juggler with the spinning plates if she so desired. In fact, although she had always been active, her "nervous energy" had increased dramatically since her divorce 10 years previously.

On one level, she was engaging in potentially healthy physical activity to stay fit. On another, she was almost obsessive about it. As she explored what was involved in her activity, she discovered some unintended consequences to action. She was so busy at work and working out at a local gym that she had little time to socialize. Her exercising was an effective way to avoid new social contacts or potential suitors, protecting her from facing fears of relationships and rejections. Although her behavior was functional in this way, it had a downside. Because she was unhappy being alone and feared a rejection from another romantic partner, Barbara's goal in therapy was to find a way to keep her protection intact, without suffocating in her emotional suit of armor. To achieve the goal, she needed to become aware of both the positive and negative functions of her (over) activity.

The bottom line here is that exploring what we avoid characteristically allows us a window into the consequences of that avoidance. Cliff's restriction on cuisine types had little impact on his life, especially when he began to explore novel approaches in other aspects of his life. By contrast, Barbara's activity was blocking her from something she said she desired. It was really worth her while to examine the full impact of her high activity status quo as a way to see what she might fear.

Another pathway to exploring what we avoid is to consider what we put into an image that doesn't fairly reflect how we are as much as how we'd like to be seen. What are the little lies I tell/believe about my history and what is their psychological value? What if others knew the real truth about me? What part of myself do I reserve with misrepresentation? What do I fear would occur if others knew the whole truth?

## Unintended Consequences

Often those strong traits and capabilities that provide us with the most goodies will, in excess, inadvertently may create the very problems we seek to overcome. Being very good at something may well work in reverse. If you are commonly seen as the life of the party, for example, it might be worth experimenting with hanging back and exploring what occurs internally, when you are not entertaining others. Stacy (aged 48) assumed that if she were not the life of the party, she would be rejected: "Nobody would invite me or want me around."

Monique (aged 50) was the most organized and efficient person both at home and at work. She garnered much praise for her skills and was proud of how well and how much she could accomplish in a short time. The downside was that she was expected to do all the work and clean up while those with lesser skills had few responsibilities.

## Consequences Versus Motivations

Effective psychotherapy often focuses on consequences more than on motives. Rather than try to understand what individuals intend to do, it is beneficial to examine what happens when they do it, especially if the behavior is repeated.

One way to become aware of our inner voices is to focus on what we don't do well, avoid, or deny. What are we trying to tell ourselves when we procrastinate or avoid something entirely? Is my fear of the unknown so powerful that I only focus on what needs to be done? Do I prefer the familiar as a way to avoid the novel? What would happen if I tried something new? What do I fear might occur?

Jay had always lived his life trying to be honorable, honest, and have integrity in all his dealings. At first glance one would wonder why he should examine such positive traits or why anyone would recommend that he do anything else. However, it is of value to explore the consequences of the admirable as well as the negative traits. As Jay discovered during a particularly difficult year at work and in familial relationships, his behavior was no longer producing the anticipated yield. He was missing out on benefits that others were receiving. He was unhappy in his life at home.

When he looked at his ways of approaching his world and other people, he saw that he was doing what he thought right, but that the responses were not always what he expected. In particular, his manager had promoted a man who had improperly claimed credit for some of Jay's work and lied and cheated regularly. In a fair world, Jay should have received that promotion. Jay discovered that his moral code and modus operandi were such that he was somehow left out of the receiving side of the equation. In an example of this in his family, he tried to intervene and negotiate a dispute between his two sisters. In that situation, he took responsibility for resolving their conflict. Of course, they both became upset with him. With some help and a serious question about why he was in the middle of such a dispute, he was able to realize that in trying to be honorable, he lost sight of self-advocacy. When he saw the consequences of his actions, he was able to reassess and slightly revise his approach. Without compromising his personal integrity, which was very gratifying to him and those around him, he managed to experiment with stating his personal desires. The result of figuring out what he wanted and expressing those desires appropriately was that he was able to live far more congruently. In this way, he did not compromise his own honor but offered others the opportunities to be as honorable with him.

## Reassessing What You Do Enjoy: Appreciating Guilty Pleasures

If you are like most people, you have some guilty pleasures. These are things you enjoy doing but believe that you shouldn't. Many of us have some television programs, films, or books or comics strips we enjoy, all the while judging them beneath us, simplistic, or even embarrassing. This is a good time to accept and embrace what is, rather than what we think should be, or what others deem appropriate. As Gilles once confessed, "I know it's stupid, but I like to watch the golf channel. I can't explain it or even admit it to my friends or wife, but sometimes, it relaxes me." Candy said that she loves children's movies. "I know it's all manipulation, but I cry like I did as a little girl when a kid onscreen is hurt, in danger or sad. I don't know; I just feel cleansed afterwards."

In our interviews, many of the Gen Xers in particular reported that they liked so-called reality television and a large number specifically said, "I know it's all fake and for show, but I watch *The Bachelor* whenever it's on. Another group described hours spent watching *Law and Order* reruns, including Alyssa (64) who said, "I think I figured out that some form of *Law and Order* is on 24/7 on cable." She explained further, "On my job, work is never done and results are very long term. There is something about having things wrapped up in an hour that is very satisfying." Others still watched daytime soaps (often recorded for evening viewing) and in 2020 TV series such as *Indian Matchmaking* was providing "guilty" binge watching for professionals who were reticent to admit their addiction to such programs.

Whatever the guilty pleasure, it may be of some psychological value to try to appreciate what it does for you or simply to acknowledge that it's truly something you enjoy without feeling guilty. Of course, for some, the feeling of guilt is part of the enjoyment—the number of men who revel in old *Three Stooges* movies is testament to that. As Warren admits, "It wouldn't be as funny if I didn't feel guilty about taking the time to watch the *Three Stooges* and laughing until my stomach hurts."

Often these guilty pleasures recall pleasant aspects of our child-hoods. Reexperiencing and reliving those feelings as adults open us to some buried jewels within. How often as a 60-year-old can I fully feel like I did as I did when I was in grade school? What would it be like to "get the giggles" again and not be able to stop? What is valuable about my inner child and what would it be like to recapture some of the childlike aspects of my personality?

# Relationships

It is not only in relationship to self that we may find meaning. Humans are primarily social beings. We seek connection with others, our lives are enriched by contact, and we seek both giving and receiving love in many forms throughout life. Even our innate competition with rivals seems related to winning love and care from those who count to us. Of course, hard-wired biological drives to reproduce and to protect our young find fruition in mutual love and maintenance of a family and social structure.

Seeking increasing intimacy in important relationships may be the greatest single path to personal meaning. To be open and honest with another requires that we have some awareness of the parts of ourselves that we are offering. It involves being present in the moment with the other person and it involves an uncommon vulner-ability—an opportunity that involves a risk to both the security and freedom parts of self. In a sense, intimacy (with self and others) may be the only antidote to the fears of mortality. One of the wonderful characteristics of passing midlife is that there is a possibility to be less image driven and more person focused. The essence of finding meaning may be available to us as we minimize the ways that we are supposed to look or act and focus more energy on being who we actually are: What *is* versus what should be. An intimate relationship is one in which we are loved in spite of or even for our scars and warts, rather than what we could be without them. Neale spoke for many when he replied, "At this age, I just don't care as much what others think about how I should be. Like me for who I am and I'll like you for who you are. No need to put on airs!"

To paraphrase the lyrics of the final song of the musical *Jacques Brel Is Alive and Well and Living in Paris,* "If We Only Have Love," it is when we offer others our little true selves that we conquer the universe.

# Exercises

## Existential Issues

Ponder the origins and growth of your tendencies toward freedom and security needs:

- Make a list of clichés that were part of your childhood: common sayings around your home, particularly instructions about how one should live or conduct oneself. Look them over and see what they tell you about the values in your home when you were growing up. Now fold a clean piece of paper in half vertically. On the left of the fold list the characteristics of an ideal you subscribed to as a high-schooler. On the right side of the fold write down the characteristics of your ideal self now.

- Compare the two lists. What do you see? Is it essentially the same or very different?

- Compare each list to the clichés listed earlier. Which of the family values have stayed with you? Which have changed?

- Consider your life choices to date, your yearnings, and see where they connect and differ. Which would you like to confront and change in the future?

- Consider the following questions: Do you seek alone time or avoid it? What do you do when you are alone? It is more pleasurable or more uncomfortable? Do you do anything to find something to keep you occupied? What happens when you get close to another person? Do you find ways to avoid it, build walls? Do you fear rejection? Do you get close quickly, typically faster than the other person?

- Jot down, perhaps in a journal, answers to the following questions:

  A. Imagine that you knew that you only had a year to live. What feelings does this evoke? What would you want to do? Do you have a "bucket list?" With whom would you spend the time? Who would you prefer to avoid? What impact will your death have on others?

  B. If you were to describe the meaning of your life on a single page of paper, what would you say? How would you like to be remembered? What do you want from life now? What do you believe would give you greater meaning?

# Part 2

**Age-Related Characteristics and Challenges**

## chapter four

# Inevitable Losses

*For we lose not only through death, but also by leaving and being left, by changing and letting go and moving on. And our losses include not only our separations and departures from those we love, but our conscious and unconscious losses of romantic dreams, impossible expectations, illusions of freedom and power, illusions of safety—and the loss of our own younger self, the self that thought it always would be unwrinkled and invulnerable and immortal.*

—Judith Viorst

How do you cope with loss? How do you come to terms with your changing appearance, the dashing of romantic and career dreams, the end of illusions about the future, your fantasies of your younger self? How do you deal with your inescapable personal mortality and the deaths of others? What new self-image emerges as you incorporate the losses into your current self-image? How do the loss-induced scars change you and set you on a clearer life path?

# Common Losses in Midlife and Beyond

In a single month, June 2007, I attended three memorial services. One was for an aged priest, a colleague with whom I had worked for many years. Another was for a former student, a woman in her 50s, whose career as a counselor was cut off just as it was blooming. The most painful of all was for a young man, who was killed in a tragic accident while celebrating his high school graduation. That triple loss was repeated for me in 2017 and 2019. In the first half of 2020, I have learned of deaths of friends and colleagues from early onset Alzheimer's dementia, COVID-19, and cancer.

The enormity of these deaths underscored for me the inescapability of loss. If we are blessed with longevity, we will mourn the loss of others.

Deaths in our personal communities typically occur with increasing frequency as we age. Ninety percent of those we interviewed reported that they had been impacted by the death of someone close to them during their post-midlife period. Deaths, however, are not the only losses we encounter when we are 45 to 65. These years can be particularly poignant precisely because they are marked by a host of both predictable and unexpected setbacks.

These losses take a variety of forms. For some, the most critical change is a loss of capacity or ability to take on as much as they had previously. For others, the physical limits are less important than the loss of dreams, hopes, and expectations. Yet others feel the loss most poignantly as they find their characteristic roles diminishing in importance and effectiveness. It may be hard to see specifically when that begins to change, but sometime during these years our usual methods of achieving success cease to be as effective.

The most dominant psychological loss is a bit more abstract, yet in some ways is even more central and powerful. It is the experience voiced by many that somehow during the night somebody slipped into our lives and changed the rules. As we move through our post-midlife years, we are likely to experience this curious phenomenon. If we keep doing everything that has always worked for us, the results become predictably less positive.

As Shobha commented, "It's like somehow nobody told me that the problems now had to be solved in base 8!" To misquote Lewis Carroll's white rabbit only slightly, "Now the harder I work, the behinder I get."

This fantasy that someone or something altered the way the universe is functioning is not easy to reconcile, because our traditional fixes of the external realities are fruitless. The only successful adaptation is to change ourselves—to adapt to "new realities."

Until Lenny hit 55, he had led what he described as "a blessed life." Lenny was born in St. Louis and moved to Ohio with his family when he was 13. His father and mother ran a small trades shop in Cincinnati for many years and with their encouragement Lenny became a plumber after 2 years in a community college. He stayed in the family business, helped it grow, and along with two brothers (a carpenter and an electrician) was financially successful, ultimately assuming leadership of the business when his parents retired. He had been married for almost 30 years and had three children. The youngest, a daughter, stayed with the family business as an accountant. Lenny and his wife had three grandchildren, who he described as "the apple tree of my eyes."

When he was in his early 50s, things began to change. He had previously adapted to change by working harder and shifting with economic trends. When his early work as a plumber on call to residences began to diminish, he found a new niche, making repairs in commercial properties. Later, he left repairs behind and moved into creating plumbing in new residences and businesses. Yet something was happening in Lenny's world that harder work and new contacts couldn't solve. Now, there were more complaints and lawsuits than ever before. Although he was never directly responsible, he was named as "one subcontractor" even when the problem had nothing to do with plumbing. The time involved in planning for depositions, hearings, and trials and the ordeal of each left him with less and less time for his actual work.

To compensate, he began to find more work, take on more hours, and hire others to work under him as he spent more time marketing his services. Yet a strange phenomenon occurred. The more he worked and the more he pursued what had always been successful previously, the less reward there was. Not only was there little financial gain for his increasing workload, but there was also little joy in his accomplishments.

Lenny's work crisis led to increasing conflict at home and on the job. He was feeling disoriented and depressed, frequently noting that something was very wrong but unable to figure it out.

During his teen years and early adulthood, Lenny learned to do things right, and he was rewarded with business success. When his hard work was insufficient, he went to his standard answer—work even harder. He always had an "I can fix it," hero mentality. However, at this stage of life, Lenny didn't need more from his life and his business as much as he needed change. Over a 4-year period, Lenny would have to learn to lose his traditional role as hero and problem solver and find a new place for himself as an elder in his world. Lenny needed to accept the losses of role and function and reorient himself to someone approaching 60 rather than continue trying solutions that worked when he was 35.

Job-oriented losses are not alone in creating discomfort and a sense that something is missing, even in lives that have been successful.

On the morning after his

50th birthday party, Eugene took the opportunity of his older brother's visit to "have the first real talk we've had in years." He wanted to know how his 56-year-old brother was coping with the aging experience. The conversation, which took place on a long walk, covered first the blessings they had experienced and the good fortune of their mother's health. Soon, however, the talk turned to the limitations and losses they were experiencing. Their conversation bridged several aspects of life; among the greatest concerns were a decreasing stamina in general and in sexual capability specifically, financial worries about the future, upcoming cutbacks at work, and health issues.

The brothers' conversation was only unique in terms of their openness. Most individuals during these years have an increasing awareness of physical, fiscal, emotional, occupational, and relational limitations. They are also increasingly aware of their changing appearance.

# Fiscal Losses

The economic downturn and near collapse of the financial markets in 2008 and the spring 2020 recession caused by COVID-19 created a great cause for concern to many who were in the decade leading up to retirement. Many of the baby boomers who were planning for a secure retirement have had to reassess their plans. Many of their 401(k) and IRA accounts were decimated, and even with a tentative economic recovery the psychological trauma remains, along with an awareness of a precarious fiscal situation.

Even before the dramatic market drops, boomers were ill-prepared to support their anticipated longer lives. According to some estimates upward of 70% will outlive their savings unless they make dramatic shifts in their saving and spending during the stretch years. Gen Xers, who have suffered from both downturns during their so-called power earning years, have reportedly even less put away to support their later years. Indeed, according to multiple insurance company estimates, their media household savings is under $70,000 in total and 40% report no retirement savings at all.

Both generations have in general been more focused on consuming than on saving, borrowing from the future to pay for the present lifestyle—a problem compounded by increased life expectancy.

Awareness of a serious discrepancy between what we have and what we will need can be more than sobering. It can feel like a betrayal. And in fact, many have felt cheated, either by people they naively trusted or by their belief in an ever-increasing stock market or housing market that would magically make up any deficits in the future.

Chan reports that she was devastated as much by the loss as by the "duplicity of my financial advisor, who put my money market funds into those funky mortgage funds and lost half of them." Now she feels that she doesn't know what to do or who she can trust with what's left of her life savings. The financial losses for Chan are greatly exacerbated by her loss of trust and confidence.

Faith and Norman also found their financial picture disconcerting as they approached retirement. They hadn't overextended their finances during the power years nor lived beyond their means. Yet, they are ill-prepared to be without a reliable income. Like so many of their contemporaries, their annual savings rate of less than 5% of their income will be inadequate. They both have opted for "re-hirement" rather than retirement until they are in their 70s.

In many ways, a financial shortfall is as much about loss of trust, unmet expectations, and broken promises than about running out of money. For couples like Xavier and Danielle, who have always lived with a "can-do attitude," the loss of a planned retirement and an anticipated lifestyle can be depressing. A couple with two good incomes and 401(k) plans, they lived at their means, spending all their income but carrying little debt except for their mortgage. As Bay Area housing prices skyrocketed, they figured that the increased value of their house and the 401(k) plans would be more than sufficient.

"I did have second thoughts," Danielle said, "when we took out our HELOC [home equity line of credit] to remodel, but the contractor and designer assured me that the house would be even more valuable with the improvements." As it turns out, in the past 3 years the value of their home not only stopped appreciating but also trended lower, and the cost of the remodel is a burden as they struggle to pay back the second loan.

## Physical Reminders of Aging

Many of our interviewees commented ruefully on several changes in their bodies and physical capacities. Among the most common were changes in hearing, vision, memory for proper nouns, short-term memory in general, sexuality, muscle mass, bone strength, stamina recovery time, figure, and ability to lose weight.

During this period, most individuals truly discover new limits to their stamina and physical capabilities. Even for those who pride themselves on being in shape, the limber, invincible feelings of a youthful body recede. Aches persist and healing becomes slower. As one of my friends exclaimed one day, "Oh God, I just made my father's [oof] sound when I sat down!"

We may feel that we are still the person we were in our 20s, but for the generation that honored sex, drugs, and rock and roll, the temptations of LSD have long ago given way to medications for acid reflux, sexual intercourse may require chemical assistance such as Viagra, and our "good rock and roll" is now known as "oldies."

The ability to stay up all night fades, as does the capacity to sleep if one has had a cup of regular coffee after dinner, pizza too close to bedtime, or a stressful day. For menopausal women, night sweats, hot flashes, and other common symptoms may make a good night's sleep elusive for them and for their partners.

Our appearance also changes. In addition to extra weight, the downward effects of gravity, and lines caused by decreased skin elasticity, there is the loss of recognition from others. Roberta recalls the day when the cute high school-aged checkout boy not only stopped flirting with her but also called her "ma'am" when he offered to load her groceries into her car. Similarly, Lee recalls the transformation when he clearly became "safe" to strangers on the street and the wary looks he knew as a man in his 20s and 30s transformed into friendly smiles from both males and females.

These losses can be consciously chalked up to "normal aging," but the unconscious feelings and personal implications are less easily addressed. As we age past midlife, there are reminders of systems slowing down and failing, coordination slipping, and the like. Let's consider just a few of the physical reminders described by interviewees:

> **Randy**: I am now the designated first baseman on my softball team—no longer the fleet centerfielder.

> **Diego**: I can still coach the kids at soccer, but I can no longer keep up with them on the field.

> **Nancy**: With my back, I can't just pick up the kids anymore. Sometimes I forget and I see stars.

> **Inez**: I have always been a swimmer and still go out to the Y three-four days a week, but now I've had repeated shoulder miseries that they can't diagnose or fix. The doc tells me, "You're getting old" and then describes his own lingering injuries. All he can do is refer me to physical therapy, which works—until I try to swim distance again.

> **Carl**: I need to remind myself that I am no longer the designated pack mule in the family. When we need to carry something, I've got to get the teenagers to do it.

> **Mark**: I can't get up on the ladder anymore. I hate that I have to call for help or hire someone to do the things I've always done.

> **Radha**: I don't like to admit it, but my nineteen-year-old daughter is a better driver than I am. She has the reflexes I can barely remember.

> **Colleen**: I just can't hear as well anymore. My sister already has hearing aids and she's "my Irish twin," only ten months older than me.

> **Peter:** I need a new hip, and I need reconstructive surgery on both knees.

Others talked about more serious problems that will limit their physical capacity. Among those interviewed were individuals who had suffered a stroke or developed multiple sclerosis, hypertension, cancer, Parkinson's disease, diabetes, or arterial or other heart conditions. Jameson had triple bypass surgery when he was only 50. He wrote, "I was lucky. The same heart condition killed my father when he was in his forties."

These physical limitations, many common as we age, are nonetheless quite hard to accept and acknowledge to ourselves and others. Thinking about new or increasing physical limitations inevitably conjures up even greater disabilities and other more serious losses of function.

Deficits in one area of life that seemed particularly difficult for the men in the survey were those involving sexual functioning. Erectile dysfunction can be embarrassing and socially limiting. Many men had opted for "the little blue pill" or similar drugs by other manufacturers as a way to hide and/or overcome their discomfort. Even more serious were prostate problems. Mort (aged 64) described a lengthy bout with prostate cancer: "We did watchful waiting for three years and then the cancer started to grow faster, so I had the surgery. They got the cancer, but the chemo and surgery had vile side effects." As he spoke more about his resultant impotence and incontinence, he tearfully added, "I may live another twenty-five to thirty years in diapers, and my sex life is gone."

Women whose hormones were depleting with menopause also described sadness about their loss of sexual capacity because of dryness or pain. Wanda, who had breast cancer and a mastectomy when she was 49, recalled, "I couldn't make love to my husband for so long after that. It wasn't him. It was my discomfort at being mutilated. Even now, I feel that I have lost some sense of my womanhood."

She was not alone. Most of us who have had surgeries have to wonder about their new identity without original equipment. Many reported a post-surgery depression related to posttraumatic stress.

Whatever the physical challenges, it is essential to accept and acknowledge them and make sound accommodations. Adjustments to the more serious health changes may be lengthy and require professional help.

## Work Life

In our careers, we also reach a point when we have to make choices much more carefully. It is no longer true that we will have time, energy, and openness to try out opportunities endlessly. Decisions made during this period are no longer simple. Each time we take an opportunity, we are aware of alternatives that are being lost.

When Roger's latest position ended because of a corporate merger, he was 61 years old. He was quite certain that because "my next career move will likely be the last one," he had to be more careful and thoughtful than he had in the past. One factor he had to weigh was whether he should seek the "crowning" position of his career or try to have more balance in his life. Roger's conundrum—deciding what was best for his work life—is a common one for professionals. As we lose our single-minded focus at work, what is the best choice for both the near and long term?

Sylvia's choice was equally powerful but a bit more direct. A breast cancer scare prompted her to reevaluate how she wanted to spend the time she had left. Although the lumpectomy and biopsy turned out to be negative, she determined that continuing as an account executive at a brokerage house was less important than spending time with her family and friends. She reduced her client load, put in far fewer hours, and let go an opportunity to become a manager.

Three years later, she is pleased with her choices. However, it's evident that she had to let go of her younger woman's dream of being a "big player." The loss of that dream was balanced by her very understandable option of seeking what was most valuable personally.

## Relationships

After an often more tumultuous period for relationships during the midlife transition, most couples settle down into fairly stable relationships. Relationships require us to relinquish the need for and insistence on changing our partners. Accepting (and, hopefully, savoring) who they are represents another type of loss—the fantasy of who they should be. Renée Zellweger's character in the movie *Jerry McGuire* conveys a destructive line when she asserts that she "loves who he could become." To quote Marvin, a client in long-term therapy, "My life improved dramatically when (my

wife) finally gave up on me as her primary remodeling project."
He related that his wife is probably still disappointed that he
didn't live up to what she perceived as his potential. "But now
she seems much more content with the life that we have and my
many imperfections." He added, "Maybe she's even appreciating
some of my shortcomings."

## Relationship Failures

For a few, relationships do not get comfortable or stable. High-
profile breakups such as those of Tiger and Elin Woods, Brad and
Jennifer, Al and Tipper Gore, Arnold Schwarzenegger and Maria
Shriver, and Jeff and MacKenzie Bezos have caused quite a stir
in the media and nervousness about divorce contagion in many
couples' homes. For a host of reasons, during these post midlife
years some decide to have a "do-over." They leave long-standing
relationships to find a new relationship or single lifestyle. We will
explore in depth why both men and women opt for something new
at this stage of life.

Divorce statistics are notoriously inaccurate, primarily because
of how they are calculated. It is generally believed that there is a
50% divorce rate in the United States. Careful examination of the
statistics indicates that the actual numbers are quite lower for most
segments of the population. Despite some statistics that indicate a
slight increase in "gray" divorce after midlife in recent years, the
number of divorces in this age group is actually fairly small. Of
those who do divorce during their autumn years, the most common
reasons are the following:

- A reduced worry about the effects of divorce on children,
  who are now becoming adults
- Financial ability to afford a divorce
- Women's ability to be in the workforce and to both support
  themselves fiscally and experience a new lifestyle
- Acknowledging that a relationship has not been working for
  many years
- An unremitting desire to be with someone else
- A recognition that with the new expectations of longevity
  an unhappy marriage can look a lot worse with a shelf life
  of another 40 years

- Fear of aging, which leads individuals to reject the lifestyle of growing old together in favor of reliving prior stages of life with a new, more youthful partner

Monique married her high school sweetheart at age 20 and at the time really believed that she was in love with her soul mate. Thirty-five years later, their two children were grown and the shift in her mind was obvious. Over the years she came to believe that she had "made a terrible mistake." She had married to escape her loneliness, which originated with a depressed mother and an absent father. Unfortunately, the man she married was in many ways very much like her parents. Her husband was moody, an alcoholic, and frequently away from the family. When he was home, Monique felt even lonelier. Frightened, she was able neither to stand up to him nor to protect her children from a childhood similar to her own.

She said, "I woke up one day and said simply, 'That's it. I can no longer live with regretting all my old mistakes. I am out of here.'" She left within a week and is beginning her new life. To be sure, Monique still seems very lonely and full of regret, but she believes that she is at least facing it for the first time in her life, instead of being controlled by her past.

## Taking the Plunge

By contrast, during these stretch years many people who have been single or out of relationships for many years begin letting go of the freedom of single life, choosing instead to be connected. It is important to note that for both personal and financial reasons even "permanent" connections at this age might involve cohabitation rather than marriage.

Lan was a true career woman. Influenced by—and taking hold of—the opportunities offered by the women's movement of the 1970s, she grew her cosmetology training into a small chain of hair and beauty salons. In the 1990s she was one of the first in her area to open up small nail salons offering manicures and pedicures to wealthy clientele. At 49, Lan owned or co-owned more than a dozen shops. She was honored by business groups in her community and was known well in civic circles. She was making a lot of money and was "living the good life without having to deal with any man at home." During the 25-year period of her entrepreneurial success, she had several relationships with men "but never wanted to settle down or be trapped into a marriage."

Two notable events occurred that gave Lan a new perspective. The first was an invitation by a civic group to run for mayor of the town. The second was her approaching 50th birthday. "You know," she began, "when they ask you to run for mayor, you really have to examine what your life is all about. And then you realize you're fifty, and there are questions about what you've become and what you left behind." When Lan came into therapy, she began by saying, "I don't know if I want to see a male therapist. I am better with women and they understand me better, but my friend [a former client] said I should see you; so here I am."

After exploring with her the possibility of seeing a woman therapist, I asked, "Well, what can I do to help?" Lan began by talking about the impressive successes in her life and then just began crying. Through her sobbing tears, she said that she was becoming aware that she would never be a mother. "I always thought that kids would just be part of my life someday, but I never found a man to parent with and now I'm fifty and it's too late." She claimed to be "Auntie Mame" to her nieces and nephews and loved spending time with them and the families. "I just got so into my work and growing the businesses that I never made space for children or a husband."

Despite her notable success, Lan was becoming aware of the loss and "the hole in my heart" that a baby would fill up. She had sacrificed family for work and now at the pinnacle of her success— running for mayor—was increasingly aware of the price and what she was not going to have in her life.

A few years later, after an unsuccessful bid to be mayor, she met and married a widower with three teens—one with special needs. She is now spending a great deal of time with him and "finally enjoying a normal family life." She misses the excitement of the entrepreneurial life and being a public figure but says, "I can maybe make a difference in [her stepson] Ethan's life."

## Relationships with Family

For most of us who took a more traditional, balanced path of work and family, this age brings less active involvement in our children's lives. While we are in our 40s, 50s, and 60s, most of the children have launched or are leaving home shortly to find their own way in the world. Weekends become less dominated by school and athletics, music, and other extracurricular events. While our children are school-aged, our own social connections are often populated by the parents of our children's peers. As children set out, there is a noticeable change in their parents' world. Although we may welcome the time back for strictly adult pursuits, there is also a sense of loss and time passing. After coaching and watching soccer, basketball, volleyball, gymnastics and water polo for many years, there can be sadness that something of value is over, not to be replicated.

When his daughter played her last soccer game in college, Louis waited only a year before becoming a volunteer referee for a youth league. He said that he liked "being around the kids and keeping in shape running down the field." Although he acknowledged it was different from coaching and going to his daughter's games, "I just couldn't pass a schoolyard on a Saturday with all those parents and kids without wanting to continue being connected to it. It's better than just sitting at home and missing her."

## The Empty Nest

The empty nest is alternatively described as "a feeling that something has been torn from my body" and a sense of "freedom, unlike anything since my twenties—only now I have my own car and some money!" It is not unusual to hear these two statements from the same person on successive meetings. This encapsulates well the seeming contradictory feelings of loss (of a child, of a role, of a parental way of being, of a certainty regarding priorities) and an opportunity to more fully be oneself.

Those who can face the loss and accept the passing of a significant era in life have the best chance of finding a new path—one more relevant to this new stage in life. Like most losses in life, adjusting to the shift is frequently slow and insidious. We do have to mourn the loss of predictability, even while we turn our attention to newer directions.

Some—by choice or necessity—do not get to let go of this role; they quickly become the main parental figure with their grandchildren or caretakers of their aging parents.

## Parents

If individuals have not yet lost their parents, they often do so at this age. We experience this both through their passing or as they enter a new dependency.

Taking care of parents, or simply recognizing their increasing incapacities, can be disquieting in many ways. When our parents increasingly show signs of old age, they become progressively less able to care for us. An aging parent might always remind you that "you'll always be my baby," but the psychological image of a protective adult mom and dad that we hold in our mind dissipates. It may have been decades since we could truly depend on them, but the reality seeps in that we no longer have a strong adult we can go to in times of stress. We are now the competent adults in our families.

Of course, some of us in the post-midlife years never had that kind of protective, caring, supportive parent. The deterioration or death of your parents is a stark reminder to your inner child that we never will have such a parent.

If we become caretakers to our parents, we also have to come to grips with them as dependent, almost as if they were children. Wes said, "I was fine with doing his shopping and paying his bills, and it was one thing to take my dad's driver's license away and become his driver to so many doctor's visits. The thing I just couldn't handle was seeing him in diapers and losing his dignity. He was this rock of a man, veteran of WWII and Korea, union guy, foreman, and now he needs help cleaning himself. I thank my stars that Val [Wes' wife] and Bridget [his sister] are nurses. They don't seem all that troubled by it."

For many boomers, it is a bit of a shock to give up being our parents' children to being our parents' "parents." In collective cultures where care for the elderly is both expected and mandated, this is far less surprising and very much done as duty and out of respect for elders. Losing parents or coping with their frailty and dependence also brings us psychologically closer to inevitable thoughts of our own mortality. When we had children, we were psychologically moved one rung closer to our own transience on the cycle of life. When our parents die or depend on us, we are moved yet another step closer to our own end and a loss of illusion in personal immortality and invincibility. Indeed, when our parents go, we become the oldest generation in our families.

Lloyd's comments resonated with many individuals: "When my mother passed, it was quite sobering to realize that now I was the oldest generation in my family and aside from one cousin, I became the oldest person in my entire extended family. You can't help but reassess how long you're going to be around when you're the old guy."

## Friends

The importance of friends remains great during this period—and the loss of friends is often felt very powerfully. As we will explore further in Chapter 7, the development of friendships is typically more difficult for men at this stage of life. Indeed, in the interviews, many men identified their spouse as their best friend. Almost none of the women did so. Of course this represents both a sex difference in interpreting the question and an underlying truth about male friendships.

> ### BOX 4.1 Men and Their Relationships
>
> There is considerable research that indicates making new friends later in life is much more difficult for men, who often describe their close friends as someone they have known since high school, college, or military days.
>
> Many are like Cal, who said, "I met my truly best friend when we were stationed together in Germany. We lived and died together with deployments and letters from home. We both stood up for (each other) as best man ... godfathers of our oldest ... and even now, whenever we talk, we can pick up on the conversation just like it was yesterday." When asked how often he and Rufus talk, he replied, "Oh, you know, Christmas and maybe a birthday—once, twice a year."
>
> For many men, aside from their wives, their friends are miles away and they have only infrequent conversations. Many men have also relied on their wives to be the family social secretary, so their contacts with other men are often her friends' husbands, who may or may not have much in common. As Wally relates,

> "I teach Spanish for a living. Most of my wife Juanita's friends are in the computer industry. Mostly when we get together, the women talk and the men make a few comments about the sports teams and the kids, but I don't really know what my smart phone capabilities are and some of these guys are designing the next generation of God knows what. Besides, what am I supposed to do, talk about how kids don't want to learn foreign languages anymore?"

Some studies link men's very longevity both to being married and to having close friends. During this stage of life it is vital to develop new connections with people of the same sex, particularly peers our own age.

There are many reasons our circle of friends begins to narrow during this age period. We often lose friends who are parents of our children's friends. We lose friends when long-term colleagues who were also friends retire from work. Some of us begin to experience the death or disability of friends during this period. Those of us who have been divorced, particularly during or after midlife, know only too well that some friends are lost because of allegiance to our ex-spouse, lack of common couples' ground, or fear of contagion. Finally, when adults near retirement some of their social group is likely to relocate to be in more gentle climates, or to be closer to adult children and grandchildren.

The loss of friends creates the need to replenish the group of people close to us. Unfortunately, this is no easy task, and in 2020 it has been complicated with social distancing and the loss of many in-person activities. Social media can be helpful, as are video calls, but they don't completely compensate for the lack of on proximity and shared interests. As one widow commented, "Virtual hugs are better than nothing, but they are no substitute for the real thing." Many others complained of "Zoom fatigue."

## Image and Externals

Among our potential losses are the images we have worked hard to create of ourselves. These are how we wish to be viewed by others or how we define ourselves. Are you what you appear to be? What happens when there are cracks in the image?

We all know that, in our youth-centric culture, looking older is undesirable. Celebrities have always gone to extraordinary lengths to cover up the visage of an aging body. Cosmetic surgery is increasingly common, as are grueling exercise programs, personal trainers, and soft-focus lenses. These are designed to minimize "the ravages of time." Among boomers and even generation Xers, the need for youthful energy and appearance has extended well beyond celebrities. In the past decade, the number of cosmetic surgeries has skyrocketed. Botox injections are routine to erase signs of aging, and it remains a far bigger compliment to say, "You look so young" than "You look so old."

Yet regardless of what we do, our bodies will age. Skin will become less elastic, lines will appear on our faces, and, as the late Nora Ephron[1] pointed out, our necks will divulge our true ages. It is notable that women, even those in positions of power, past a certain age will frequently wear scarves to avoid showing their necks.

We associate youth with vitality, strength, beauty, and other highly regarded values in North American culture. Naturally, as we age, we suffer losses to our younger self-image. These dents in image all involve what Judith Viorst[2] calls "necessary losses." She notes that the fading of youthful beauty is experienced as—and is, in fact—a loss. It represents a personal loss of power and of possibilities. According to Viorst and others, there is mourning to be done for the losses of our youthful, sexier appearance; our energy levels; our vision and hearing; and our dreams of being an ingénue in a hit movie or starting third baseman for the Boston Red Sox, saving the planet, losing those extra pounds, flossing religiously, reading all the great books, or just sleeping through the night without waking up to urinate.

Our roles and the influence of our achievements can also be lost. Among these potential losses are those wonderful external

---

1   Ephron, N. (2006). *I feel bad about my neck and other thoughts on being a woman*. Knopf.

2   Viorst, J. (1986). *Necessary losses: The loves, illusions, dependencies, and impossible expectations that all of us have to give up in order to grow*. Fireside (Simon and Schuster).

definitions that mean so much to individuals as they develop and are often central in one's route to success. Some of us are particularly impacted by the loss or the modification of culturally honored definitions. Cathy has to relinquish her role as the perfect parent; Letty, her standing as the first woman dean at her university; Kazuo, being the one whose patent made his company successful; Keith, being the youngest full colonel during peacetime.

Each of these honors represents significant success, but Keith, at 55, is just another colonel being forced into retirement; Letty has recently stepped down as provost to allow another woman to succeed her; Cathy's children are grown and out of the home; and Kazuo is retired from his company, where new hires don't even know his name. For some, these losses are tragedies; for others, they are opportunities.

## How I Learned to Stop Kvetching About the Losses and Appreciate the New Blessings

That each of our losses comes with built-in opportunities is not always obvious, because they are options we had put aside as unpractical or as having a greater risk of failure. The developmental task of these years is to find, acknowledge, and face those unknowns. As explored in the previous chapter, it's essential for us to decide to face the anxiety of the unknown and eschew the safety and stagnation of the status quo. We will be pushed to do so, because the losses make maintaining the status quo a deteriorating spiral, requiring increasing energy for decreasing gains.

As the major writers in developmental psychology and aging have opined, the road to human development is paved with renunciation. There is no growth, only stagnation and entropy, without letting go of patterns of behavior that have heretofore served us quite well. Just as the infant has to forego the symbiotic bond with mother to explore the world for greater freedom, so must the post-midlife person give up old ways to—hopefully—discover newer and deeper passions for this stage of life. Some of the losses inherent in this process are separations from those with whom we have shared intimacy; others involve the conscious and unconscious losses of earlier definitions that our images of ourselves depend on—our romantic dreams, impossible heroics, and illusions of security and freedom.

To embrace the future, we have to let go of the past, even though it has worked so well for us for so long. It is a lifelong process and is particularly important as we realize that the hourglass of our lives has turned over, and we have lots to do before the sand runs out.

As Jean Piaget[3] theorized, we move from periods of consolidation and stability to transitional stages in which we must challenge the stability and opt for the unknown. These stages offer the opportunity for a richer life full of growth in exchange for the termination of life as we know it. Daniel Levinson[4] writes that during a transitional phase such as the one between midlife and old age, our task is to review and evaluate the past and determine which aspects to keep and which to reject as we consider our future dreams and wishes. Much from the past must be left, rejected, and mourned, while the seeds of the future are being planted.

Perhaps the difference between us and the hermit crab is consciousness. When the crab leaves one shell to find another, there is a period of vulnerability followed by the opportunity to grow in a new protected environment. The crab that stays in its old home will surely neither grow nor survive.

# Refusing to Age

Indeed, one thing seems quite clear. Those youth seekers among this generation—the ones who make every attempt to go back in time, to remain 25 or 35—are potentially the biggest losers. They liked what they were at 35 and want to keep replicating it. They find their partners growing old, and they leave them for younger ones. Their children go away, and they create another family with young children. They don't like their careers, so they start over. Each choice of course has some potential positives, but there are great losses of opportunities to be fully 55 when one insists on remaining 35.

---

3   Piaget, J. (1967). *Biology and knowledge.* Chicago University Press.
4   Levinson, D. J. (with Darrow, C. N., Klein, E. B., & Levinson, M.). (1978). *Seasons of a man's life.* Random House.

# Exercise

Make two columns on a sheet of paper or computer screen. On the left-hand side, take a short inventory of your own losses in the following categories:

- Physical (health, appearance, and abilities)
- Emotional (awareness of feelings and what may be out of tune with you now)
- Spiritual (time outdoors or in nature, meditation, or religious services)
- Work (what is no longer yielding the best results, changes in your official or real role)
- Home and family role (empty nest, young children or boomerang kids at home, and needs of family elders)
- Other losses (death, moves, etc.)

In the right-hand column and opposite the entries of losses, list the new opportunities that you have or could have in each of these categories.

Seriously consider the skills, passions, and desires that you quite appropriately set aside when you were younger and whether they can be recaptured or brought to fruition in new ways.

# chapter five

# Sixty Is the New ~~Forty~~ ~~Fifty~~ Sixty

> *Those who cannot learn from history are doomed to repeat it.*
>
> —George Santayana

What is it like to be approaching signal birthdays like your 50th or 60th? What do you think about being at an age that seems older than you feel? What's it like to have your contemporaries age so? Would you prefer a chance to redo the decade of your 30s or another previous era in your life?

It's not an easy path to maturity. Whether we're approaching our first day in a new grade in elementary school, entering high school, going off to college, starting a career, committing to a relationship, becoming a parent, or retiring, we have concerns that balance or even overwhelm the sense of excitement of doing something new.

Each step into facing the unknown elicits a healthy, useful anxiety. This *existential* anxiety has both a beneficial side, energizing our emotional and psychological growth, and a counteracting side, pulling on us to return to well-known, safe ground, to repeat what we have already done and feels comfortable to us. When 6-year-old Seth is screaming that he hates first grade and wants to go back to kindergarten, he's voicing the prototypical dilemmas of his parents and grand-parents, who know so well how to be 35 but are less certain about embracing 45, 50, and 60.

As part of our interview, we asked people to identify an age they most identify as. These reference ages, described in Chapter 2, were most frequently in the 30s, roughly two thirds their chronological ages. What does this tell us? One of the ways I may cling to my younger self-image is to avoid noticing the incremental shifts in that face in the mirror. If I am shaving the same face each day, then perhaps I do not see myself aging. I can think I am just as good as when I was 35. Most importantly, I know how to be in my 30s. I do that quite well. What I don't know is how to master, or find meaning in, being 60. If I can find a way to stay 30 in my mind—if not in my body—I do not have to face those disturbing unknowns.

Consider the plight faced by Barry, who had a 30-year career as a military officer. He retired to take a lucrative position in indus-try and was quite successful before stepping down and leaving the business to a younger colleague.

Barry was always the hero in his career. He retired as a decorated colonel and later became a successful CEO. He reports modestly, but with justification, that he was loved by his troops and workers and always kept their interests first.

At age 64, he has to face a harsh reality. His military career is over, and although he remained a board member, he is no longer needed for day-to-day work in the company that he served. One would guess that after such success and a long career, Barry would be looking forward to days on the golf course and settling in to enjoy his grandchildren. Yet, when we met, he was looking "desperately" for another challenge, another leadership position in the midst of a recession, because that "retired guy" life does not appeal to him.

Throughout his working life, the world came to him and brought him new jobs and new challenges. In each, he was able to succeed by enhancing his skill set. Barry was "the knight on the white charger," helping everyone else and succeeding personally in the process. He knows well how to be 35 or 40. In fact, the age with which he identifies is 37. What he doesn't know very well is how to focus on his personal internal needs. Although he has mastered growth from the outside in, he doesn't yet know how to grow from the inside out. In a sense, Barry has always considered himself an expendable resource to be used by his wife, children, grandchildren, country, and businesses. Having been the hero for so long, he knows little about how to be the wise elder—a far more appropriate role at this stage of life.

Barry is not alone in being drawn back to the familiar instead of approaching the new challenges that life offers (and the attendant fears). It isn't easy to acknowledge the loss of capacity or the loss of willingness to play the game. However, the alternative is even more daunting. Until we let go of being 30, we cannot begin to deal with the possibilities and challenges of being 50 or older. The progression of time, losses, and age-related challenges is inevitable. Postponing them probably means they will recur, and we will have to face them ultimately, perhaps with less capacity.

## Déjà Vu (Again)

Barry could progress successfully into another venture and lead another company. He has that skill set. He could again be the hero, but what are the personal ramifications? One consequence is that he would not have to refocus his attention on the internal life, his personal shadow, that he has successfully kept underattended while he was out in the world of doing things right and reaping the rewards. The seeds of that inner life and of the passions, skills, and interests that he set aside during his earlier years to achieve success are still there. If they receive the proper attention now, they could grow into something quite important. However, without the proper appreciation and nurturance, they might wither and disappear. Barry's inner needs were left dormant both by conscious design and by unconsciously allowing his laser-like attention to focus on worldly success.

Barry was fortunate. Although he originally entered psychotherapy to get help in dealing with feelings of anxiety and sadness about not having a new work opportunity, he warmed quickly to the understanding that something else might be more important to him. Barry's less developed sides were in the areas of nurturance and art. In therapy, he expressed an increasing need to be able to express his emotional side in creative ways. Another aspect of his life that was under-expressed involved verbal expressions of love for important people in his life. He had always been comfortable expressing love to his wife but was far less so to others, especially his sons. With the therapist's encouragement, he made a conscious effort to reach out to his grown sons and grandchildren and expressed verbally for the first time how much he cared for them.

He reported back with pride that he was not put off by their initial discomfort at his new behavior. He said that he also had to stay on task and express his loving feelings "and reassure them that I was not at death's door." Over time, he discovered that they all became more affectionate with him. He was most happy that when he left them, his sons gave him a hug instead of the usual, near-formal handshake.

## The Trap of Assumed Security

Like Barry, most of us dealing with the reality of aging hearken back to the psychological sense of security in keeping the status quo. Unfortunately, this is a trap at two levels. First, the status quo provides only temporary security before devolving into stagnation or entropy. Second, it keeps us from the age-appropriate challenges that help us break out of our security-oriented rut.

The impact of this psychological trap is to pull us back to redo things we once did so well—I can still shoot the three-point shot, reach the back line, and rush the net, remember trivia on my feet, drink what I please, and stay up all night. I can hop on a plane, fly across the country, make a smashing presentation in the afternoon on the West Coast, return on the red-eye, and be back at work in the morning. Oh, and let's not forget, I'm always ready and eager for lovemaking.

Is it worth accepting that we aren't as energetic, quick, or competitive as we once were if that acceptance gives us a far more well-rounded life? Or maybe the more salient question is whether it's worth practicing that kind of acceptance *before* the first heart attack.

Gus was like many type-A individuals. A hard-driving sales representative, he rose to high ranks from a working-class background. He worked his way through junior college and university night classes and finally earned an MBA in another evening program. He reports that he was the only one in his neighborhood to escape and do really well. At 58, Gus was as motivated and hard driving as he'd been in his 20s. "I worked hard, played hard, drank hard, and ate Big Macs on the run since I was sixteen." Gus's lifestyle choices came to an abrupt halt when he suffered a heart attack while carousing with a prostitute in Las Vegas.

Only after the cardiologist got his attention and told him clearly that the next time would be his last did he alter his lifestyle.

Consider the following questions:

- Do you want to be known for your competence despite a tendency to forget proper nouns here and there?
- Can you make it on time even though it takes you longer?
- Is it okay that you need more frequent bathroom breaks?
- How do you determine your needs to move forward most effectively?
- What will the nature of your personal challenges be at this life stage?

From a developmental/psychological perspective, we are better off facing the tests of our stretch years head-on rather than hiding from them in the safety of our past. That may be more difficult, but the challenges of our post-midlife years provide fertile soil for our optimal growth. This was indicated well by former vice president and Nobel prize winner Al Gore, who responded with a chuckle to Lesley Stahl's announcement of his impending 60th birthday on *60 Minutes*: "Well, first of all, sixty is the new fifty-nine."

## Are You Really Fifty or Sixty?

Like Mr. Gore, you have surely heard or read the opinion that 60 is the new 40, or 50. The premise behind this assertion is our added longevity, and the youth-oriented expectations of these generations have made our age different from the experience of previous generations. It's claimed that when our parents and grandparents were 60, they were older in their ways than the baby boomers who are now hitting the big six-oh. It seems like a compelling assumption.

Let's consider the evidence for this proposition:

- In the 1950s people entered "old-age" homes at the average age of 65. Today's average new residents are older than 80.
- Boomers are healthier than their parents were at this age and expect to live longer.

- The boomer generation's youth-oriented expectation of active lives is still present. Most 45- to 65-year-old interviewees had a reference age in their 30s. We probably do feel and act younger than our forebears.

As generations, the boomers and gen Xers have been extremely youth oriented, but are we truly functioning as 40-year-olds when we reach 60? More important, do we really want to? Perhaps it's one of those "it seemed like a good idea at the time" notions that turns out to be less positive than it initially seems.

From the perspectives of psychological development, maturity, and satisfaction, trying to be 40 when we are 60 might not be such a good idea. If we try to redo our 30s when we are twice that age, there is a chance we will do neither well. Indeed, how can you move on to the new you when you are clutching the old you as if for dear life?

## Trying for a Redo

It is likely that people who keep acting 40 when they are 60 are locked into a developmental lag that has as a primary goal avoiding the challenges and fears of their stretch years. When he was in his late 50s, Chet's youngest son went off to college. Having been a very involved father to his three children, he faced dealing with an empty nest and living with his wife of almost 30 years without the buffer of their children. He opted almost immediately to divorce and marry a woman with three younger children. In his words,

> You know, I know how to be a father and to be with kids and do school and soccer games and all that stuff, and I'm very good at it … I just didn't want to face Chris and me getting old together and having to be around sixty-year-olds. I know I must seem like a middle-aged cliché to leave my wife for a younger woman, but by keeping in shape and with a little help from pharmaceuticals, I can keep up with her and the kids and I won't have to get old so fast.

Chet chose to be less mature and to avoid the transition to older age. He is not alone in choosing the presumably safer, known course over the fear of the unknown. In some ways, he has been successful in making his 60s a repeat of his 40s, but there is a growing downside for him:

> I still see Chris, and I miss her a lot. I can't say that
> Lisa really understands me in some basic ways. It's
> like she knows a part of me, but Chris really knew all
> the parts, and she accepted them. I worry now that
> Lisa will find out about my less virile sides, and be
> disappointed. And I really miss my old friends. When
> we get together, some say they envy me, the younger
> woman and the sex, but I envy them more with their
> new perspectives on life.

As Chet and many others are beginning to understand, 60 is not all that bad. It offers new challenges and opportunities for growth. Indeed, if we're doing it right, 60 is the new 60—not the new 40 or the new 80. Opting to act younger or older will likely come with a substantial psychological price.

Of course, we're not the first generations to try to minimize our age. America has long honored youth over age-related wisdom, although we do tend to prefer a father figure when it comes to presidents and CEOs. Ours might be the first generation in which being seen as younger is less humorous and more imperative. The boomers may still enjoy seeing Joan Baez, Pat Benatar, Bob Dylan, the Jerry Garcia-less Grateful Dead, and Cyndi Lauper out of nostalgia (if not the current quality of the music), but there isn't as much room for a premier comedian like Jack Benny, who perpetually celebrated his 39th birthday.

## Appearance or Essence?

It seems that there is a discrepancy between looking younger, feeling younger, and being younger. In most Western cultures, a younger appearance is equated with looking better. Because of this, many focus on the facade. Flourishing antiaging industries would make Ponce de León drool with envy. The incidence of cosmetic surgery more than doubled between 1990 and the first decade of the 21st century and its growth is accelerating. According to the 2019 annual plastic surgery procedural statistics report, "There were 17.5 million surgical and minimally invasive cosmetic procedures performed in the United States in 2017, a two percent increase over 2016."[1] Americans spent between $16 and 17 billion on such procedures in 2018. In 2019, people in the 45 to 65 age range accounted for one half of those surgeries. In addition, there are a host of specialized exercise and diet programs, skin potions, anti-wrinkle creams, meditation techniques, medications, and self-help programs that are also supposed to do the job. The big business of a more youthful appearance assails us with print, electronic, and online media advertisements.

At 56, Rita is willing to try all these methods to keep herself "in the game." Divorced by her choice from her second husband after 20 years of marriage, she has dedicated the past 5 years to getting her body to look more like it did when she initially met him as a 30-year-old. Since she turned 50, she's had several cosmetic surgeries to "correct" her crow's feet, lips, stretch marks, and the effects of gravity on her breasts. In addition to surgeries, she has twice had Botox injections. When we first spoke, she was discussing some newer procedures in the upcoming months. In addition to the surgeries, she was using skin treatments, massages, and exercises for several hours daily. Her diet was carefully measured by a personal coach/dietician.

Rita described her reason for leaving her husband, "He was just too old in his appearance and attitude. ... He seemed happy to be a grandfather to his daughter's [from his first marriage] children." She added, "I need to be around someone more youthful and fun-loving." She has consistently dated men in their late 30s and early 40s. Her current boyfriend is her former trainer and, like her, is a health food and exercise aficionado. She laughed, "I am that cliché, a true 'cougar,' and I have no intention of stopping."

For Rita, the goal was not to be a post-midlife woman. She was dedicated to reliving the earlier years of her life. From her self-description, she seemed happy doing so. In a quieter moment however, she admitted, "I know my friends think I'm foolish, but I don't relish the idea of being an old woman, alone in the world except for dozens of cats. I have no great ambition," she adds, "I just want to have fun."

---

1   https://www.plasticsurgery.org/documents/News/Statistics/2019/plastic-surgery-statistics-full-report-2019.pdf

# When I'm 64

Not everyone desires a return to the halcyon days of their young adulthood. Maggie (aged 59) stated, "Don't get me wrong. I loved my twenties and thirties. They were glorious, mostly, but I have no desire to revisit them."

Carmen declared, "Sometimes, I miss the romance, excitement, and fear of trying to find my handsome soul mate, but even if he walked in today, I wouldn't trade in my twenty-fifth-anniversary husband. He's bald, out of shape, and less interested in physical activity than I'd like, but he's always coming up with new ways to love me."

What's compelling about Carmen's notion is that redoing her successes at twenty or thirty would simply be a replay, with a diminishing return. Why do something again when you can try for the excitement (and the fears) of the novel challenge?

Carmen's new challenges involve exploring anew her spirituality, focusing on relationships with friends and family, and a small home-based arts and crafts business.

It's not just how we see ourselves. The challenges of age and appearance can be imposed on individuals in a discriminatory way. Although Greg doesn't look 60, his opportunities to continue on a familiar path are limited by his chronological age.

A successful entrepreneur for 3 decades, he finds himself at 60 with a diminished investment portfolio, few opportunities in his area of expertise, and a track record dominated by a business failing in the 2020 economic recession. Although he understands that he may well have an opportunity for a new venture in his future, he is almost desperate in his attempt to continue to operate as he has historically: "I'd just go in and push it to the limits, 24/7, until we sell our creations to a network or media group." Greg may in fact have another big hit in him, but he doesn't have the energy or capacity to abuse his body with sleepless nights and irregular meals the way he did as a teenager. He acknowledged that he is not healing quickly from a pulled muscle, has digestive problems and an enlarged prostate, and has been diagnosed with sleep apnea.

Age has become a limiting factor for Greg, in part because of social factors and in part because even as he looks forward, he is applying backward methods for success that will minimize his likelihood of success.

Javier, like Greg, took a hit to his wallet and ego when the company he built and served as president for was merged with a large publicly traded company. Although he received a generous severance package, he had to adjust to being out of work at age 63 with no immediate prospects. He took some time to consider his options and then went looking for a new position.

A year later, when offered a position in a related industry, Javier faced a difficult decision. He could downsize his lifestyle or he could take the position and a substantial salary. On the one hand, he could do what he had successfully done before. He was confident that it would turn out well financially. On the other, he was not excited about doing what he had done for the prior 35 years. He was longing for something different, "something more meaningful." A part of him yearned for new challenges that didn't have anything to do with building another company.

Javier was facing the quandary of dealing with being 60-something or trying to remain 40-something. The question he was struggling with was both philosophical and pragmatic. To stop being a high-income earner meant that he would have to significantly alter his family's lavish lifestyle. The dilemma for Javier was which loss (lifestyle or self-growth) he was willing to accept. After many lengthy discussions with his wife and children, he opted to forego the offer from the new company.

## Same Jewel, New Setting

By contrast, Brenda is pushing new limits as she approaches 60. She is approaching new possibilities with skills that are age appropriate.

When Brenda was 19 years old, she was already pregnant with her second of four children. Although she was married to her high school sweetheart at the time, she felt like a single mom. "I had full responsibility for the kids and a low-paying job running a cash register at (the local supermarket). Me and Billy were both going to night school after our jobs and just switched off the child care most weeks and my mom helped when she could."

Brenda completed school as a licensed practical nurse (LPN) and later went to nursing school. She and Billy divorced in their late 20s, and she was left with the childcare and full-time work. Despite all that, she saw to it that her children succeeded in school, and "all four went to college, which was my dream for them." She married again at 35 and took on two stepchildren. When she was 55, her husband retired with a reasonable pension after 35 years with the county. He got involved in a community action committee and developed a fundraising plan to help send local children to summer camps and then college on scholarships.

Brenda retired soon after and began to look for her own passion. At first, she tried to join her husband, but she found the work less satisfying than nursing. She also dabbled in quilt-making, scrapbooking, hands-on grandmothering, and a few other expected projects. She related, "Nothing really grabbed me. I mean, they were all okay, but not very exciting for me." Asked to focus on what she had not been able to do when she became a mother and nurse, she quickly replied, "I wanted to be a lawyer when I was a little girl, but you know in those days, there weren't many girls who went to law school, and I was always broke." At 57, she began studying for the LSAT and found her passion returning. Now as a 1st-year law student looking forward to her 60s, she indicates, "I don't know if I'll ever be a practicing attorney, but nobody loves my classes as much as I do; I love learning the law and all it means." She also confided, "I like the books and the studying partly because I don't have to take care of anybody else. This is all for me, and I do love that."

Brenda is still nurturing her husband, four children, two stepchildren, and 10 grandchildren, "but for the first time in my life, I am giving to them on my terms."

## Be Your Age: Where Is Lamont Cranston (the Shadow) When We Need Him?

Why is it important to be 50 or 60? Struggling with the human condition by meeting the challenges of our life stage is a pathway to spiritual and psychological growth. This doesn't mean resigning ourselves to walk, talk, or think like grandpa when we turn a certain age. It's simply beneficial to face the natural tests offered by aging: focusing more on our inner lives, pursuing long-lost skills or desires, and opting out of the rat race and into our personal emotional triathlon.

Satchel Paige, the legendary pitcher in baseball's former Negro Leagues and then a major league performer at an age when his contemporaries were long retired from athletic prowess, once opined, "You don't quit playing because you get old. You get old because you quit playing."

To modify Mr. Paige's sage words somewhat, you don't have to stop playing, but you might enjoy a new game or a new way of playing the old ones. Carl Jung[2] theorized that as we age, we are better able to explore the "shadow"—his term for the underdeveloped parts of the self. Psychologist Diane Ehrensaft[3] indicates that the discovery may be somewhat gender related; that is, the characteristic shadow challenge and growth for women (a refocus on the *doing* parts of life) are different from those for men (the *being* aspects).

What are these new challenges for the post-midlife years?

## Common Themes

Regardless of a host of individual differences, some issues are familiar to nearly all of us after midlife. Entire chapters in this book are dedicated to some of these. For example, the inevitable losses we face were delineated in Chapter 4. Later chapters address shifts in relationships; financial, retirement, and vocational considerations; the influence of time and time management; mortality; and spiritual yearnings.

It may be easy for 20-somethings to put things off for tomorrow and 30-somethings to postpone personal gratification to support their growing families, but during the stretch years we need to make such decisions far more consciously. As we become increasingly aware of our mortality, we realize far more poignantly that any choice we make now automatically eliminates alternatives. Thus, if we opt to be 40 when we are 60, we need to understand that we forfeit being 60 to do that.

## I'm an Adult. Now What?

How might we miss out on the opportunity to make these age-60 decisions thoughtfully? It's a deceptively simple question: "Now

---

2   Jung, C. G. (1933/2001). *Modern man in search of a soul.* Routledge.

3   Ehrensaft, D. (1987). *Bringing in fathers: The reconstruction of mothering.* The Free Press.

that I'm all grown up, what do I want to be?" For many of us this is the first time as adults that we get to visit that particular query.

The apparent yet deceptive simplicity of the question makes it harder to hold in mind for many reasons. It requires that we slow down and give ourselves a chance to wonder about and ponder our current goals. Doing this requires that we review our life choices and explore what we might do differently. It also demands that we explore what aspects of the status quo we want to relinquish to opt for more novel ways of being in the world. This is often surprisingly quite anxiety provoking. It may require that we experiment with alternatives, some of which may not work out as well as we had imagined.

Tammy married in her mid-20s and by the time she was 35 had three children. A woman with "tireless energy," she was able to hold down a full-time executive position and be the primary caretaker for her growing family. This went well until she was 40 and had a series of setbacks. Her company consolidated its management, and she was left reporting to a man she disrespected and disliked. No matter how hard she tried, "he held me down and passed me over each time a promotion or even bonuses came around. Mel [her husband] was supportive, especially when he took up being the primary cook and cleaner at home, but he just couldn't make up for the way I was feeling."

She described a midlife crisis that began with her high school reunion:

> I went back to Atlanta and my twenty-fifth reunion. I probably shouldn't have done it, but I did a lot of comparisons with my former classmates. At some time during the weekend, I had a few drinks and was dancing with my high school boyfriend. He was a good dancer then and still was very smooth. We went out to the parking lot and had a few hits of marijuana and I kissed him in his 'Vette.' I came to my senses a little while after that and declined his invite to come back to his room, but the whole thing really troubled me and made me wonder about my whole life, job, marriage, kids, everything. By the time I was on the plane coming home, I felt like I was in a freefall. What did I want? Who was I? Was I really questioning my whole life?

Within 13 months of her return, her mother passed away. Tammy resigned her position in her company, took a new job with a former boss in a small start-up firm, bought a brand-new Jaguar (her "dream car"), and was hospitalized with a debilitating illness. She said, "The work was hard, but at least I didn't feel suppressed, and I just threw myself into making it a success and let all those other questions go out of my mind—until now." Now 55, she says the questions from that weekend have reemerged:

> Did I really want to be with my ex from high school? What would my life have been like if I were the wife of a blue-collar guy who was a great dancer but had little ambition beyond owning his family's supply business? What would my life be if I hadn't gone off to Vandy and got my masters at Chicago? Was I happy in my marriage and with my family? What is my life all about anyhow? Do I like working, and what will I do when my husband retires from his teaching job and I retire? I started to wonder what I would do with my time if I was not working. I never had any real hobbies or anything like that.

Tammy became depressed and was prescribed antidepressant medications. She decided it was time to be in therapy. When she came for treatment, her opening statement was, "I am either falling apart or going through menopause and facing an empty nest." As treatment continued, she began to explore a number of issues around her desires in life, especially questions about the meaning of her life. As she did so, her depression dissipated and she began to think more about what she wanted from Mel, from her children, and from herself. She also set a reachable goal for her work accomplishments.

Tammy's story has its unique elements, but she was experiencing many of the concerns of the generation as a whole. She needed to adjust to losing her dreams at work and her mother's passing. She had to come to grips with a family growing older and her desired relationship with her husband, and she had to reconsider her past romantic fantasies. To find more meaning in her life, she had to explore what was best for her now and in her future, rather than what had always been her way of doing things.

Two phases are universally encountered during these years. We can consider the 1st decade (45 to 55) of this period the late summer–early fall season. During this time span we rediscover our personal history, figure out what we've left undone, and address these concerns to consolidate our gains. In the latter decade (56 to 65), the "autumn" decade, it is best to use our resources to plan for and head off in new directions, finding the shadow sides of our life and discovering fulfillment in pursuing the aspects of self that are most precious and/or less developed.

One of the most prominent results from our survey was how individual the aging process was during this transitional period. Although we could easily measure general trends across the boomer and Xer generations, each person had a personal trajectory. So, although the actual stages were consistent, their timing was related to how individuals managed prior life stages.

## Individual Distinctiveness

Contrasting his life at 55 to that of his late 30s, Nobu said, "I am reasonably energetic, far more patient, less competitive, more sensitive to others, and even smarter about my choices." Mary Ann, in the midst of menopause at age 51, stated, "At times, when the hormones are really low, I am achy and old and my mind is like mush, but most of the time I feel pretty good and accomplished." She confides that she can't wait to be through with "the change" so she can be like her sister Marilyn, 8 years her senior, "who is truly soaring." A new grandmother, Marilyn has begun a small thriving business in her home and is on the road to financial security.

## Personal Uniqueness

Although some of the issues that we encounter between 45 and 65 are universal, the most important tests are our personal challenges for success. To a large extent, each new transition is regulated by how well prior developmental stages and transitions have been surmounted.

Even at 55, Lois is dealing internally with unresolved aspects of her adolescence. This manifests in an almost knee-jerk negative reaction to anyone she perceives as an authority figure. Because of this, her career path has come up against several premature ceilings. In addition, her personal relationships have been volatile. Lois can be as angry about something that happened 30 years ago as she is about something she perceived as a slight that happened 5 minutes ago.

For Lois, and many others who have some of their psyche locked into prior conflicts, the success of her post-midlife transition will be impacted by her capacity to work through and overcome some of those unresolved "adolescent" conflicts. Each new transition stage creates an opportunity to revisit the misfortunes of the past and to repair them in the present. Lois was finally able to assess the impact of those prior developmental breakdowns, contain her adolescent insecurities, and overcome them in psychotherapy.

What will mark your personal echoes from the past and yearned-for future directions? What parts of yourself will you emphasize? Which parts deserve less attention?

If we've focused our lives on doing things right and successive accomplishments, these years may be the time to reset our vision on the *being* aspects of our lives. If our past has been focused on the *being* aspects, *doing* might dominate our future. Finding fulfillment involves finding and exploring those aspects of our lives that we left underdeveloped.

Do you have an artistic or nurturing side that has been fallow? Has caretaking overwhelmed your desire to find out what potential you have for business success? Is there a career that has always intrigued you but that you haven't yet pursued?

If you've given up a goal earlier in life as impractical, now may be the ideal time to try it. Maybe for the first time in life, you can afford to pursue this dream. Perhaps you have gone as far as you can in your chosen pursuits and now is the time to begin a whole new challenge. Have you decided that it's finally your time and that others' needs will be more secondary or that you've done enough for yourself and now is the time to give back?

Whatever our personal goals, they are colored by unfinished business from our past and our unique ways of going through life.

## Trailing the Crowd

What are the implications of being "a late bloomer" for these years? Unlike Javier, who was running a major company while in his early

30s, Nick describes himself as "the last guy on the block to do anything." He spent 3 years after high school doing odd jobs around his
neighborhood, then went into the Coast Guard, and finally went to
college on the GI Bill in his mid-20s. He married later than his friends,
only starting to truly date when he was over 30. Now at 55, he has two
children who are not close to leaving home. He joked, "My fifteen-
year-old daughter might experience the empty nest before I do."

Having done everything in life at later ages than his cohort,
and still living in the neighborhood in which he grew up, Nick is
likely to deal with the issues of being 55 or 65 at an older age. His
trajectory may be similar, but the speed at which he arrives at each
goal is quite different from his "whiz kid" peers.

In understanding ourselves and our peers, it's essential to consider personal relevance as paramount. As we eschew our familiar,
well-beaten paths, each of us may look toward a unique, less traveled one. For Roland, a tradesman his entire life, being in his 50s
meant that he finally had enough free time to fulfill a dream to be
in a rock and roll band. He began with a new guitar and advanced
lessons. At this time, he is enjoying his new band with a couple of
friends and "[their 42-year-old] 'kid' drummer."

JoEllen spent 20 years in her position as a tech writer. At 48, she
decided to follow her passion to become a marriage counselor. She
returned to school part time for her master's degree and at age 55
earned her license to finally do the work she felt she "was made for!"

# Conclusion

To take to heart Santayana's observation about the dangers of repeat-
ing history, we do not need to reexperience or reinvent our personal
histories. Instead, we need to use our history to invent a new future.
It's a great start if we consider our prior decisions as right for their
time. Should we choose to simply stay in our long-term comfort
zone, we will stagnate and lose opportunities for new growth. The
new question is what is right for us now?

There are some benefits to dealing with life as we age. As the late
singer-songwriter John Prine observed,[4] older trees are stronger and

---

4   Prine, J. "Hello in There." https://www.google.com/search?client=
firefox-b-1-d&q=prine+hello+in+there+lyrics

older rivers get wilder. Similarly, the late Robert Mondavi frequently observed that wines from old vines are more mature and more complex. So it should be for people. There is great advantage to us in meeting the challenges of our 50s and 60s rather than continuing to travel the route of our 30s or early 40s.

# Exercises

Take some time to jot down on paper or on your computer answers to the following questions. You may find it additionally useful to refine and enhance your memories by reconnecting with others who shared the time.

- What do you consider the best times of your life? What were the most troubling?
- What made these times special? What challenges were you meeting during these times?
- What skills were you bringing to these challenges? Were they physical? Emotional? Problem solving?
- What is similar between these times and skills and your present time and capacities?
- What do you see as the biggest issue you have to confront at your current age?
- What have you tried to date in order to make progress on this?
- Which of your previous skills can you use? Which are now unavailable?
- What new skills, understandings, and emotional capacities would be useful?
- If you assume that you made the right decisions earlier in life, what are the right decisions for this life period?

# chapter six

# Relationships After Midlife

*What a wretched lot of old shriveled creatures we shall*
*be by-and-by.*
*Never mind—the uglier we get in the eyes of others,*
*the lovelier we shall be to each other;*
*that has always been my firm faith about friendship.*

—George Eliot

Our interviewees and the literature are clear. For most individuals in the 45- to 65-year range, relationships take on increasing prominence in life satisfaction and distress. Primary relationships are highlighted and friendships shift as the career push recedes from the energy apex and children leave home.

## Primary Relationships

Despite the significance of parents, children, siblings, extended family members and friends in our lives, the most significant relationship in most of our lives is usually the one with our partners. Unlike our affiliations with blood relatives or adoptive parents, our primary relationship is one that we chose.

# Bifocals

When there are two people at the table and there used to be more, they get to look at each other with a new lens. When shelter-in-place took hold during the 2020 COVID-19 pandemic, enhanced togetherness or enforced isolation intensified relationships and interpersonal stress. Some couples were thrust into a 24/7 presence with partners for the first time. Others were forced into long-term separations. Adjustments had to be made.

In general couples and individuals reported that things that were good in their relationships got better and things that were problematic got worse in an accelerated time frame. For many, the forced closeness and seclusion from others led to a reassessment of the relationship.

Pandemic influences may have intensified the experience of being a couple again after years of being a family, but many in the post-mid-life age range get to view anew what holds them together and what might increase distance.

## When Things Are Good

For some couples more time together leads to new discovery or a heightened sense of the connection that originally brought them together. Betty spoke of a new appreciation and love for her long-time partner: "I always thought that Brian was a good choice for me. He was kind and unflappable," she laughed. "I'm the one who goes into an uproar, but now, I've been finding that he does feel things deeply too. He just needs some time to tell me about it. So now that we have more time, I get to hear what he's all about, and he's even better than I thought." Brian replied, "Well, B knows I love her, but she tends to fill up the airwaves, so I didn't get much chance to think about things when she and the kids were goin' at it. Now the house is quieter and peaceful, so I can tell her more what I think about. It's never been a problem for me, because I'm usually the quiet one, but this is better."

## Growing Old Together

For many, the idea of growing older and staying together is more than just a romantic ideal or religious imperative: The relationship with their life partner is the pathway to pleasure, a way to find meaning and a place to flourish together and separately.

Many interviewees talked about their partners as someone they needed no pretense or posturing with. Some admired a partner's ability to "let go without leaving." They enjoyed the shared history of the family they created and frequently noted that agreeing on so many issues made life much easier. In addition, at least for men, long-term marriage has been linked to health and longevity.

One factor, described well by Elise, seemed to make a big difference in keeping long-term marriages healthy and growing during this period. She acknowledged that she had "finally stopped seeing Saul as a remodeling project and just tried more to enjoy him for who he was." They both claimed that it made a huge difference in marital satisfaction.

## Growing Apart

For others, the view across the breakfast table is disconcerting. As the more functional aspects of the relationship, such as parenting and building careers, diminished in importance, a loss of interest in their partners was exposed. For them the highlighted feeling is disconnection. The good news is that by the time most couples have managed the midlife transition that precedes this phase of life they've made the decision about staying together happily, staying together as the best option, or ending the relationship. The task of the stretch years is to learn how to deepen relationships and to come to terms with what makes for more profound happiness and meaning.

However, some couples continue to struggle with their long-term discontent. Wayne "discovered" that his primary interest in Diane was as a mother to their children.

> Don't get me wrong; she was a great mom. She still is, even with the kids gone, but she's never been interested in sharing much with me or in intimacy. Since the kids left, she's volunteered as a teacher at the church school. I think if she could, she'd choose to be a nun. I tried to get her to go to counseling with the priest and a professional marriage counselor, but she's just not that interested in adult relationships, at least with me.

Similarly, Malia reported, "Once the kids left, the house seemed cavernous. So, I went out and got a job, and now I have an interest in a man at work. He makes me feel young and attractive, and for the first time in years I look forward to seeing someone who is not anything like Brett. I think I only married him because he'd be a good provider and husband, and now I want to have some excitement."

Although Wayne and Malia both divorced their partners after long marriages, their issues and decisions are more characteristic of people in the midlife transition than is common between 45 and 65 years of age. In fact, Wayne married another woman within 10 months of his divorce. He laughed when he said, "I hope there's nothing to astrology. My new wife has the exact same birthday as Diane."

One impact of being secluded together during the pandemic was that some couples, who already felt discontented, began describing a sense of feeling trapped. When this was accompanied with anxiety, depression, and alcohol consumption, the discomfort has led to breakups and even domestic violence.

## You're Not the Girl/Boy I Married

There's an old joke about why men and women are unhappy in marriage. Women are unhappy because they expect their husbands to change, and they don't. Men are unhappy because they expect their wives to stay the same, and they don't. During the course of a long relationship, events, situations, and people mature and shift. Sometimes the changes are close to what a partner desires. Other times, it goes in the opposite direction, but the behavior isn't as much a problem as the discrepancy between the behavior and personal expectations. In every marriage, there is more than one subjective relationship. How you feel about and experience your partner is inevitably influenced by your own beliefs, values, perceptions, and expectations.

In many cases, the person with whom we fell in love and married represented more about an image, or projection, held in our minds of a proper partner than specific characteristics about the person per se. When we are in long-term relationships, those often unconscious, images progressively give way to reality. For fortunate individuals, the real person is as or more lovable than the romantic fantasy. However, that is not always the case.

Indeed, it is especially those aspects of romantic endearment early in a relationship that may become most troubling later. His "spontaneity" that once was so attractive, becomes in time experienced by her as "impulsivity and irresponsibility." This occurs without any change in his behavior. Similarly, her "gift for organization and neatness" later becomes seen by him as a "rigid and controlling." This evolution in judgment is far more influenced by expectation than actual behavior. As the discrepancy between expectation and reality widens, satisfaction decreases.

When we realize that our partners are not the persons who resided in our heads, we engage them in a power struggle—to get them to be what we hope they will be—in short, to become our fantasy of a man or woman, instead of the less than perfect real person who is sharing our bed.

These power struggles and discrepancies cycle throughout a relationship and can be more evident when one spouse interrupts the status quo by being drawn to new endeavors or insights.

What does it mean to my partner when I have the urge to find myself anew (or for the first time)? What happens to my marriage when I decide to leave my current position and go back to school to learn new skills or seek a new career? What are the implications when my partner decides that the answer is a new religion or a different political party, one that is very difficult for me to accept?

Paul, a 51-year-old business owner, decided to sell his business and seek out new adventures in the nonprofit sector. This entailed retraining and a sharply reduced income for several years. Not only was his wife not consulted in the decision, but her status and lifestyle were threatened to be sharply curtailed by what she called "his sudden madness." The resulting renegotiation of their relationship's unspoken agreements took almost 3 years before they could successfully compromise.

When Denise turned 50, she felt a renewed calling to the religion of her childhood. Her husband (aged 58) was startled that she would go off and abandon him and was quite vociferous about his negative feelings about the particular church, often referring to it as a "cult."

Denise's devotion to her religion and spiritual matters was likely very positive for her, but it was not something that could include her husband. Instead, he felt rejected, hurt, and angry at her desertion of him. When she committed to a significant tithe, it seemed to him a potential threat to his anticipated retirement age, and he gave her an ultimatum, demanding that she choose between her church and the marriage.

# Divorce

Not every couple works out the relational fissures during midlife. For those who don't, there is a post-midlife phenomenon called the "30-year divorce." What is particularly interesting about post-midlife divorces is that women frequently generate them, and they often come as a surprise to their husbands.

Some of these women report opting for a less fettered, single life, others for passion and romance with a new male or female "soul mate." Others talk about conflicts or resentments they have had for decades that were unresolved either because they carried the conflict inside expecting their partners to realize it was there or because he disregarded her numerous attempts to inform him.

Men at this age tend more than women to depend on being in an ongoing relationship, and for that reason are less likely to initiate divorce. Men who do instigate divorce after many years of marriage are primarily those who are still working out their unresolved midlife or earlier issues. Worrying about aging and maintaining a fantasy about staying youthful themselves, they are often drawn to a much younger partner. Failure to face the fears of their current age and stage of life propels them retroactively into prior stages and holds them in a long-term psychological status quo. Such a commitment to redoing a previously successful stage of life may temporarily reduce their fears of the unknown, but it only postpones them.

The major reasons given by women for a divorce in the stretch years are physical or emotional abuse, infidelity, addictions, or taking out a new lease on life. Some, for example, reported "falling out of love" or "loving, but not being in love" as the reason for leaving. The latter group often focused more on the fault of their partners than on their own complicity. Divorces are more common for those who have been divorced previously.

It is predicted that people currently in the 45–65 age range are going to experience an increase over previous generations in post-midlife divorces for a number of social reasons:

- We have learned to focus on personal happiness and have a reduced sense of obedience and duty.
- Women of these generations are less financially dependent on their husbands.

- Our added longevity means that we may be with our spouse for another 30 to 40 years. Forty years of anticipated unhappiness is daunting, especially compared with a new beginning with someone else.
- Because as a group we married initially at older ages, we get to that critical decision point later.
- Problems like depression and a financial downturn may build during these post-midlife years and contribute to wanting to leave a bad situation.
- Comfortable career and family roles along with other external reasons to stay together are lost.
- Divorce is more acceptable and easier to obtain in this generation than prior ones.

# The Divorce Process

Separation and divorce are lengthy processes, during which individuals progress from being married to being divorced to being single again. Regardless of the reasons for the divorce, there is typically a period of mourning, if not of the person, then of the dream and expectations of a kind of life. Elisabeth Kübler-Ross's stages of grief[1] (denial, anger, bargaining, depression, and acceptance) over the loss of a loved one map pretty well with grief over the loss of a marriage.

How do you deal with all the anger, sadness, hurt, and fear to move ahead as a single person?

When Michelle first came into therapy, it was about 3 months before her divorce became final. Her husband of 27 years had betrayed her with affairs through much of their married life. Ultimately, he chose to leave her for a much younger woman within a year of losing his job and their youngest leaving for college. When I first met her, she was furious with him and to some extent with men in general. She repeatedly said, "I really believed in 'happily ever after,'" and explained, "I know it's the best for both of us ultimately. After a while I couldn't trust him and living that way was miserable, but I still feel like I am marred somehow, you know damaged goods with scars that are ready to show if a new guy gets too close."

---

1   Kübler-Ross, E., & Kessler, D. (2014). *On grief and grieving: Finding the meaning of grief through the five stages of loss.* Scribner.

A year later, Michelle was feeling somewhat differently. She spent the year focusing on herself and her personal needs. She took part in activities that she previously eschewed because her ex didn't like them. She made some good friends and found greater satisfaction in her work. She felt less like "damaged goods" than a woman who might well find happiness in another relationship. In fact, after a few false starts on online dating sites, she was considering going out with a man she met through mutual friends. She described the prospect as "exciting and scary."

Although that first date didn't turn into a relationship, she felt a great sense of accomplishment and was pleased about her own experience. She pursued what was for her an active social life, and 2 years later she became involved in a "very satisfying" longer-term relationship.

## It's Just a Matter of Time

Some couples report that the relationship was just long dead, and the divorce or separation was merely the obituary notice. It's not uncommon for couples in chronically unhappy marriages to wait until the children are grown before instituting a divorce, believing that a divorce at that time will have less impact on the children. Often that is an accurate assumption, but, as psychotherapists and marriage counselors know well, divorce can hurt adult children, too. Divorce can provide relief and an opportunity to grow separately for couples who agree on the need for it, especially if they part amicably and without important secrets.

When Bernadette and Phillip divorced, they continued to live under the same roof for almost 2 years. They described themselves as "friends" and praised each other's parenting. They cited financial reasons for not separating physically, but it also served them psychologically to separate slowly. When they finally sold their home, they moved into apartments in the same neighborhood. Even after beginning romantic relationships with others, they kept in close contact through more than just the children.

## Traumatic Breakups

If affairs were used to cope with unsatisfying marriages, the adjustment to a post-divorce lifestyle may take longer. Marriage counselors and couples therapists generally believe that although the normal run of couples work is about 2 or 3 months, the amount of weekly therapy time grows to 1 to 3 years if an affair has occurred.[2] Because an affair and other forms of betrayal impact our ability to trust, it takes a long time to be able to be vulnerable again in our marriages or new relationships.

## Financial Fallout

Divorce may leave emotional scars, regrets, and a need to quickly learn a host of new skills. Two years out of a divorce after a 25-year marriage, Theresa said, "Basically I am still a babe in the woods when it comes to money. My ex took care of everything from taxes to bill paying to making large purchases. When I bought my new car at fifty-five, it was the first one I bought on my own." There are other financial challenges in her future. She is expected to make a proportional contribution to her youngest children's college expenses, and her income is limited.

Although the divorce settlement provided for Theresa to get her master's degree, her job as a career counselor pays less than $70,000 per year, a low figure for her San Francisco cost of living. Furthermore, with the pandemic crisis, she received no cost-of-living raise this year and is threatened with a cut in salary due to the economic downturn. "Sometimes," she says, "I wonder why I instituted the whole divorce thing in the first place. The grass looked greener over here, but I didn't realize that a lot of the greenery was weeds."

Her experience is not unique. In many ways, divorce is the most damaging financial downturn for everyone concerned.

## New Relationships

Even for those who had a problematic marriage, it's common to reconnect in a new primary relationship soon after divorce. According to Elizabeth Enright, a writer for AARP's magazine, more than 75% of women in their fifties found a new significant love relationship within 2 years. Eighty-one percent of men in their 50s did

2   Shapiro, J. L., & Patterson, T. (2018). *Real-world couple counseling and therapy*. Cognella.

the same. In fact, 26% of all interviewees in her study were dating before their divorces were final.[3]

## The Post-Midlife Single World

Pedro, whose wife left him and their children and home "suddenly" is now 4 years into his separation and is just beginning to see some financial stability. He has also just begun to date using a couple of online services. He reports that dating is as anxiety provoking as it was when he was a teenager—a common experience of divorced people. Basically, they have the dating skills they had when they met their ex-spouses; of course, those skills are 25 to 30 years out of date.

"I met this one woman," Pedro explained, "who was a veteran of the dating service and wanted to get right down to the big questions—no playing around. I understood that she didn't want to waste time on someone who was just dipping his big toe in the water, but I was on my second date in thirty-three years. I could barely find the lake."

As it turned out, they became friends, not romantic partners, and she has been helpful in mentoring him on the pitfalls and pleasures of online dating. "Although she was a good guide, I couldn't help but feel like when I went out with a woman who was also divorced, we each had our own invisible duenna sitting between us at the dinner table. You know, like the annoying relatives who invite themselves to dinner and clearly disapprove of everything."

Not all singles in this age group are hooking up or hanging out. Almost 40% of the singles in our survey reported that they hadn't had a first date in the past 12 months. More than 30% reported that they hadn't had any romantic or sexual contact at all during the previous 6 months. Most of these individuals hadn't given up the idea of meeting someone and developing a long-term relationship. They just reported that they weren't ready or, like Clarence, felt "I need to get out of my small social circle and figure out how to date these days. My daughter [aged twenty-four] tries to give me advice on where and how to meet women, but I think her perspective is threatening and wrong for me."

---

3   https://divorcecoaching4men.com/blog/3-women-initiated-divorces

## There's Nobody to Help Warm the Bed

One post-divorce problem, which is generated by loneliness and affects men more than women, is trying to reconnect prematurely. Those who do often bring the same problems into the new relationship that they experienced in the old marriage.

Roland had been married three times, each for 5 years. He was always the one who left both his marriages and between-marriage relationships, because the woman "became totally dependent on me." He described a great fear of "dying alone" and had always been in a primary relationship since he was a teenager. Because of his abandonment fears, he usually had a new relationship lined up before he left the previous one. When I interviewed him in February, he had been alone for less than a month, yet admitted to a "great pressure" to reconnect with someone. Naturally, when a man is desperate to find someone, he is likely to look for someone just like or apparently opposite from his ex. In either situation, any relationship he enters will replicate the prior relationship, with him playing the same role, or the one of his ex-partner.

By April, he was already planning to wed for the fourth time, with a woman who—like his previous three wives—was very dependent, with financial and alcohol problems and her own history of poor relationships. His desperation led him into exactly what would inevitably end up the same way as his prior relationships. In fact, the new marriage was over before Christmas the same year.

## Someone Needs to Take the Lead

One couple in our survey was very interested in talking about their "courtship." Frederick, aged 64, said, "I married my high school sweetheart. I was in a very bad marriage, full of alcohol, affairs, a bankruptcy, and misery, ending with her incarceration for credit card fraud. I actually divorced her while she was in jail. Then I just went into a prolonged celibacy until I met Debby. I have to admit, I was very gun-shy, and she really took the lead."

Debby laughed and said,

> That's not the half of it. I actively pursued him into submission. We met online on [one of those popular dot-com personals sites]. I was on about five of them and was dating a new guy or two a week for almost

three years. Then he popped up and there was no pretense, no ego, just a straightforward description of who he was and a lot of fear. So, we had a coffee date and I really liked him, but as those things go, a lot of times it's one message and you never hear from him again. I just kept up the emails and invites. He always responded sincerely and at length, but he never initiated anything. My girlfriends said, "Let it go; he isn't into you." But I was determined, so I invited him out on a date and then for a weekend down in La Jolla with my friends—separate rooms of course [laughing], and he did sleep in his own room until Sunday when I just wouldn't leave his place until he began to realize that I was serious. Only then did he become very passionate. We haven't been apart much since."

## Sex and Romance

The 78 million Americans referred to as baby boomers came of age during the era known for sex, drugs, and rock and roll. Our rock and roll is now commonly described as "golden oldies," and with the exception of now legal (in many states) marijuana, boomers have replaced most of their recreational drugs with prescription medications and over-the-counter cures for ailments and loss of physical and sexual vitality. Yet for individuals in this age group, sex has remained remarkably important. Almost 80% of men and 70% of women in our survey considered their sexual lives one of their top current interests, concerns, or pleasures. Among interviewees, both boomers and Gen Xers, in or out of relationships, listed their sexual life as one of the more problematic aspects of their current lives.

This may reflect several social trends that impacted this cohort of current 45- to 65-year-olds. They came of age just after the sexual revolution, women's liberation movement, and a huge shift in cultural mores. It seems that having been part of far more active sexual expression than prior generations, they are loath to set it aside when they are past midlife. Of course, most of those surveyed placed their age of identification 20 or more years younger than their chronological age.

As Janice (aged 62) said, "After living through the Woodstock years, it was hard to imagine settling down and giving up sexual freedom like my mother and grandmother did when they were approaching menopause."

## The Pill (Redux)

When the birth control pill became readily available in the mid-1960s, it ushered in a new era of sexual expression. Freed from fears of unwanted out-of-wedlock pregnancies, a generation of young people in the late 1960s and the early 1970s truly believed in "free love." Sexuality without consequences became an accepted norm. Virginity became less valued than experience, and the pleasurable aspects of sexual intercourse superseded the primacy of reproduction for large parts of the population.

With women as free as men to experiment in these ways and with a corresponding growing emergence of women as full partners in the workplace, America in the sixties[4] was opening itself to sexual liberation. This era progressed until the early 1980s when the proliferation of sexually transmitted diseases such as herpes, chlamydia, and AIDS ushered in a new awareness of the limits and dangers of "free" sexual expression. The short period between the advent of oral contraceptives and the awareness of AIDS was an exceptional era in human interaction.

Just as one pill ushered in for this generation a sense of sex with fewer limitations, another pill has impacted them at their current ages. Viagra (the little blue pill) and its competitors such as Levitra and Cialis, a host of generic drugs and a host of alternatives marketed by health food stores, vitamin shops, and online sites, provide a sense that sexual intercourse need not diminish with age. Indeed, it is difficult to watch a television network news program without being presented with advertisements for erectile dysfunction medication, replete with a speed-talking voice indicating a host of side effects.

Both of these chemical solutions to social concerns have occurred concurrently with the increase in divorce and shifting partner

---

4   The era of the 1960s is usually dated from 1965 to 1974 and the 1970s from 1975 through the early 1980s.

relationships. Few in these generations have been unaffected by family or personal divorces. The fantasized promise of greater fulfillment with a new partner may have influenced some of these divorces. This effect has been magnified for members of Generation X, who came of age when these social changes were already normative, rather than novel.

## Single and Sexually Active After Midlife

Single interviewees reported irregular, but not inconsistent, sexual activity, albeit with various partners.[5] Many found dating again at this age disquieting at best and were treating dating not as an ongoing pleasure but as a means to a goal—like a job search—something you did until you could stop. It is no surprise, then, that people in their 50s and 60s are the most active on some internet matchmaking sites.

In 2006, Barbara Kantrowitz introduced her *Newsweek* column "Sex & Love: The New World" with the words, "More middle-aged people than ever are single, and they're finding the rules have changed. STDs and internet dates. Aging bodies and kids at home. Who knew?"[6]

Census figures indicate that approximately one third of adults in the 45 to 65 age range are single; most were married previously. They are frequently described as a group of people looking for another relationship. In Kantrowitz's words, "Many of these singles are on the prowl."

A 2003 AARP[7] survey indicates that this group is sexually active, with more than one third reporting sexual intercourse at least once a month. Of course, some of them are cohabitating in a monogamous relationship; others are also in exclusive, if not live-in, relationships.

---

5  One resource for this population is a major study headed by Dr. Xenia Montenegro: Montenegro, X. (2003, September). Lifestyles, dating and romance: A study of midlife singles. *AARP The Magazine*. Another is a 2020 book: Hatfield, E., Rapson, R., & Purvis, J. (2020). *What's next in love and sex*. Oxford University Press.

6  http://msnbc.msn.com/id/11300387/site/newsweek/

7  Montenegro, X.P. Lifestyles, dating and romance: A study of midlife singles. *AARP*.

In the AARP study and similar studies as well as our own survey, more than 60% of single men and close to 40% of single women desired more regular sexual activity.

Dating after a long relationship is daunting for most. We face issues of finding a date, turning down dates, fitting another person into a possibly complex living situation, and dealing with each other's personal histories.

Laura, a successful corporate attorney, divorced her husband when she was 45. She avoided dating completely for a few years and then slowly began to ask her friends to introduce her to an eligible man. She was not short on crucial criteria. In Laura's words, "He had to be tall, athletic, have a full head of hair and no back hair, preferably Catholic, educated at least to the master's level, have a six figure salary, own his own house, and be able to keep up with me intellectually and physically, have no kids at home, and live within one hour drive time [to her San Francisco home]." For a couple of years, she was somewhat secretly pleased that nobody met her criteria. Then, slowly, she began to look over personal ads with one of her colleagues at work and ultimately posted a profile on a few online sites and with a professional singles organization of alumni from high-tier undergraduate schools. She also went to a few singles dances designed for her age group.

Finally, she agreed to go on a dinner date with Ben, a man she met through work. He met a few, but far from all, her criteria.

> So, I went out with this guy whose family owns a couple of restaurants. And to tell the truth, he really made me laugh. I had a great time. Then he takes me home, no kiss at the door, and tells me he'll call. He waits almost a week and calls to ask me out again to this fiesta downtown on a Saturday afternoon. Against my better judgment and because my friend insisted, I went and again I had a great time. We made a whole afternoon and evening of it, and when he took me home, he asked if I wanted to go to a football game on Sunday. I said yes, and he politely kissed me goodnight.
>
> Again, we had a great time, and we went to dinner afterward at one of his family restaurants. So now I'm wondering all evening if this is "the third date" when

you're supposed to have sex or it's over, and I am tense and less of a conversationalist than normal for me.

So when we get back to my house, I invite him in and we have a glass of wine, and I sense he wants to stay and I'm feeling the same way but don't know what the protocol is, so I finally started to ask him about his past relationships and tell him about my ex, and we ended up talking until three in the morning. So, he just naturally stays and we cuddle and do some things, but no attempt at intercourse. I don't know what to make of that, but don't want to bring it up. I knew he had to leave on Monday morning early, so I didn't expect much in the morning. When I awoke, he was already gone and my heart sank, until I went into the kitchen and found a flower in a vase and these great rolls, I love from the local bakery that he left for me.

At this point she appeared to be confused about what to do next. "I just don't know what the protocol is." Slowly, almost with embarrassment, she added,

He doesn't meet most of my standards. He's not a professional, but he's a successful businessman. He's not tall; I think we're about the same height when I wear my normal heels. He's older than I was looking for, not athletic, kind of roundish, and balding on top. I think he's Jewish, and I've never been to his house, but I think he's very connected to his children and one might be living there. I enjoy his company, and he listens to me and understands more about what I do than some lawyers.

When they next met, she discovered that he was 10 years her senior and did in fact, have two children living with him, and like her, he hadn't had much dating experience since his marriage ended. Unlike her, he was the one who was left in his marriage. Both of them had spouses who cheated during their marriages, and both had been warned by friends to be careful and to get tested for STDs.

Those are just some of the complications involved in dating in one's 50s. Laura and Ben were cautious and developed a longer-term relationship, but some of the single boomers engage in dangerous sexual practices. Roughly only 60% in the AARP study reported using condoms for protection against diseases, and as Linda Fisher of AARP indicated, the number of AIDS cases for this population has grown sevenfold in a 15-year period.[8]

One trend is the increase in the percentage of couples who cohabitate rather than remarry. This is seen increasingly among seniors and is drifting into the stretch years as well. There are a lot of reasons for this trend.

## Cohabitation

There is a dramatic increase in the number of single individuals in this age cohort. In part, this reflects the increased freedom that women have in being able to live on their own. Another reason is the increasing phenomenon of people cohabitating instead of remarrying. Recent census data indicate that among households headed by a person 45 or older, almost twice as many now, compared with 1995, have two adults who are not related or married to each other. In fact, the percentage of married American adults of all ages is now below 50% for the first time.

In general, people who have been divorced and connect anew with partners in their 50s or 60s are less likely to think of relationships as being for life. Some of these are people whose divorce was particularly painful or problematic. Others have financial reasons to keep apart legally, if not emotionally and sexually. Of course, for the older group in this cohort, long-term gay and lesbian couples were not allowed the opportunity for legal marriage and cohabited as singles out of necessity, if not preference. In fact, since same-sex marriage has been legalized (2015) nationwide, people in this age group have been early adopters of the opportunity.

Talia has been in a monogamous relationship for 10 years following a divorce and several years single. She has three grown children. She acknowledges that she and her mate are "in it for the long haul" and "seriously committed," but she is also very cautious about any financial comingling. In her divorce, she "lost everything, except the inheritance I got from my grandparents. It was like the worst

---

8   https://www.aarp.org/research/topics/life/info-2014/srr_09.html

of those stories you hear on daytime TV. I got the kids and the house, and he got all the savings. He was supposed to pay alimony and child support, but that stopped after a couple of years when he moved to Australia. The kids and I haven't heard from him since except my daughter gets an occasional postcard or email." So, her way to protect herself in her new relationship is to keep finances separate, simply share expenses with her "soul mate," and focus on leaving something for her children.

## Hot Autumn Nights

Couples who cohabitate, those who remarry, and those in self-described good relationships all report similar levels of sexual satisfaction, at least after 5 years into their current arrangement.

Several people have said that when sex is good in a relationship, it's a small part of the pleasure. When it's bad, it's a large part of the problem. Not so, according to our interviewees. Sex and sexual pleasure were reported to be primary pleasures or had primacy for many in this age range. Although the nature of the romantic and sexual expression changes and the propagation imperative becomes inoperative, most of the interviewees and years of clinical observations indicate that sexuality is alive and well during these years. Individuals talked about experimenting with their partners in ways that had disappeared when the first child was born. They were more vocal with their partners about what was pleasurable. Lovemaking also took on a more languid, less acrobatic quality. These couples often described special weekends away that rekindled both romance and sexuality.

These couples also described sexual accommodations they made as they became older. For example, individuals reported making more active attempts to deal with a loss of sexual capacity or desire and health-related concerns. They more commonly used erectile dysfunction medications for men and lubricants for women. There was also an increase in prescriptions for antidepressant and antianxiety medications to alleviate a drop in sexual desire. Rose reported that once she hit menopause, sexual intercourse became less comfortable and even painful. She and her husband of 30 years talked about it and were able to experiment with other ways of pleasuring each other that allowed connection, closeness, and fulfillment without penetration.

Sally said that when her husband was around 60, he lost his ability to get or maintain an erection that would allow for intercourse. "We tried Viagra," she indicated, "but I found it off-putting and he would get a headache when he used it, so we reverted to the kinds of sex we had when we were teens and afraid of pregnancy or getting caught by my parents. It's still fun." Blushing, she added, "Well, we both do some things that neither of us would have considered cool when we were teens."

Not everyone reported such comfortable accommodations. Some individuals were quite frustrated at their own or their partner's declining capacity for sexuality. One of the cosmic "jokes" about the human condition is that no two people with the same level of sexual desire are ever allowed to live together.

It's a reality that sexual desire can diminish with time and can even shut down completely. More frequently, it was the woman in a couple who lost desire or inclination. This can lead to frustration on the husband's part.

When his wife declined to have sexual or affectionate interactions with him for more than a year, Felipe complained and requested that she go to a sex therapist with him. She declined. Later, when they were in bed and he made advances, she queried, "Do you really want me to do something that I don't want?" Felipe surprised both of them when he responded, "Occasionally I do!"

Similarly, Robert said, "I understand that she isn't interested any longer, but she's putting me in a freezer with her and I'm not ready for that. I want to be close to her and to love her in physical as well as emotional ways."

Others found that the medicinal cures were less helpful or contraindicated. For example, some of the most commonly prescribed antidepression medications (Selective Seratonin Reuptake Inhibitors, SSRIs like Prozac and Zoloft) lift depression and can increase desire but can have the unfortunate side effects of reducing sex drive, inhibiting orgasm, and causing weight gain. Similarly, erectile dysfunction medication can interact poorly with certain other medications or physical conditions.

# Loss of Sexuality in a Relationship

As important as individuals in this age group reported sex to be, it is no surprise that they experienced a lack of sexual expression as an important relationship loss.

As Juanita reported, "When we stopped having sex, it was like there was a hole in my relationship. It just wasn't the same without sharing the bed together. I could even understand his sleeping in the other room, but at least he could hold me and be with me before he fell asleep." She was not alone in expressing the loss of something significant in the relationship. Whether it was related to self-esteem, needs for human touch, deep connecting with a partner, fears of physical decline, or mortality, the loss of a sexual relationship or a major change in sexuality was associated with several experiences of loss.

Several individuals reported four issues related to such losses:

1. *The importance of remaining sexual.* Recent evidence seems clear that a regular sex life fosters better overall health and potentially longevity. Indeed, many men talked about a sense of "skin hunger" that compelled them toward connection with partners.

2. *Sexual incapacity and new relationships.* For those who were dating, loss of sexual capability becomes a daunting embarrassment and concern. As Jerome said, "I just think it'd be a huge problem to talk to a new partner about my erection problems. I actually wonder if anyone would actually want to pursue a relationship with someone with my disability."

3. *A partner's sexuality.* Some interviewees talked at length about their partners' aging and changes in appearance as factors in recalibrating their personal sexual responsivity.

4. *Return to a virginity.* Finally, of course, there is a group of individuals especially in the older half of this age group, who gladly eschewed sexual contact. More often women, they either never enjoyed their prior sexual experiences or experienced sexuality primarily as a means of procreation. That being something in the past, a celibate life was more desirable. These individuals were content to remain in a relationship that was not sexually active or to be single.

# Friendships

There is far more to successfully meeting our relational needs than romantic and sexual relationships. We are social animals, and we need others in our lives. One of the most compelling results of the survey was the importance of having friends and acquaintances who share our interests and offer us connection and companionship.

This is a time, like the teen years, when friendships again become very important. Women have often developed and maintained a relationship network through their earlier stages. Typically, this is less true for men. One of the major challenges for men is to develop new relationships with others who share sentiments, interests, and activities and to pursue these. Those men who do, often for the first time since school or military days, find these friendships particularly nurturing. The increase in outside friendships also takes some pressure off the primary relationship to meet needs. In the survey, many men named their spouse (or sometimes ex-spouse) as their best friend. Almost none of the women did that.

Friendships at this age can be mutually supportive or caretaking, but in general, adults seek friends who share their interests. This is a change for many whose previous adult friends were the parents of their children's schoolmates or those who shared a workplace, dorm, barracks, or community organization. These new friendships and some that have lasted for decades tend to be more interesting, more based on shared experiences, and more nurturing than functional.

# Exercise

You can do this exercise alone, separately with a partner, or together. Divide a fresh piece of paper into quadrants. On the top place your name and label the two vertical columns "What I Like" and "What More I Expect." On the left side of the page, place your partner's name and label the horizontal columns "What They Like," and "What More They Expect." Then list those issues according to the box titles. For example, in the A box, place those positive aspects of the relationship you agree about.

The boxes can provide a quick picture of the discrepancies between what is expected and what meets consensual reality in your primary relationship or friendships.

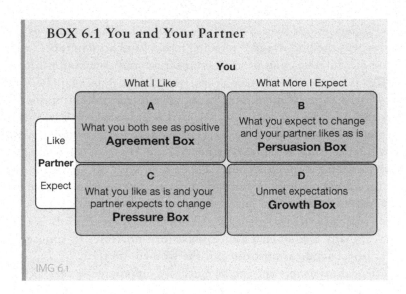

The idea here is to increase the size of the A box, what you both like and agree on, and decrease the size of the D box. The B box contains areas of the relationship in which you want to try to change your partner or your reactions to the way they are. The C box contains things your partner wants you to change and you like as is.

Because it's an extraordinarily difficult and unrewarding enterprise to try to change another person, the key conclusions you can draw involve things you can change in boxes B, C, and D.

For items in box C, it might be wise to consider how you can alter your expectations and make compromises. In box C, you can look at which of your behaviors you can change and negotiate for other considerations with your partner. Box D contains the areas of dislike for both. This is the area of things you might want to try to accept and open lines of communication about.

Let's consider one example of this in the brief example completed by Larry and Aiko. When they completed this exercise, they had been married for 22 years and had two children. Aiko was 53 and Larry 50.

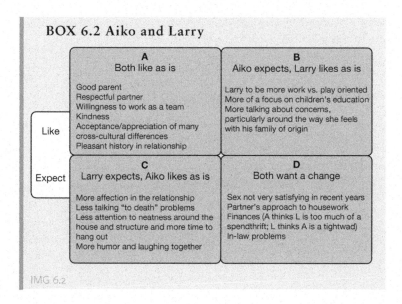

BOX 6.2 Aiko and Larry

|  | **A**<br>Both like as is | **B**<br>Aiko expects, Larry likes as is |
|---|---|---|
| **Like** | Good parent<br>Respectful partner<br>Willingness to work as a team<br>Kindness<br>Acceptance/appreciation of many<br>cross-cultural differences<br>Pleasant history in relationship | Larry to be more work vs. play oriented<br>More of a focus on children's education<br>More talking about concerns,<br>particularly around the way she feels<br>with his family of origin |
|  | **C**<br>Larry expects, Aiko likes as is | **D**<br>Both want a change |
| **Expect** | More affection in the relationship<br>Less talking "to death" problems<br>Less attention to neatness around the<br>house and structure and more time to<br>hang out<br>More humor and laughing together | Sex not very satisfying in recent years<br>Partner's approach to housework<br>Finances (A thinks L is too much of a<br>spendthrift; L thinks A is a tightwad)<br>In-law problems |

IMG 6.2

A brief glance at this chart indicates that Aiko and Larry's relationship is quite positive on balance. They have some disagreements stemming from family-of-origin issues and could use some help with financial, in-law, and declining sexual satisfaction challenges, all of which they got in couples counseling.

It also would serve them well to accept and be more tolerant of their partner's differences. For example, Aiko could find a way to talk more concisely about things that matter to her, and Larry could learn to listen more actively and respond better to her needs to connect via talking. Aiko could offer Larry some chances to be affectionate and to enjoy more before they finish all the work. Larry could relinquish some of the role of the "fun parent" and allow her some space to play that role if he picked up more of the homework monitor role.

They both could focus more on all the things that are good between them and enhance the A box as they diminish the D box and reduce the B and C areas.

# chapter seven

# Gender Differences

## Myths, Realities, and the Shadow

*Different though the sexes are, they inter-mix.*
*In every human being a vacillation from one sex to the*
*other takes place,*
*and often it is only the clothes that keep the male or*
*female likeness,*
*while underneath the sex is very opposite of what it is*
*above.*

—Virginia Woolf

I t is increasingly clear that gender identity—a person's conception of oneself as male, female, fluid, both, or neither—is far from binary. It may also be somewhat changeable over the course of a lifetime. For reasons of understanding gender identity during the post-midlife years, we will describe stereotypical male and female characteristics.[1] Like all stereotypes, this one must be adjusted to your

---

1   These differences are presented in this chapter as stereotypes for points of clarity. We know that there are greater differences within each gender group than between them. Thus, in some relationships, the perceptions may be not only different, but reversed.

own personal experience. Particularly during the second half of life, gender identity and gender roles may have a much broader definition.

# Why Can't a Man Be More Like a Woman? Shouldn't He Be?

One of the stickiest topics of our time reflects the question of whether men and women are truly different in their desires, needs, and behaviors. To what extent do any differences between the sexes reflect biology (nature) or social conditioning (nurture)? After all, isn't there more psychological variation within the group of women (or men) than between women and men? Indeed, if we examine the bulk of biological, social, and psychological studies, we are drawn to an inevitable conclusion. All of us have both traditionally masculine and traditionally feminine traits and capacities.

During the procreative years, sex-related differences are magnified, with women typically taking on more nurturing aspects of family life than men. During the stretch years, this often changes. After our childbearing years, our gender-related selves are more linked to rediscovering the less known, more hidden sides of our personalities. For most men, for example, the less understood parts are what were commonly seen as softer, more introspective feminine traits. Conversely, women at this age typically refocus on the more masculine parts of their self-growth.

# Me and My Shadow

It is a classic premise of Swiss Psychiatrist, Carl Jung that at midlife and beyond, psychological growth involves increasing awareness and acceptance of one's "*shadow*" side. Far from something ominous, the shadow represents those parts of self that have gone underdeveloped for decades while individuals have been busy creating successful lives for themselves. Jung stressed the reintegration of the opposite-sex components of our personalities. The late 40s to mid-60s offer a golden opportunity to reflect on and recapture those skills, traits, desires, and aptitudes that have received less attention.

## Being and Doing

Psychologist Diane Ehrensaft emphasized the typical difference between men and women in how they master their environment. She describes for men the "doing" (action/mastery) parts of life as typically dominant, whereas for women the "being" or receptive parts are more central. Success in later life should involve something of a reversal. Those who have concentrated their energies primarily on action are better served during the stretch years by an increased focus on receptiveness and vice versa. Thus, for traditional men to be successful in later life, they have to pay less attention to the doing action parts of life and discover more about their inner worlds and the process of being.

In his personal description, Kurt wrote that he was always known as "a man's man." A former marine and mechanic, he rose through the ranks to ultimately become a partner in a construction business. During his time as an owner, he was frequently a hands-on supervisor on large jobs. He was divorced twice and called himself "a hard drinker." Three events occurred within a 5-year span while he was in his 50s that combined to change his perspective: Both his father and his business partner died after long illnesses, he had a heart attack, and his pregnant granddaughter was tossed out by her parents and came to live with him.

> I figure God had sent me enough messages about how I was living. I had to give up the booze because of my heart and because I couldn't have it around to tempt Melissa, because she was just like me. She was really messed up and I knew I had to give her a steady home while she was pregnant and the baby, when he came. I'd never been religious, but my therapist said it was a "Come to Jesus event," and I guess I figured she might know more than me. So, I started making a home for Melissa and T.J. I got into cooking for her and staying up talking about all sorts of things. We even cried together about her dad—my son—and his alcohol problem and rages. I couldn't believe that she wanted me to go to the doc with her, and we picked out all kinds of stuff for the baby together. We must have seemed quite a pair, her with all the piercings with a guy forty years older. I can only imagine what

> the store clerks thought ... It's like I began to see life
> and death from a new perspective and started to enjoy
> what was happening instead of always looking for what
> was wrong, putting out fires.

By contrast, the stretch years for women are often marked by a recapturing of less receptive, more dynamic, action-oriented aspects of life. Many authors have noted that many women "soar" after menopause. This soaring describes the more active leadership role that women may play—a role our culture generally rewards and honors more.

Carolina, a homemaker for 25 years, celebrated her 50th birthday by going alone for a week's wilderness adventure. When she returned, she told her husband that she had decided to go back to school and finish the four classes she needed to get her BA, and then she thought she'd like to get involved in an active way with her brothers in the family business inherited from their father.

> I just felt like I wanted to do things and get involved
> in the world out there. I had raised the kids and kept
> a good home, and now it was my time and I was going
> to take advantage of the freedom. ... The surprise was
> my husband's reaction. All he said was he'd support
> me in whatever ways he could, and we should sit down
> and re-divide the chores to make it work for me. ... It
> scared me a little. I was ready to fight with him, and
> instead he just said, "Go for it!"

Not every woman gets that kind of reaction from her husband, especially if he feels abandoned or rejected by the new plans. This is particularly true if the change in plans is not considered mutually but appears instead as a sudden jolt to the relationship. It's one thing to find one's partner revising the life script in ways that enhance herself and benefit the couple's relationship; it's quite another when the shift blocks out the partner without input.

Many women in this age group are like Patricia: "I expected my husband would be closed to or argue against my new plans for life, and so to avoid unpleasantness I just did it without telling him or getting into an argument." Only later, after much marital grief, did Patricia come to realize that her way of avoiding conflict by working unilaterally actually produced more conflict—about the event itself, and even more about the secrecy.

# Inside Out or Outside In

Another gender difference to consider is how men and women stereotypically understand and process their perceptions and worldviews. For women it's often an inside-out process. Women take in their perceptions and use their inner senses to understand what is going on in others and in the world around them. By contrast, men operate more from an outside-in approach, processing their perceptions based on external factors and only slowly internalizing the event, feelings, and reactions.

Nowhere is this seen more clearly than in how men and women care for children. Watch a woman approach an infant. She picks up the baby and rolls him into her breasts, providing comfort, warmth, and security. By contrast, her husband holds the baby up, making eye contact, or with the baby's back to his chest, or up on his shoulder. This offers the child a sense of a shared world.

Differences can also be seen in how mothers and fathers play with and discipline children. In play with moms, the child directs the play. The mother follows her child's directions by being the Sheriff of Nottingham dueling with her little Robin Hood or making believe she is eating the mud cookies "baked" by her child. In this way, mothers offer opportunities for creativity, imagination, and self-expression. When dads play with children, the father directs the play. He will tell the child, "Hand me the crescent wrench and I'll show you how to loosen this nut." This teaches the child teamwork and how to be part of something larger than themself.

Mothers typically discipline adjusting moment by moment based on their perceptions and understanding of the child's inner state. Fathers tend to discipline by established rules determined by outside influences or agreements, such as curfews. Obviously, the greatest value for the child is to experience both approaches.

During the stretch years, these tendencies begin to shift. Women start to add a greater sense of outside-in processing, and men develop more of the inside-out methods. The more successful we are in adopting methods characteristic of the opposite sex, the richer and fuller the second half of our lives will be.

Numerous in-depth studies, including the MIDMAC[2] studies, suggest that only about 25% of women and 40% of men until age 49 have fulfilled a special dream in the prior 5-year period. During the stretch years, however, 36% of women report such an achievement, while the percentage of men drops to 28. Whereas for men the instigator of a transition crisis is related to career or other external factors, women's crises are often related more to internal physical or psychological issues.

Seeking solutions, women are far more likely to talk it out with others, to be open about their unhappiness and solution seeking, and to be introspective. They are also far more likely than men to look for answers in religion or other spiritual pursuits.

## Women Soar, Men Decline. Reality or Myth?

There is both experimental and observational evidence that after menopause, women's lives become richer and fuller. Examples abound of women starting new careers, opening or expanding businesses, and rising to higher levels of an organization as they age. As Cecilia described herself, "I wasn't really expecting it, but I have more energy and a greater variety of interests, and I have that amazing sense that nobody can get away with telling me what to do anymore. I just won't put up with that any more or suffer fools at this point in my life."

There is a corresponding set of examples of men who spend several years of their employed life in "retirement jobs," holding on in noncreative and often nonproductive ways or those who don't know what to do with themselves after retirement. They can be seen in slow decline without the prop and excitement of work.

In looking at the trajectory of male and female experiences through life, it becomes obvious that success after midlife comes from taking the less traveled personal path more. Women who soar find and develop the aspects of their personalities that had lain

---

2   Brim, O. G., Ryff, C. D., & Kessler, R. C. (Eds.). (2004). *How healthy are we? A national study of well-being at midlife.* University of Chicago Press.

dormant until this age. Similarly, men who are able to develop their less competitive, more receptive sides appear far happier than those who keep going as before or who simply "sit down," either before or after retiring. They tend to live not only better but also longer.

This is not true for everyone. Many men find ways to soar as they approach retirement and well into their retirement. By the time C.J. was 50, he was in a dead-end job. He couldn't leave the work because he needed the income and health insurance, but in his words, "It was mind-numbing." Instead of trying to change the immobile work environment, he began to explore and expand his off-the-job world. Mostly C.J. decided to get to know himself better by a combination of classes, training programs, reading, and psychotherapy. The result was that he enriched his nonwork life to the point that his on-the-job hours became more enjoyable as well, or at least less aversive.

Similarly, while her friends and sister flourished into their late 50s, Margo became more dispirited. She related, "I am still struggling with becoming invisible. You know when my hips disappeared and my neck started to get that turkey look, I could no longer charm anyone and was like a lot of old women. I just became a nonperson."

## The Shadow Knows

Gender alone does not explain successful adaptation at this time. In our survey, we found that women who held down challenging careers and learned how to succeed in the more masculine-oriented business world mirrored the characteristic male pattern more than the female style when it came to post-midlife challenges. Similarly, men who were more receptive and less competitive in their earlier lives had a more feminine challenge at this stage. Thus, it is not gender per se that produces thriving or failure during this period. It's the way men and women understand their personal histories and try to capture their underdeveloped selves—Jung's *shadow*. To the extent that we can turn to and expand those capacities that until now have been dormant, we can all soar during this period and after retirement.

## Women After Midlife

What is unique to women as they leave midlife? Are there predictable patterns for women of this generation? What is consistent for the approximately 37 million American women who are now between 45 and 65 years of age?

Wall Street Journal columnist and author of *The Breaking Po!nt: How Today's Women Are Navigating Midlife Crisis*, Sue Shellenbarger[3] writes persuasively about a woman's midlife crisis—a stressful or turbulent psychological transition that occurs most often in their late 40s and early 50s.[4] She estimates that upward of 15 million women are having or about to have such a crisis. This means that more women than men are experiencing a crisis during this transition. The MIDMAC study supports her observations.

According to Ms. Shellenbarger, the increasing complexity of women's roles and opportunities (financial muscle, skills, and confidence) to act out their frustrations promotes this dramatic shift. During their stretch years, women are more likely to become aware of and be willing to express their frustrations as a way to resolve both internal and external life changes. Their enhanced skills, opportunities, and resources also enable women to make career, avocational, and relationship changes.

## Common Losses

One commonality among women is a sense of loss related to changing relationships. Most women comment on the evolving aspects of long-term relationships.

By this age, a large number of women have separated or divorced; some are widows; some have grown apart from long-term spouses; and others have decided to give up the single independent life. There is no preparation for these changes. Most women in our study grew up with the happy-ever-after myth of marriage and family.

Even the best relationships are challenged by common life changes such as midlife transitions, shifts in work, empty nests, sandwich

---

3  Shellenbarger, S. (2005). *The breaking po!nt: How female midlife crisis is transforming today's women*. Henry Holt.

4  Because the stretch years had not been categorized as a separate developmental life stage before this book, many authors have written about midlife as extending well into the 50s or even until retirement. Although there is disagreement about the label, the phenomena that Shellenbarger and others identify are consistent with those of this book.

caregiving, and changes in self-esteem as the importance of earlier activities, such as childrearing, begin to decline.

Another loss is a sense of financial security. As retirement approaches, many women become keenly aware of the limits of their savings and pension benefits. A large majority of the interviewees were at least somewhat worried that they will outlive their finances. This can have a debilitating, even depressing, impact on their life outlook.

Minnie reported, "I do not want to end up being supported by my daughters. I know they would do it, but to me, it's a failure." She added later, "I wish I had learned more about finances when I was younger. I just let my ex-husband do all the investing and taxes. It was easy for me then, but now I am running to catch up and I don't have time left to save enough, to invest enough, or to leave my job at all. ... At least now I have an advisor I trust. My son-in-law is a CPA and he has great incentive." She laughed, "If it doesn't work out, he thinks I'll end up living under his roof!"

Other losses involve expectations or psychological identity. As Althea mentioned, "I always thought of fifty-year-old women as old and in the way (like my mother). All the old women I knew were crabby and demanding." Now that Althea is 50 herself, she is struggling to reconcile those perceptions with her real-life experiences. Like Margo, Althea partially defined herself (and other women) by looks when she was younger.

## Women Finding a New Equilibrium

As women dealt with these issues, they identified three stages on the road to a new equilibrium and recommended some paths through these:

1. *Lose the old stereotypes about aging women.* If you hold notions of hags, hapless or helpless individuals, or eternal mothers, you might find yourself both resentful of slipping into such a role and scared of losing the best aspects of yourself. A number of women expressed anger, rebelliousness, even indignation at being invisible or being offered unsolicited senior citizen discounts. Suzanne Braun Levine eloquently described the stage in her 2004 *Ms.* magazine

article, "The Fuck-You 50s: We're Loud, Proud and 37 Million Strong."[5]

While the anger and frustration may serve you for a while, there is a danger of being trapped there. In some ways it is easier to continue being angry at society in general than to evaluate your fears of aging and change your self-perception and your life.

Tara exemplifies this. At 62 she is still furious at the inequities she experiences between men and women. She has been a political advocate for women's rights for much of her life, and for almost 15 years has been dedicated to fighting gender injustice. In fact, she's made a difference in her local community. Yet on a personal level, she is as angry today at her ex-husband, as she was on the day he left 15 years ago. In the process of carrying the fight for equality, she has, in her own words, "partially managed to become the 'crabby old lady' I was trying to escape." In addition to her justifiable anger, it would serve Tara to get in touch with her fears. By being lost in the singular perspective, she has alienated her old friends and her children, something that bothers her a great deal.

When Mina turned 50, she said, "At first I just denied it. I kept thinking of myself as forty-something." Laughing, she added, "You know like forty-eleven!" Then she began to notice a host of gender-related inequities. "I was feeling old, and men I was meeting were my age and they were acting much younger. I was dating a man who was almost sixty, and he was able to go out with younger women, including me I guess, without question. I got really upset that old men were sent out to pasture [stud] and old women went unseen and unnoticed and unvalued. Well, I'm telling you now that I am not going to take it lying down. I am going after that promotion at work, and I am not going to let [her new boyfriend] Leo push me around because he thinks I make less than him."

The anger served her. She was able to use it as a motivator to reassess and to seek new directions. A year later, Mina related, "Not really happy about it, but I just had my fifty-first birthday. Leo made

---

5 Levine, S.B. (2004) The Fuck-You 50s: We're loud, proud and 37 million strong. *Ms. Magazine*, Winter. See also, Levine, S.B. (2009). http://www.suzannebraunlevine.com/2009/05/19/defiance-daring-and-an-awakening-of-authenticity-welcome-to-the-fuck-you-fifties/#sthash.xGJehJQ8.dpbs

it special. As I wanted, it was just the two of us and a nice weekend. He listened when I told him no party, no surprise party, no big celebration. He was very cute. He told me how he really liked how I made more than he did and how much he respected my career."

2.  *Accept post-midlife realities and set new priorities.* A new understanding can evolve from the process of experiencing and overcoming the emotional pains that emerged from the losses of this stage of life. Going through the pain of loss to emerge with a new sense of self seems like yet another ordeal related to menopause. Yet it's important to experience these losses to be able to find a new life course.

It may be as natural as it was for Olivia, who said, "I was very unhappy about not being able to have any more children, even though I really didn't want any more and pushed my husband to have a vasectomy, years ago. Then just as I was becoming post-menopausal, my daughter had her first and I went from mom to grandma in an instant. That was the best!"

Pam had a far more difficult transition:

I railed against becoming an old lady for two years without stop. I had a face-lift and even went so far as to consider a boob job and cellulose thing. I was like a woman on fire, running this way and that. I was ready to bite off my husband's head if he disagreed with me about anything—especially when he said he didn't want me to get the boob job. It took me about a month to take in what he said in that conversation about how he liked the way I looked. I just figured that if I was having hot flashes, he should be experiencing it too. So then one day I am in the office, and my thirty-two-year-old son tells me that I have more energy that he does.

That revelation began Pam on a path to rediscover what she wanted in her life, rather than stew about what was wrong in her life. She began to accept what was going on in her life and fight less against the tide of age. She found some peace and some excitement in being who she was instead of what she wasn't.

3.  *Carve out a new lifestyle as an elder.* There is a great role for the wise older woman, but it isn't one that just comes

naturally. One has to pass through that "slough of despond" to emerge feeling freer. I have always admired Jenny Joseph's poem "Warning" and the great title (taken from Joseph's poem) of Sandra Martz's book[6] *When I Am an Old Woman I Shall Wear Purple* for capturing so well this shift, allowing women to move from the "musts" of youth—"pay our rent and not swear in the street, [a]nd set a good example for the children"—to the irreverence and freedom of older age, including going out in slippers in the rain, picking flowers in other people's gardens, and "learn[ing] to spit."

# Men After Midlife

By the time a man has reached his stretch years, he has become increasingly aware of disparate forces pulling at him. He is probably at the higher rungs of his career ladder, and by now he knows how to get work done and done well. His management skills serve as "project Velcro." He seems to be the man in the aphorism "If you want something done, ask a busy man," and as he attracts additional responsibilities at work and in his community and as the jobs pile up, his typical response is to work more diligently. He is beginning to learn about effective delegation but hasn't yet mastered the worry that others won't do the job as well.

As he looks more at what he wants from his life, he is apt to realize how important it is to find more in his friendships. Up to this point in life, women have been far better than men at developing and nurturing social networks. Most men have been driven by cultural norms of independence, personal competence, and success. There has been little time for connecting with others in personal ways.

As midlife recedes, men become increasingly aware of their need for more shared experiences and feelings. They also may want to connect more with their children and grandchildren. It can be a problem if the adult children are launching and seeking independence at precisely the time Dad wants to connect more. It can also be problematic if the one and only person a man wants to connect

---

6 Martz, S. (1991). *When I am an old woman, I shall wear purple.* Paper-Mache Press.

with is his wife, who is being driven to test herself in new ways and has a more powerful stake in the world outside marriage and family.

The central fear for men is rejection, and the remedy is acceptance and intimacy. Often, when men reach this age, they are experiencing real loneliness.

Reggie (aged 58) was referred to therapy by his physician after his depression and erectile dysfunction had not responded well to medication. By the third session, Reggie was talking about how he felt isolated at work and home and didn't know what he was living for.

> My wife has always been my best friend, but now she is off exploring herself with friends and it's just me and the dog most weekends. ... I work mostly with overseas markets with people in Japan and Korea, and I go over there maybe twice a year. There's nobody else at my level (vice president) in the division, and the only people who really know what I do and what's important are the competition. It's just a lonely life. I had a dream the other night that I was that Russian cosmonaut who was up on the space station alone for like three months. I'd go nuts if that was me.

When I asked him about friends, he said,

> My best friends are a guy I knew in business school and this girl I grew up with in the old neighborhood. The thing is, he lives up north and we get together with the families maybe twice a year and maybe he and I get to take a weekend. It's good. We talk about everything: work, wives, kids, politics—even where we want to retire. I don't get to talk much with Gina anymore. My wife is real jealous of that relationship—I gotta tell you we have always been like brother and sister, but she's still against it and when we get together as families, there's no chance to really talk.

Reggie has two adult sons and said that he was close to them and liked them both as men. He reported that time with them and their own families was always nice, "but I'm still their dad; it's different, they have to love me." When I asked him what it would be like for him to have a close friend on a regular basis, he half joked, "you mean besides you [his therapist]?" Then his eyes teared up and slowly he said, "I would just feel like I belonged, like I wasn't such an outsider."

## Shifting to the Inside

Like many men, part of what Reggie is seeking is greater intimacy in life. This of course entails knowing better what is going on in his inner life. Knowing ourselves allows us to be aware of what we are offering others, and to gain a far more complete sense of what our lives are all about.

Thus, the goal for most men at this age is to find the aspects of their lives that are more characteristic of the feminine sides: feelings, relating, caring, and expressing those softer emotions. Any shift in life patterns is necessarily anxiety provoking. It's a good example of leaving the status quo of many years and experimenting by facing fears of the new and unknown. Yet that is the antidote to loneliness, isolation, and the sense of a lack of meaning.

Not everything about being in touch with the inner self is positive. At work, for example, it may involve becoming aware of fears and the reality of being replaced by someone more up to date, less expensive, or sharper. In addition, we may discern that our careers are less able to produce meaning in our lives.

When we open ourselves to our inner feelings, we have both the opportunity and the imperative to examine and come to grips with our relationships with our spouse, children, and friends. Finally, we cannot help getting in touch, perhaps for the first time, with our mortality and fears of incapacity and death.

With all those negatives, why shouldn't a man exercise as much denial as possible and keep his nose to the grindstone and shoulder to the wheel? Surely, a flat nose and rounded shoulder are easier to tolerate than facing the unknowns in life.

Walter, the CEO of a public company reported,

> Last year we had the best profits in our history and this was during a time when the rest of the industry was in the toilet. And this year looks better. My bonus was almost obscene last year. So, what am I doing in therapy, worrying that I don't know my kids or wife

anymore? Me and the missus hardly relate at all except to fight about spending money, and I can't even remember having had a true vacation (not some big event at an elaborate resort) with just the four of us.

Later he added,

I guess I do know why I'm here. I'm so into the financial riches, now I want some of those other riches, like when I was a kid and we went to the lake for 2 weeks.

# Tuning In

Most men in American culture grew up wanting to be good boys. This meant pleasing parents and authorities, filling in the squares, and playing by the rules of the moment. Success usually didn't mean following one's personal bliss. It meant doing what others wanted and expected. Yet after midlife, those methods yield diminishing positive results.

The answer (the road less traveled), which has two components, may seem somewhat contradictory and almost anathema to the lives we've been living. Each involves facing some unknowns.

1. *Desires and the prime directive.* The first question a man needs to answer is what he wants—not what he needs or what's best for his company, his wife, or his kids, but what *he* wants. This question, let alone the answers, often comes as a shock to men of this age.

This is not to suggest for a moment that it is ever appropriate to desert our families or do things that might harm them or others. It requires that we add a new dimension of self-awareness to the prime directive of protect and provide. It isn't easy because it may well bang up against a decades-old desire to do things right.

Mario expressed this concern well, "So you're telling me it's okay to be selfish and go get that red sports car and have an affair with a young woman or just go off by myself and sail away?"

Mario's leap from a sense of duty to an opposing sense of devil-may-care indulgence serves a very useful purpose. By casting self-awareness as selfishness, he has to reject it as an option. The risk of abandonment for being inappropriate is too great in his mind to even consider what it would be like to pay additional attention to what was happening inside.

When Mario was encouraged to think "smaller" of things he might desire, things that wouldn't upend his life and that of his family, he first became anxious and then, with encouragement, slowly began to describe a trip that four of his friends were taking to a sporting event at their alma mater. He wanted to go but dismissed the opportunity because he thought it would unduly burden his wife. Finally, he decided to broach the idea with her. To his surprise, she thought it would be a great idea. She also suggested that he take their son along, but he held fast and replied that "going with Scott to see the school was another trip. This is just for the old guys." Again, he was surprised when she said that made sense and told him she hoped he'd go.

It wasn't that he needed permission, nor was she doing anything except providing encouragement. The significant thing was that he allowed himself to focus on something he wanted and to tell her that he wanted it.

While on the trip, he and his friends talked a lot about the old days and what they missed today. One of those was a lot of approbation for Mario's singing voice as part of the school a cappella group. Soon after returning, he told his family that he was interested in getting back into music and was going to join a local amateur barbershop quartet. Naturally, his kids teased him about "that kind of music," but when he did join the group and they had their first performance, his whole family came to the concert. Mario joked, "It's a good thing too; they were about one fifth of the audience."

By focusing partially on desires instead of full time on needs and responsibilities, Mario, like many men his age, was able to find something of personal value and reconnect with some of the past joys that he voluntarily gave up to be a responsible adult.

2. *Legacy.* Knowing more about who we are and what we want may lead directly to questions about our legacies. How would you like to be remembered? What do you want to be known for? What do you want to give back? What would you like in your obituary or on your gravestone? It'd be quite a surprise if someone answered, "I wish I had spent more time at the office!"

As adolescents and young adults, we matured and mastered, as well as it suited us, how it was to fit in, to be part of the group, and to be the best we could be, within our realm and skill set. At this time of life, it's time to review the sacrifices we made to succeed and to revisit some of those aspects of ourselves that we left behind to facilitate the earlier journey. What was formerly considered extra baggage might now include passions, emotions, skills, and self-questioning.

It's time to reassess those aspects of self and add future dreams, challenges, and hopes, to strike out on a new path that suits you now, rather than the one that others prepared for you and was useful to you as a younger man.

## What the Guys Recommend

In a recent group for men of this age, the participants drew up a list of suggestions to help others progress toward that new path:

*Notice that you are changing and not just becoming less physically adept or can't remember names as well as before.* Accept the new you as a step in the right direction. If you are more emotional, explore what it's like to express more tenderness and caring. Verbalize more with family, friends, and trusted others about what you're experiencing during these stretch years.

*Appreciate the complexity in life.* As a younger person, nuances were sometimes best left behind as a way to foster action. Try to stay open to various ideas and opinions. See the validity in others' perspectives as a way to better develop the subtleties in your own.

*Recalibrate your priorities.* Make a time chart to explore how you actually spend your time and think about allocating more time for the "wants" in your life. One of the participants made a list of his priorities and experimented by cutting the bottom two off the list to see what would happen. "It worked so well," he said, "I cut off two more and then two more. It's amazing how much time I saved by having a local kid mow the lawn, and for a few bucks a week, I bought myself time for gourmet cooking."

*Focus on friends, both old and new, particularly guys.* Spend more time with others who appreciate who you are and who you've been. I was recently at a 60th birthday party, and the theme of the speeches honoring the birthday "boy" all began with statements such as "I've known George since 1970 and he has truly enriched my life." One person began, "I guess I'm the new kid on the block. I met George only three years ago, and I'm honored to be here with so many of his older friends and family. I knew the day we met that there would be a close friendship, because we instantly saw we had so much in common."

*Reconsider the big questions in your life and focus on the spiritual and transcendent sides of yourself and your beliefs.* Spend time considering why you're here, what your life means, and what you want to say, do, or leave before you die.

*Recognize both your uniqueness as a man and how you are like many others.* One fellow quoted comedian Lenny Bruce on this point: "I got to keep in mind that 'there's a schmuck inside of everybody,' not just me."

*Make peace with your enemies and friends.* Make whatever amends are possible. Apologize to others and ask for their forgiveness. Even more important, offer forgiveness to others even if it is unsolicited or just in your own heart. Verbalize your appreciation for others for what they mean to you and for what they offer you as a person. One man reported, "I tell my wife at least two, three times a week how much I love her and how much I'm pleased that we've made a life together."

## Denouement

For both men and women, success in this period involves rebalancing. For those whose lives have been focused internally, there is value in adding an external perspective. For those for whom the external world has been primary, it's of great value to include the internal aspects of life.

# Exercise

On a sheet of paper or computer, answer the following questions:[7]
For women:

- What do you want to know about men as they are during the stretch years?
- What do you want men to know about you during the stretch years?

For men:

- What do you want to know about women as they are during the stretch years?
- What do you want women to know about you at this age?

Once you are satisfied with your answers, ask a friend of the same sex to answer the same questions and compare the answers. You may want to discuss similarities and differences in answers. After that, ask your spouse or a friend of the opposite sex to answer the questions and compare answers.

What new information does this provide for you? How can you use this new information to better your relational life?

---

7   This is written for heterosexual couples. If you are in a same-sex relationship or identify as gay or lesbian, you can alter the questions accordingly.

# chapter eight

# Children, Parents, and Lifestyle (the Economic and Time Sandwich)

*While on the little league field with my seven-year-old son, I suddenly realized: my glove was the second oldest thing on the field.*

—46-year-old father

What does it mean to be a parent in today's world? What marks parents today as different?

In prior generations, there were a couple of near certainties. By the time parents settled into a post-midlife pattern of life, their own parents were gone or their care was well established, and for the most part, their children were reared and launched. Terms like "sandwich generation," "boomerang kids," and "boomerang seniors" were yet to be coined. In those recent days of yore, our parents grew old and became grandparents as midlife receded into old age.

Presumably, after midlife there will be time to be alone again as a couple, to make the big savings push for retirement with school and college tuition relatively complete, and to have fewer day-to-day family responsibilities. Those are some of the expected trade-offs coming to fruition for the nuclear family.

Those presumptions might not be true for members of the baby boomer or X generations. Our children are fewer and often much younger; our parents are just becoming elderly. A divorce will have touched most of us, and we might be in a step- or blended family. A greater number of us have been in nontraditional relationships or remained unmarried.

What are the implications of these changes?

## The Sort of Empty Nest

The losses experienced, the bereft feelings, and the refocus on our primary relationship when the last child leaves home were explored in earlier chapters. But what happens when the parting is partial or evolves into another type of dependency? Three related social trends—the economy and employment situation for recent grads, a now commonplace extended adolescence into the late 20s, and the increasingly later age for marriage and childbearing—have combined to extend our offspring's dependency. This means that when we are in our late 40s to mid-60s, we may well still have children either at home or at least financially dependent. On top of that, our parents' and possibly grandparents' extended longevity might make them physically, emotionally, or financially dependent on us.

The term "sandwich generation," referring to adults who care simultaneously for young children and aging parents first appeared in a *New York Times* article in 1978.[1] As evidence of the complexity of our era, in 2001, the AARP added the nuance that many are also caring for their grandchildren, placing them in a "club," "Dagwood," or "triple-decker" sandwich.[2] Furthermore, a 2010 *Time* magazine article employed a new term—boomerang seniors—in reporting a Census Bureau study of the trend of aging parents who have moved in with their adult children jumping 50% between 2000

---

1  Brozan, N. (1978)  Grown child, aging parent: Help arrives. *New York Times*, Section C, p. 1, 5/10/1978.
https://www.nytimes.com/1978/05/10/archives/grown-child-aging-parent-help-arrives-grown-child-aging-parent-help.html
2  https://assets.aarp.org/rgcenter/il/in_the_middle.pdf

and 2007.[3] By 2017, *USAToday* reported that according to Kaiser Health News, this trend was expanding with extended longevity.[4]

This can stretch our fiscal and time reserves thin at the juncture in life when our own retirement planning needs are calling.

Elena and Ricky Ortiz, a couple who came to consult with me, were emblematic of this sandwich generation predicament. They lived in a modest home in Northern California; had a reasonably good income for the area; had two children in college; were financially contributing to the care of Elena's aging, infirm mother who lived 2 hours away; and were trying to catch up on their savings for retirement. With a combined after-tax income of $140,000 and a dedicated work ethic, one would think that would be sufficient. However, their fixed expenses, tuition, and cost of Elena's mother's care totaled more than their combined income. Box 8.1 offers a quick look at their family budget for 2018 through 2020.

### BOX 8.1 Fixed Expenses for the Ortiz Family

|  | Monthly | Annually |
|---|---|---|
| Mortgage, taxes, and insurance | 2,700 | 32,400 |
| Mother's care contribution | 2,400 | 28,800 |
| Auto costs | 850 | 10,200 |
| Food necessities | 600 | 7,200 |
| Clothing/work-related expenses | 600 | 7,200 |
| Medical expenses | 1,200 | 12,000 |
| Tuition | 6,000 | 72,000 |
| Total |  | **$169,800** |

It's clear that there is nothing in this budget for the estimated $40,000 in home repairs, vacations, or adding to their retirement savings. Instead, they face a minimum shortfall of over $20,000 annually. They will be in the red for at least 2 more years and will be reducing their nest egg by a substantial amount until the children

---

3   Kluger, J. (2010, February 11). Be careful what you wish for. *Time*.
4   https://www.usatoday.com/story/news/2017/03/30/kaiser-boomerang-seniors-aging-adults-move-near-mom-dad/99788434/

are fully launched. Their personal values are such that they feel they should also help the children get a master's degree, if they want one.

If the college costs seem at first glance to be a major budget-buster, they are actually lower than what many families face. Indeed, in 2020, the average costs for resident students in public institutions are close to $26,000 per year, and close to double that for private schools. In fact, some of the top-tier colleges in the United States estimate approximately $70,000 per year in total costs to attend. Both of the Ortiz children are going to public institutions and have some financial aid in the form of scholarships.

Elena and Ricky are not alone. According to a 2013 Pew Research Center report, they are among the 15% of "Middle aged adults" that are raising children or supporting an adult child while providing financial support to an aging parent.[5]

Are you in that group? Will you be at some time in the near future? How much more complex is your family situation than you anticipated?

## Complicated Families

It is now commonplace for aging boomers to have a late child or a second marriage with young children in the home. Step- and blended ("his, hers, and ours") families may make for humorous sitcoms, but in the real world, they present many serious practical and loyalty considerations.

### A Blended Family

When Allan (aged 48) married Victoria (aged 49), they had seven children between them. Neither divorce was particularly adversarial, and they all still lived in a small rural community. Allan's ex-wife was quite well off financially and there was no problem sharing expenses for their three children. However, Victoria's ex had a gambling addiction and contributed little time and money to his four

---

5 https://www.pewsocialtrends.org/2013/01/30/the-sandwich-generation/

children's upbringing. This was exacerbated when he remarried a much younger woman and quickly had two more babies.

Consider the issues for Allan and Victoria around the support of their children. Contemplate the potential problems when one set of children has newer and better clothing and play gear than the other and the potential resentment that could be caused by Allan using his income to try to equalize it for Victoria's children. What are the implications when some of the children living under the same roof are free to attend any college that accepts them while their stepsiblings are limited to local public institutions?

The resentment materialized when Carrie, Allan's ex-wife, purchased a new automobile for their eldest daughter. Trying to be as fair as possible, Allan was able to give a 10-year-old vehicle to Victoria's son, the next oldest child in his blended family. In a high school environment, where a teen's car is a major status symbol, this drove a potential wedge into the family. This was not a situation where anyone acted with malice. Instead, the generosity of both Allan and Carrie came with inadvertent problems.

Although they have been able to work things out, it has been hard on everyone in the household. Not only were they blending two families, but there were also intrusions by the other parents. From a socioeconomic perspective, they were a bicultural family living under one roof.

Feelings for step- and biological children that naturally differ also cause difficulties. When Joy said with some guilt, "I know all the kids should be treated equally, but I just have a softer spot in my heart for my own," she was giving voice to a most common, and quite understandable, phenomenon. What about the situation in which one set of children live full time with the blended family and the others rotate in and out?

# The Sandwich Generation

Much has been written on the impact of being in the sandwich generation. Rosalyn (aged 52) is married with three children (aged 12, 14, and 16). Last year, she experienced something quite unexpected. Her mother, who had always been a healthy, vibrant woman, went into a hospital in her hometown and came out with severe complications from surgery and a staph infection. Rosalyn flew to Illinois and, after some professional consultation, decided to fly her mother west to live with her in California. She was able to get some in-home care for Evelyn, but the majority of the substantial caretaking fell to her. Not only was the healing and treatment difficult and time consuming, but her mother was also showing symptoms of early dementia. Rosalyn described the event as "a train wreck, and my three teens and Terry and I have to pick up all the pieces. Well," she added ruefully, "mostly me!"

Rosalyn's situation was particularly difficult because there was neither warning nor planning. The fact that her 14-year-old son was learning disabled and needed substantial tutoring, which Rosalyn provided, compounded the challenge. The only extra assistance was from her brother, who was able and willing to help financially with their mother's care. However, he was living overseas and unable to provide any hands-on help.

Many of our generation are in this sandwich of needs. According Gina Shaw, in a 2013 WebMD article titled, "Stuck in the middle with you" almost 45% of Americans between the ages of 45 and 55 are "sandwiched" between aging parents or in-laws and their children under the age of 21.[6]

The majority of individuals view it as "just something you do." They aren't angry with anyone, nor do they describe themselves as victims. In fact, Rosalyn and many of her peers reported that they were quite proud of the job they've done with both sides of the sandwich. Unfortunately, almost all described feeling guilty because of what they could not do for their parents and children.

Most reported that they had received some advice and assistance from local community service organizations for the elderly and had quickly moved up the learning curve on available options. Regardless of the information available, the costs for elder care have skyrocketed with the inflation in health care generally, and most in our parents' generation do not have sufficient long-term care insurance. This means personal, social, cultural, financial, and psychological factors may limit our options.

## What to Do With Grandma

We face numerous considerations when our parents become older and less capable of caring for themselves.

---

6   https://www.webmd.com/healthy-aging/features/stuck-middle-you#1

What assistance are you able and willing to provide? Is it financial? Is it a living accommodation? Does it involve organizing their care in home or elsewhere? What is the nature of your relationship with your parents? Who does the responsibility fall on?

Historically and within many cultural groups, many of these questions had automatic answers. When Isabella's husband passed away, her oldest daughter moved in with her and provided care and homemaking for a decade before Isabella passed away. Other families expected aging relatives to move into their children's homes. They would perhaps build a new wing or room or rent an adjacent apartment. Often, they would convert a bedroom deserted by an adult child for Grandma's or Grandpa's use.

Many of the individuals we interviewed described exactly those scenarios in the current generation. When Jose and Christina had their third (of eight) children, both sets of grandparents relocated to their small town. Christina's parents had their own place close by, and Jose's parents moved in with the family. All four of the grandparents were active in the family's life and helped out quite a bit until they no longer could. In time, the help from aging grandparents turned into help for them. When Jose was 58 and Christina was 56, his parents and four of their children were still in the home to support financially, emotionally, and, increasingly, physically. They also had a son who was out of the home but needed continuing financial help while his struggling small business became viable.

They have made it work, at least in part because Christina's parents were able to save enough money to support themselves and help with college tuition for their grandchildren. In fact, the only retirement funds that Jose and Christina can count on are those from their home's equity and their anticipated 25% share of her parents' estate.

## What If the Choices Are Not Viable?

Jose and Christina's family made it work because of the mobility of the grandparents and their willingness to help each other out. For many of their contemporaries, it isn't so easy. The Martin family lived for several generations in the Northeast. Both Elaine and her only brother Matthew grew up and went to school near Boston. After graduation both married and their job opportunities took Elaine, her husband, and their two sons to St. Louis, Missouri, and Matthew and his wife and daughter to the Silicon Valley in

California. Their parents had lived their entire lives in the greater Boston area and had only traveled out of the Northeast to visit their children and relatives who relocated to Florida.

Although the family was separated geographically, they described themselves as emotionally close-knit. The first crisis occurred when Grandma Martin had a bout with pneumonia. When she returned home from the hospital, her breathing was still labored and she needed portable oxygen for some time. Soon thereafter, her husband fell on the ice while shoveling snow on their front steps and broke his leg. Elaine and Matthew came to the rescue both times, but when they had to go back home, the elder Martins were angry that their children would not stay and care for them directly. Both of the adult children tried to convince the elder Martins to move closer to either St. Louis or San Jose, but the parents adamantly refused to consider any move.

After Grandpa Martin passed away, there was another series of visits and phone calls. Mrs. Martin again refused to move to be near her children and grandchildren, preferring instead her friends and her geographical comfort zone. Elaine made almost monthly trips back to her mother's home, each time feeling worse about her mother's reduced ability to care for herself. Ultimately, Matthew and Elaine moved their mother into a progressive facility, where she currently resides.

Many seniors are, like Mrs. Martin, quite unwilling to move. This can place a different kind of burden on their children who are in their own post-midlife years. While having Grandma in your home may be a real challenge, having her away is also difficult.

What can you say when your dad tells you, "I'm not moving anywhere they don't have kielbasa," despite reminders that he isn't allowed to eat sausages anymore?

Can you put your parents in a facility? Can you allow them to stay in their family home when they have difficulty in the kitchen? Can you find the courage to have your father's driver's license taken away? Driving is one of the last vestiges of freedom many elders cling to.

Can you afford to give up your family room for elderly parents? Felicia and Han experienced this problem when Felicia's mother came to live with them full time. The loss of their privacy and almost constant contact with the older woman put a heavy strain on their marriage. In addition, they had to face her discomfort with and criticism about the way they did most things, especially parent their two adolescent daughters. These problems only exacerbated the stress of the financial drain.

## Other Family Needs

It isn't always parents or seniors who need care. When their parents died within a year of each other, the full-time care of their schizophrenic brother Tim fell to Troy, Holly, Shelly, and Meg. Although their parents had tried to leave enough to provide for him financially, Tim needed a home and people to spend time with him. They found a good facility for Tim and developed a schedule for weekly visits. They had to face the hard reality that the inheritance they had expected from the sale of their parents' home would have to be dedicated to Tim's facility.

This family had a uniform commitment to their brother's care. Although Meg, who lived near the facility, did the most, all four contributed financially and visited. It isn't as equitable in other families.

Emily's ill sister had to be cared for in Emily and Todd's home. Although her brother had promised to contribute, his checks came sporadically and unpredictably. Emily's other sister was barely able to care for herself and her child. The financial and care burden was difficult for the couple, and as Todd admitted, "There was a moment when I didn't know if I could keep doing it. Emily was stressed out, my sales were down, and we got an empty envelope of 'help' from Gerry. I called him and told him there was no check in the envelope, and he came close to accusing me of taking it."

When we take in a brother, sister, niece, nephew, grandchild, or in-law, the commitment is often considerable. Any additional person in our household will alter the delicate family homeostasis and force development of a new balance. Not only do the finances have to stretch further, but also space and interpersonal relationships get more complicated.

In some families, siblings have quite different resources and capabilities. In the Carlisle family, the oldest son, Max, was quite able and willing to provide money to help his aging mother, but he did not allow her to even visit his home because of the way she treated his wife. His younger brother, Craig, was able to handle her budget and spending, but he had no room in his small home for another resident. The two sisters, Sherry and Brandy, were willing to provide hands-on care and drive their mother to doctors' visits but unwilling to have her in their homes. All of them agreed that too much time around their mother was "toxic."

Hanging over all the Carlisle siblings is what will happen when their mother, now in her 80s, can no longer live in her own home.

# Dealing With the Top Half of the Sandwich

There are no hard-and-fast rules for taking aging parents or other relatives into a nuclear family. However, experts agree on some guidelines:

- First and foremost are a series of conversations with your spouse. Remember, they aren't related to your parent, do not feel the same level of guilt, and may not have been treated well by the parent. They may also have different values about caring for family. These conversations and negotiations may be extensive and require some significant compromise.
- Consider the impact on the children in the home. Adolescents may have some considerable embarrassment or difficulty with a grandparent who is intrusive or omnipresent. Younger children may feel rejected when the attention they desire goes instead to an elder.
- Talk in advance to all of the family members about what is to happen and get them to buy in as much as possible to the family-oriented values.
- If you are not an only child, have a serious discussion with your brothers and sisters. Try to get agreements for others' contributions. Among these are sharing the financial burden and providing time off for you. Caring for a disabled parent shouldn't mean that you can no longer get away for a weekend or a vacation. Who will cover, for how long, and where?
- Get control over the finances of elders as early as possible. When people get to a certain age, they can become anxious and suspicious about their money. Certainly, if dementia is an issue, you need to make these plans even if you have to institute a conservatorship. It's important to know how much is available and to make plans for how to spend it. If your

parent doesn't want you to have that information, consider a trustworthy fiduciary custodian as an intermediary.

- Protect your parents' nest egg; it's a sad fact of life that fear-spreading scam artists prey on elders.
- Be transparent with your siblings and any other stakeholders. Keep good records of spending and how the funds of the estate are being drawn down. It's common for those not in the know to believe that their inheritance is being tampered with or put at risk by the caretakers. Providing transparency, frequent updates, and continuing discussions about what is happening is the best antidote.
- Anticipate when and if the parents' funds will be depleted and make early plans for specific out-of-pocket contributions.

# Boomerang

Pressure comes from the other direction as well. An estimated 15% of children over the age of 25, once done with school, either stay at home or move back in after a taste of the far less comfortable outside world—and the trend is accelerating as unemployment and underemployment remain high. There has been a significant, hopefully temporary, spike in the numbers of adult children living with parents during the 2020 pandemic.

Morgan was a good student at a small liberal arts college. She and three roommates rented a house near campus for their junior and senior years and did a nice job of managing their resources. Although Morgan had always worked summers and part time while going to school, her parents and student loans covered her tuition, room and board.

When she graduated, she had a fruitless job search in her college's town. After 6 months with only a few temp positions, she moved back in with her parents and is overqualified for the part-time job she has while she looks for permanent work. After submitting "about a hundred job applications that fell into some black hole," she is considering a return to school for a master's degree. She isn't able to both pay off the remainder of her existing student loans and pay rent on her limited income. Although Morgan describes her parents as "cool, for their generation" and says there are no real conflicts, she would like more independence and less scrutiny. So would her parents.

## I Am Almost 60 Years Old and I Know Where My Kids Are ... 24/7

Rashad's family struggled financially while he was growing up, and he had to work to pay his way through college, a process that took almost 7 years. When his first son was born, he swore that he would pay "whatever it took" for the children's education. Despite sacrifices, he and his wife have made good on that promise. Their two oldest have graduated from college, and their youngest is now a junior in high school.

Rashad has been looking forward to having an empty nest, refocusing on his marriage, and catching up on retirement savings when the youngest leaves for school. A number of events have conspired to make that less likely, at least in the near future. After graduating, his son returned home to attend graduate school at a local university. His fiancée (also a grad student) also moved in as a cost-saving measure.

"It's far less expensive than being in his own place," and as Rashad describes, "We have his old room anyhow. We don't really need a guestroom or whatever." Shortly after their son moved back in, their daughter and her husband separated, and she, with her 7-month-old, also returned to the family fold. Again, Rashad reported that his granddaughter is "great to have around, and my daughter is getting back on track." In the meantime, he and his wife have felt they needed to increase their income, and both are working longer hours.

## Catching the Boomerang

What can we do when our adult children want to return home for emotional and financial support? Most experts agree that we must institute new rules. It's natural for these returnees to fall into an old pattern, having their parents take care of them as if they were still adolescents. It's important to signal clearly that this time it's different. Your 20- and 30-something children may be welcome in your home, and in many cultures are obligated to stay until they begin their own families, but a free ride is ill-advised.

- First of all, it's important to emulate those essential parenting skills of firmness and fairness. One way to send a clear message that this is different is to underscore that this is a one-time transitional event based on an identified need. A time limit is optimal if you can set it legitimately. Morgan's parents, for example, set the time as three years to get the master's degree and another 6 months to find a good job. When the time was up and she was still not fully able to support herself, they encouraged her to share an apartment with roommates until she could get her own place. As her dad admitted, "It killed me to take a tough stand with her, but I knew she needed a little push and it would be best for her in the long run."

- It makes sense to charge some affordable rent based on your adult child's earnings. When returning children feel that they are contributing to the household, they are far more likely to assume an adult perspective, giving much more to their parents and feeling much better about themselves. It's important to recognize that most boomerang kids are returning because of necessity, not for an easier life. They are quite likely to feel guilty unless they feel that they can do something to compensate their parents. If rent is not feasible, some duties around the house are effective. If debt is involved, be sure to help them work out and stick to a repayment plan. Bailing them out or forgiving repayable debt may not be a real gift to them in the long run. Similarly, if credit card debt is a problem for your child, help them work out a repayment plan, switch to a debit card, and live within their means. It's one thing to subsidize your boomeranger's room, board, and possibly tuition, but they should be able to earn enough to pay for their recreation.

- Ground rules should be set to include clear adult responsibilities for the boomerang child. These should make a real impact on the parents' time demands. It's customary for returnees to take on chores that they would have to do if they could afford to live on their own, such as meal preparation, laundry, and cleaning. Jalen lost his position as a sous chef when his restaurant closed during the 2020 pandemic. He moved back with his parents and took over all the shopping and meal preparation for the household. The "joke" in his family is that they will keep him on because they never ate so well.

- It's also wise to clearly state, perhaps in the form of a contract, those values-based ground rules that indicate whose house it is. Some families, for example, cannot tolerate a fiancée moving into their son's bedroom. It is best to lay out rules on being a respectful family member in advance. Perhaps your son was accustomed to a certain level of drinking or carousing in college dorms. That may not be acceptable while he lives under your roof. The best rules are ones that the parents also abide by. Of course, it's important to avoid unreasonable rules for adults, such as curfews.

## This Rule Above All

We want and feel obligated to take care of our children, even as adults, but we also need to take care of ourselves. Remember that safety instruction we hear before a plane takes off: "If you are traveling with children … please put your oxygen mask on first." If we sacrifice our own financial future to get a child's financial future squared away, we are potentially hurting our children as well as ourselves. Most financial advisors today insist that their clients maximize their retirement contributions before paying down their children's college debt. Our 25-year-old presumably has 40 earning years ahead of her; we might have 10. Our children are able to take out a loan to fund their education, but nobody will give us a loan to fund our retirement. The closest we can get to such a loan is a reverse mortgage; a bank-friendly device that often provides poor terms and ultimately takes our home from our estate. Remember that if we end up dependent on our children as elders, it will not be good for us or them.

## Helicopter Parents and Boomerang Kids

With fewer children in the home due to the trend of smaller families, greater awareness of the potential dangers to children, and our desire for our children to be successful, there is fertile ground to become overinvolved in managing our children's lives. Some of the 45- to 65-year-old parents have been aptly named helicopter parents. The label describes parents who not only hover over their children's every experience but also actively manage their children's lives at school, play, and even their launching.

It's one thing to avoid lead-based paint on toys, force a recalcitrant child to wear a safety helmet while rollerblading, and insist on seatbelts. It's quite another to have 24/7 cell phone access; be involved in college registration; rewrite their school assignments; do their battles with administrators, coaches, and professors; and get in the middle of a conflict with an erstwhile boyfriend or errant roommate.

Although the goal of helicopter parents is to make their children's lives better, they may inadvertently do the opposite. Instead of being better able to cope with life's events, the child, even as an adult, can become increasingly dependent. This is a prescription for lower motivation and capability to grow into normal adult responsibilities. Although it may seem contradictory, firm, reasonable standards and increasing expectations foster greater independence and growth in our children. When Alicia moved back home with her parents at age 26, she indicated that her mom's calls to her boss to negotiate for her "ruined my reputation at work, and I had to quit." She also said that her mom had frequently called her former live-in boyfriend to pressure him to be better to her. It was not much of a surprise that Alicia appeared to be far less mature than her 26 years.

If you have been a helicopter parent and want to decrease your child's dependence, sit down soon with them and explain that you have done a lot for them, but it's time for them to take over; you plan to be a support in the future, but not on the front lines. This won't be easy. Your child and your strong need to take over will test your resolve to follow through. In the long run, however, it's a far better gift to your child to hold the line.

# I Need a Village to Care for My Family

The most commonly cited estimate is that roughly 30% of all post-midlife parents are caring for unmarried children under the age of 25. About a third of that group is also caring for their aging parents.

This challenge includes demands on time and money. Many of the interviewees described cutting back on work hours, and income, to provide the care. Martina said that after several years of working for her company, "they offered me the promotion and position I had always dreamed of, but with my mother now living with us and the kids still in high school, I don't think I can take it unless Hector [her husband] can pick up the slack at home and give up some of his work." In the face of lower income and increased expenses for such needs as medical equipment and doctors' visits, families can really become strained. For this reason, let alone the loyalty issues and feelings of being torn, it is essential that couples make all decisions related to caring for their family jointly and carefully. Unilateral decisions about what one "has to do" can destabilize a relationship, when stability is essential for making such a difficult situation work optimally.

After many hours of discussing the options alone together, spending time to think, and then consulting a therapist as an independent third party, Martina and Hector made a very big decision about how to deal with her new job offer and the needs at home. Hector cut back at work, going on the family track, and focused more on their children, Martina arranged for her sister to pick up the driving and medical needs of their mother, and Martina became the primary breadwinner in their family until their children graduated from high school.

## Sandwich Exercise (Hold the Mayo)

If an economic and time sandwich is in your present or future, a number of considerations are germane. Answering the following 12 questions is a helpful exercise.

It's useful for you and your partner to write down the answers independently. Once you've answered them separately, share each question one at a time. See where you are on the same page and where you disagree. Consider what compromises you can make to come to a unified agreement that is comfortable for both of you.

1. When are the children on their own and no longer financially dependent?
2. At what age do the children have to rely on themselves to support their lifestyle?
3. What is best for the children: having opportunities and advantages we did not have that are equivalent to their peers or teaching them a stronger work ethic?
4. How is our parenting different from our own parents'?
5. How will we set time and financial commitments for aging parents?
6. What relationship priorities supersede the guilt and shoulds of others' values or priorities?

7. What do I/we want at this time of life?
8. What are our needs for retirement and how can we fund it?
9. Do either or both of us want to expend the time and energy necessary to try to increase income or would we prefer to move to a less expensive area?
10. To what extent are we hiding behind our omnipresent caretaking as a way to avoid facing our own, more personal issues?
11. Am I hanging onto responsibilities and dependence for fear of the empty nest?
12. What are the known and unknown anxieties that might arise for me to face and address? What losses will accompany the extra caretaking and how will we deal with them? Is our personal growth and freedom at risk? What is our relative valuing of guilt, obligation, and altruism?

# chapter nine

# Time Is the Essence

*Time is the coin of your life. It is the only coin you have, and only you can determine how it will be spent. Be careful lest you let other people spend it for you.*

—Carl Sandburg

Most of us living in North America have been blessed with a comparatively easy life. We have lived in an era when shortages have been inconvenient rather than desperate. Our parents and grandparents may have been children during the Great Depression, but despite the Great Recession of 2008 and the 2020 pandemic, our own lives generally have been more comfortable than those of our ancestors. At least for those in the economic middle class and above, there have been opportunities for upward mobility and a better life. To some extent, even traditionally disenfranchised groups have made positive strides during the boomers' and Xers' lifetimes. However, most experts agree that those in the generations coming of age in the early part of the 21st century, especially minorities, are less likely to have the advantage of that upward trend. In fact, many are expected to have more challenging lives than their parents. Of course, immigration and the acculturation process will also impact the trend line.

The opportunities for a better and longer life are not limitless. To the best of our knowledge, time is the only truly limited commodity in life and therefore the most precious. Regardless of how long we live, we know that our personal era on earth will end. Somewhere around midlife, this temporal limitation in life becomes salient. After midlife, the personal hourglass is turned over and the sands seem to run through ever faster. There is a growing and more persistent urgency as the subjective experience of passing time accelerates.

- How do you spend your time?
- Does it reflect what's most important to you?
- When is the last time you were bored?
- Is life "passing you by?"
- When do you have time to do what you want, instead of what you have to?
- Do work and chores expand to fill all available time?
- When is it *your* time?
- What do you still need to accomplish for success, happiness, or the future?
- Do you need to heed the warning from Carl Sandburg about being master of your own time?
- To what extent has the COVID-19 pandemic affected the way you spend your time?

Your answers to these questions will provide a glimpse into those aspects of your life that you may want to expand or change.

If what you most cherish is time with friends and family, creativity at work, hobbies, or your community, your time allotments should reflect that increasingly. One of the keys to success during these years is to stop putting off for later what is best for us today. It's time for a conscious acknowledgment of how to best spend our time.

This is very different from how we best allocated time in our 30s. While building families and careers, we expanded our working time, often to build a better future for ourselves and our children. Just as it was appropriate to defer gratification when we were younger, it is now time to defer less and enjoy more. This post-midlife shift in time allotment is essential to living fully during these years.

Yoshie described it well, "I'm proud of our kids and the nest egg we built, and I've had a productive career, but now is our time to enjoy the fruits of our labors. We don't want to wait until we are too old to enjoy what we've got." Her husband added, "I want to play with and enjoy my grandkids, on the floor and in the yard, not viewing them from an old folks' rocker. It's like the man said, 'Use it or lose it.'"

## Time Is Prime

A little older than the oldest boomers, Carole and Eddie have some valuable perspectives on time to offer. A married couple in their early 70s, they made a momentous decision when they were in their early 60s to cease doing anything unnecessary that they didn't enjoy. They cut back dramatically on their work as university professors. Keeping the teaching and scholarly work that they both relished, they eliminated the frustrating, higher-status administrative aspects of academia and stopped teaching summer school. Free for almost 4 months a year, they spent more time with friends and began living for a month at a time away from their home. They also greatly reduced time with people who they found more of a drain than a pleasure.

The redistribution of time did have a cost. To pay for this life change, they live more simply and frugally, no longer drive new cars, and go easy on unnecessary expenses. It was a worthwhile trade-off. For Carole and Eddie, clearly "time is prime!"

## New Dreams, New Lifestyles

Not everyone can or would make the same choice, but people who make a reasonable assessment of how they spend their time after midlife will use the latter half of their lives more fruitfully.

Are you determining how your time is spent? Would reorganizing your time allotments be valuable? Is there a dream you'd like to follow? What sacrifices would you be willing to make to reprioritize and rebalance how you spend your time? What fears do you avoid by staying on a frantic schedule?

Miriam's lifelong dream was to travel to Europe. Many factors kept her from doing so earlier in her life. She had responsibilities to her husband and children. For many years, she cared for her aging parents and in-laws. Then, when she was 60, her husband died. She turned down the options of going back to work full-time and moving in with her married daughter as a childcare provider and grandmother-in-residence. Instead, she mastered a computer for the first time, researched carefully, and then took off for 3 months of travel with only what she could carry in a backpack, staying in private homes, elder hostels, and inexpensive pensions. When the 3 months became a year, she returned home long enough to sell her house, move in with her daughter's family for six months, and plan a second trip to Europe. When she isn't traveling these days, she is writing a book on "how to travel well as an old lady on a limited budget." She confessed that she didn't think the book was very good, but "whenever I write about my experiences, I get to relive them."

## Using Our Skills in a New Way

Most of the interviewees were interested in reducing stress and responsibilities. For the first time, status and honors were secondary to quality of life. Some of the interviewees were cutting back at work and handing off some time-intensive, less enjoyable aspects of work to ambitious younger workers. Many also spoke about shifting into a mentor's role at work or in their communities. A large number began new or reestablished former creative activities such as music and artistic pursuits.

Not everyone reduces responsibilities. Lewis and Karen actually increased theirs, rededicating themselves to community service after an early retirement. Lewis had considerable administrative skills from his 30-year military career. Karen was an experienced community organizer. For the past 6 years, they have worked together directing a major charitable organization. Not only is their nonprofit successful, but they truly enjoy working together.

Pointing to Karen, Lewis said with a boyish grin, "I get to hang out all day with this good-looking babe that I keep falling for." Lewis said he always had the idea that he'd die on the battlefield in uniform, yet he found that the new service career was just as meaningful and rewarding as his years of military service. Both of them claim to be inspired by the work of former president Jimmy Carter, "whose efforts for peace and work with Habitat for Humanity since he left office have overshadowed his presidency."

## Different Strokes

A great deal of the way we use time has to do with what aging means to us. Those who consider age 60 or 65 the time to retire and be "put out to pasture" were more likely to be interested in pastimes and hobbies than in new initiatives; whereas those who think of this age as the beginning of the next period of life often allotted their time to new endeavors that will keep them active and involved. Looking ahead to retirement, Dychtwald and Morison present four general, but not permanent, paths: continuing to work or re-hirement; exploring leisure time through adventure, travel, or being grandparents; living for the moment and enjoying life, regardless of finances, including many who take on new income producing opportunities; and struggling to make ends meet and experiencing retirement less as "golden years" and more of unpleasant old age.

These approaches to post-retirement age begin with planning earlier, especially in midlife and the ensuing 20 years until 65. The most significant aspect of this for 45- to 65-year-old men and women is that they have considerable say in how they want the later stages of life to be.

One group of individuals was different. Uninterested in changing or in looking at the options newly available in their lives, they simply continued to act 30 or 40 in a 60-year-old body. These individuals actively competed with younger colleagues, kept on the same trajectory that was set for them when they were in their 20s, and sometimes left marriages to find younger or like-minded partners who would support these efforts. By allocating their time as if they were 30- or 40-something, they risk failing to rebalance life to correspond to their chronological age. In doing so, they miss out on post-midlife possibilities.

## Tempus Fugit

Have you noticed that now you've completed the climb of the first half of your life, the clock is moving faster? Do you feel like you're on a temporal downslope? Like most things, time rolls downhill faster than it goes upward. Of course, this sense of time speeding up is a purely subjective experience.

Ray described this perfectly when talking about his daughter's impending college graduation: "I know eight years have passed, but it seems like she was just entering high school last year, and now she's finished university." Loretta, his wife, replied in a more complex way, "I agree with Ray that it seems like just yesterday when she went off as a freshman to high school, but her last two years in college have also seemed like ten, because of all the demands in her life the past several months." They both reflected on the difficult job market into which she graduated and commented, "We may have her back for a while until she gets something," intimating that there may be a subjective reversal of time in the near future.

Loretta's reflection of the variability of the experience of time isn't unusual. Urgencies, particularly those that involve our children or health, can seem interminable while they're happening. Yet from another perspective, the time it takes for our kids to go from diapers to having their own children seems to go a lot faster than 20 or 30 years.

## So Little Time, So Much to Do

Another aspect of time is that at ages 45 to 65, most of us think we can get as much done as we did when we were younger. This phenomenon can lead us to overfill our plate with demands, leaving little time for reflection or pleasure. The highly successful men and women we interviewed believed that they could keep up with those much younger. In fact, we do slow down as we age. This doesn't mean that we are less effective or accomplished; it simply means that we act and react slower, both physically and emotionally. It also means we get to linger more, contemplate history, more carefully weigh options and savor the good times.

Professional athletes have to learn this lesson, usually by the time they are in their 30s. They have to play smarter and take shortcuts to be successful against younger more athletic opponents. Five-time Olympic swimmer Dara Torres was something of a marvel, competing into her 40s and racing successfully against much younger competitors. Satchel Paige pitched in the major leagues in baseball when he was in his 50s; Gordie Howe was playing hockey at a similar age. They may not have been as dominant as they were in their earlier years, but they became better attuned to the rhythms of the game and are able to conserve energy. In recent years, two of the oldest pitchers in baseball, Tim Wakefield and Jamie Moyer, were slow-pitch specialists. Neither relied on power to accomplish the job of getting batters out.

It is easy to see how athletic prowess wanes quickly with age. Consider the fate of female gymnasts who appear to be on the career downslope soon after reaching puberty. However, athletics serve as a model for almost every field of endeavor. By the time we are in our 40s, characteristically, we switch from field work to management, both because we can through promotions, and because those are the skills that we can best use after midlife.

J.T. described his work as a computer programmer: "When I was thirty, I'd come in at noon and stay till past midnight to get the job done. I just threw my energy (and a lot of caffeine) into completion. Recently, I work smarter. I still keep late hours, but I actually stop in the middle of writing code and pick it up the next day." What seemed telling was his comment "You know, I think my output is actually better in quality if not in quantity."

Aja related, "I've been with the postal service since high school Christmas jobs. In the old days I drove a truck and delivered mail. Now I am in the office working the desk. The pay is better and I'm not exhausted after work."

## Don't Put Off to Tomorrow What Can Be Done Today

What does this proverb offer us today? It relates to avoiding procrastination at work as before, but it takes on an additional meaning during these stretch years. It begins to relate to pleasure as well.

Crystal, a 62-year-old retired teacher, described it like this, "It's as if when I turned forty-five, the hourglass turned over, and the sand was now dropping the other way. I had the deep sense that when the sand was gone from the top, it would not be turned over another time."

Like Crystal, we are increasingly aware that time is running out. For most, this means using the remaining time well, especially the time when we have sufficient health and vitality. There are, of course, folks in their 90s who still perform quite well, but these years can provide an awakening for most of us. In Crystal's words, "If this isn't my time, when will my time be?"

## Using Time

Consider for a moment that this is the time for you to refocus on more enjoyable options. What have you been putting off because your "shoulds" use up your time? When you are on vacation, how do you spend your time? Do you shift from serving one master at work to serving family and friends, or do you kick back or engage in activities that you otherwise miss?

For Miriam, who made her second half of life an exercise in travel, Crystal, who is focused on her new grandchildren and a new romance, and Joseph, who is "trying my hand at being a novelist," the years between midlife and retirement provide an opportunity to pursue what they desire more than what is required of them, the realistic focus of the earlier part of their lives.

## Leftovers Are Good, but Not Seven Days a Week

What would it take to change your priorities? Getting control over your calendar is a crucial first step. When you look at your calendar, what do you enter first? What if you put your pleasurable items in first and built your work life around them—the reverse of what people typically do? "Responsible" people fill up their calendars with mandatory, time-consuming tasks and get to keep what's left over.

Sadly, most of us realize that there is no, or precious little, time left. So, we postpone pursuing our bliss. As a couple therapist for many years, I often recommend strongly that the first thing to go on the family calendar is date night. This is the first priority, not something left as a chore that we try to squeeze in between other demands.

One of the exercises psychotherapists sometimes offer clients is to answer the following question: If you only had a year to live, how would you spend it? It's worthwhile to consider your answer. It's a rare person who, faced with the end of life, says that she would opt to spend the remaining time on chores or demands at work.

## Here and Now or There and Then

For a good part of life, we are planning for the future. Years of schooling and work have been geared to learning what we need to be successful in our culture. Although there are many moments of immediacy and poignancy, most of us have learned the essential importance of delaying gratification.

To some extent, the post-midlife years involve a continuation of this planning. The years from 45 to 65 are often the prime earning years. Not until these years are the majority of individuals able to put away sufficient funds for retirement and preparation for their senior years. As might be expected, there is a tension between this need for future security and the realization that these years of life are also the era we have been planning for previously. It's time to harvest and enjoy the fruits of our labor. In the words of a wise man, "It's good you have been saving for a rainy day, because it's starting to drizzle."

This tension, like those discussed earlier, is both a macro, over-arching struggle and a moment-by-moment experience. One thing is certain: If you are to begin to reap the benefits you have been saving for, you need to be more fully present psychologically.

## No Time Like the Present

Living fully requires stopping, at least temporarily, the frenzy of life and the planning for the future to experience living in the here and now. It is vital to come into full contact with all your senses to savor the experience of living.

Being more fully aware in the present isn't easy for most of us to do. Consider the words of Alonzo, "I know I should just slow down and enjoy my life, but I have no time to slow down. There's so much to do and so much to plan ahead for. You know how much I love to ski, right? Well even when I'm skiing and truly enjoying it, I'm checking my phone and thinking, when will this be over so I can get back to work and errands?"

Alonzo's focus on what's next minimizes his experience of the present. He could reduce this conflict by eliminating the skiing and just stay at work—a seductive solution to many—but that's the opposite of a healthy, growthful approach. Far more beneficial would be for Alonzo to find a way to be fully aware of skiing when he is on the slopes and equally conscious of work when he is on the job.

Mandy said something similar in response to a suggestion that she take a "real" vacation for a change—one without her cell phone and laptop. "How can I just go off and take a vacation when there's no coverage for the dogs or the office and there's laundry to do and the garage is a mess and needs to be cleaned out ... besides," she added, almost with relief, "Joe [her husband] can't take that kind of time off anyway."

From an existential perspective, the emerging question is what Mandy would have to face on a real vacation. The pull of the status quo for her is particularly potent. We are drawn to keep doing what we have always done and to avoid the unknown. Most of us who have been immersed in careers inside or out of the home are more oriented to doing than to being.

This is about more than stopping to smell the roses; this is about using the precious time and physical capacity we have left to cherish these moments. We are best served if we use the time to engage in things that we truly enjoy and that allow our creativity to emerge. Although the actual behavioral changes may be quite small, the personal meaning of these changes is significant.

Vivian talked about how until she was in her late 50s her life was always her reacting as best she could to what the world brought her. She related a history of both very good and very difficult times and of how she was proud that others could always rely on her resolve and resourcefulness. When asked what changed, she laughed heartily and replied,

> You're gonna think this is silly, but one thing is now I go to movies by myself. I used to wait until I knew what everyone else wanted to see and organize the event. Just last week, I told my husband and my best friend that I wanted to see this one movie. Neither of them wanted to plan to go, so I just went on my own. I never would have done that when I was younger. ... I also decided that I'm not going to any more formal affairs for my husband's work. I hated them for years, and so now I'm going to the movies instead.

For Vivian, doing more of what she enjoyed and avoiding what she disliked was part and parcel of the privilege of aging. It may seem a small shift to others, but Vivian's newfound freedom for self-care is making a real difference. Vivian's cousin Madeleine had a much more dramatic shift just around her 60th birthday. Discovering that her husband had resumed a sexual relationship with a long-time mistress, she decided that living alone was better than being in a relationship that involved betrayal. Within a year, she divorced, moved to a new city, and began working in a part-time job that she had long desired.

When asked what prompted the abrupt life shake-up, Madeleine replied,

> It wasn't really that abrupt. I'm just now doing what I want, not what he wants or my parents wanted or my kids want. You know, I used to spend all my waking hours being Mrs. K. Now I'm doing what's good for me, and you know what? Every day, I enjoy the sunshine and the rain and being alive, puttering around in my little garden, reading, and meeting new people. I've even started to date a man in my ballroom dancing class. The weird thing is now that I'm independent, Kenny keeps trying to get me back. I guess now I am interesting to him too.

You have certainly had many experiences of living in the here and now. Consider those times when you were absorbed in something, your thoughts, a walk, or some "mindless" task like sanding a table. On how many occasions have you emerged from such a task only to be surprised about how much time has passed? When you're absorbed in something, it involves you fully. When you're really listening to music, watching a movie, or reading a novel or "in the zone" of physical activity, you're not focused on how or when it will end and lead to the next task. Although you may wait for and appreciate the crescendo of the cannons at the conclusion, you don't listen to or fast forward through the rest of the 1812 Overture. It's the same with a good novel. The ending may be a delight, but only if we are lost enough in the characters to make it mean something to us.

This is the reverse of watching a pot of water and waiting, apparently endlessly, for it to boil. There is little interest in the experience of watching or of the water heating up or beginning to bubble. All of our interest is in it getting to a boil. This is the opposite of the time contraction experienced in being absorbed.

# Living Life Versus Planning to Live Life

Gestalt psychotherapist Fritz Perls was wont to counsel that a core of self-knowledge was to lose our minds and come to our senses. There are several advantages to following his advice:

- When we are absorbed in our experiences, we are living more fully.
- We feel more alive and enjoy life more.
- We get into the flow or process of our experience instead of the specific outcomes or content of tasks, which by definition are more time limited.
- We become more aware of ourselves and of the world around us.
- We are able to get closer to our spiritual selves.
- We are more likely to do the right thing instead of being diverted into doing things right.

Among philosophers and psychotherapists, there is a line of thought referred to as *phenomenology*, a tenet of existentialism. Our subjective perceptions and the meaning we give to those perceptions are central to living more fully. From this perspective, personal meaning in life is enhanced from living each moment as fully and with as much wonderment as possible. As many psychotherapists remind us, "To be alive and responsive to yourself and others, you have to show up."

As we come to understand during these years, our best-laid plans might not yield us what we expected. By focusing on our subjective experience, we will increasingly be in touch with what is in our lives rather than what *could have been*. Of course, this potentially opens us up to more pain, but as the existentialists will argue, "'tis better to suffer the true pains of living than to suffer worse by avoiding life."

A well-known biblical passage speaks to both the importance of being in sync with a time in life and the fact that there are indeed different seasons in life:

For everything there is a season,
And a time for every matter under heaven:
A time to be born, and a time to die;
A time to plant, and a time to pluck up what is planted;
A time to kill, and a time to heal;
A time to break down, and a time to build up;
A time to weep, and a time to laugh;
A time to mourn, and a time to dance;
A time to throw away stones, and a time
to gather stones together.
A time to embrace, and a time to refrain from
embracing;
A time to seek, and a time to lose;
A time to keep, and a time to throw away;
A time to tear, and a time to sew;
A time to keep silence, and a time to speak;
A time to love, and a time to hate,
A time for war, and a time for peace.[1]

This ancient wisdom focuses us on being present for the sowing and the reaping rather than on struggling against the tide to plant in autumn and harvest in spring. To do otherwise will be frustrating, and we may go hungry.

# Exercises

A. Imagine you have 1 year to live. What would you do during that time? With this unique focus, what would you allow to fall into the background and what would you bring forth as essential? How is that different from how you currently manage your life?

B. What stops you from living now as if you had but a year? Consider the extent to which you inhibit yourself from doing what you want in normal (non-fantasy) situations and whether the reasons are wise or simply represent inhibition. Review the timeline chart you drew in Chapter 2.

---

1 Ecclesiastes 3:1–8.

Focus on the portion of the chart that is to the right of the X indicating your current age into the future.

- What goals are best set during the time remaining in your life?
- What will get in the way of pursuing your desired goals?
- Which goals are best dropped?
- Which excuses will you use to keep from the desired goals?
- What isn't on the chart that you would like there?
- What aspects of your life have you been putting off?
- If you have been planting until now, what might you harvest? What can you stop doing now to save for later or as a legacy? What do you want to sow anew?

C. What boundaries can you set on others' influencing your activities, thoughts, and ways of relating?

D. If unexpected unemployment, illness of you or a family member, or if COVID-19-related reduced income and seclusion has altered your plans, how can you catch up without losing a sense of being present as well?

# Part

**Planning for Retirement**

# chapter ten

# Retirement Planning

## The Financials

*The stark truth about managing our money these days is that we are mostly on our own.*

—Ron Lieber[1]

Disclaimer: Anything as important as retirement planning should be done with a trusted financial planning professional. The ideas presented here are best used only heuristically. Your individual circumstances will likely not fit exactly into any general model.

The stretch years lead up to and end essentially with retirement, although depending on one's work life and physical and economic factors, actual retirement may come somewhat earlier or later. During these years, you will have to prepare and plan for the next stages of your life. What you do now will determine the quality of your retirement, or even whether you will be able to retire at all.

There's little question that the concept of retirement, borne on the previous generation's life expectancy, pension plans, expanding economy, and promises is rapidly vanishing. The fantasy of a permanent vacation for the rest of your

---

1   Lieber, R. (2008) Five basics for building a solid financial future. *New York Times,* May, 17, 2008, B, p. 1.

life will be out of reach for all but the wealthiest few or those with an alternative, nonconsuming, or "off-the-grid" lifestyle.

This shift in retirement expectations reflects the economic realities of shrinking pensions, longevity, the devaluation of self-funded retirement plans, such as IRAs and 401k's, and on the "ever-youthful" boomer mind-set. It may also be an undesirable way to live out our senior years. Indeed, surveys indicate that only about 20%–25% of people approaching retirement envision a lifelong vacation as a favorable endeavor.

The good news is we will live longer and healthier, have more opportunities for variety in life, and new challenges to surmount. The "other" news is that those goodies come with a price. Most notably, for most of us, age 65 will fade as a marker of retirement as we continue to work for some time after that arbitrary age. Very simply, living longer will cost more.

The big financial questions today are "Will I outlive my money?" "How will I support myself in retirement?" "My assets are all in my house. How will that support me?"

In this chapter and the next we explore the predictable concerns and lay out some methods to plan for a personally satisfying retirement. Although the financial and psychological aspects of retirement are interlinked, we will explore financials in this chapter and psychological considerations in the next. Some foreseeable detours on the way to a fiscally successful retirement are identified, and strategies to surmount these blocks are described.

# Retirement

For most of human existence, there was no thing called retirement. Individuals worked in their communities until they died. The nature of the work might shift over time, but nobody was expected to have time off to enjoy the fruits of their former labors.

The concept of retirement, outside of care of elders by their families, is a relatively new concept in human history.

## When Can I Retire?

The first known retirement age of 65 was set in the late 1800s by Otto Von Bismarck in Germany. When he set the age of 65 for retirement, he wasn't being very generous. Expected life span at the time was just 45 and only about 3% of the population lived to benefit at 65. In 1935, when Roosevelt's Social Security plan adopted the same age, the average life expectancy was only 61. Only a minority were able to use their benefits for very long.

Today, with an average life expectancy in the 80s, it is inevitable that Social Security benefits will have to be adjusted to avoid failing while the boomers and especially the Xers are alive and aged.

It is hard to remember that extensive pensions were available only for a single generation of Americans. Sully was one of the fortunate ones. When he retired from General Motors after 25 years, he was under 50. He passed away at age 91, predeceasing his wife by 2 years. In sum, they received monthly pension checks from GM for over 40 years (well more than he had actually worked for the company).

Such retirement packages and other "loyalty" benefits for all but the highest level of management and some civil servants are rapidly disappearing, and are unlikely ever to return. As people today start reaching the magic age of 65 (67 or 68 for younger boomers and gen Xers), they will have to rely on other sources. Of course, at least for the older members of the generations, there will be some Social Security benefits, but these were always meant as a safety net to provide food and shelter. They were never intended as a path to the good life, nor a way to spend one's days in relative leisure. Indeed, when it comes to retirement, it is not much different than it was in Bismarck's day—except we are older and healthier. The bottom line is that we have to provide for our own retirement and some portion of our lifelong health care.

For today's generations, with an average life expectancy in the 80s, Social Security is typically only one component of retirement planning. Increasing life expectancy along with the decline in defined benefit pension plans for middle-class workers, a proliferation of nuclear and alternative (versus extended) family configurations, divorces, and smaller families in general make comprehensive retirement planning essential.

# How Can I Retire?

Since the 1930s and through the 20th century, there was a three-pronged approach to support the retirement years:

1. a pension;
2. Social Security benefits; and
3. personal savings.

In the 21st century, most individuals will not have traditional pensions, will likely see a reduction in Social Security benefits, and will realize that a longer life requires a more substantial cushion. In addition, among those currently in their stretch years, there is an additional burden of debt, accrued while financing their education and present consumerism. Among those interviewed, a majority were as yet insufficiently solvent to support themselves. The average 60-year-olds reportedly have approximately \$135,000 saved for retirement, a number far below the estimated \$1.1 million considered by financial advisors to be sufficient. In 2019, a TD Ameritrade retirement survey concluded that at least half of retirees will be unable to maintain their pre-retirement lifestyle.

Indeed, many who were confident or already retired a few years ago found their savings, IRAs, 401, 403, and 456[2] plans decimated by as much as 40% in the recession that began in 2007. Those who stayed in the market and did not cash out at the bottom have seen the numbers recover and rise only to have a similar downturn and potential rebound in 2020. Most significantly, such market volatility has shaken their confidence.

In fact, in our survey, only 7% of responders described a savings plan and long-term strategy of living within (or below) their means. That minority had set a retirement date and had a plan and funds available to support that strategy.

## Current Retirement Planning?

- Twenty-two percent of interviewees had no long-term plan and could easily outlive their savings and benefits.
- Twenty-one percent were saving aggressively with the hope of catching up.
- Fourteen percent reported no plans to retire. They reported that they planned "to work until they dropped."
- Twelve percent, more often women, had already begun or planned small businesses that they could do at or close to home.

---

2   The numbers of these plans 401, 403, 457 all refer to U.S. tax codes for deferred taxation.

- Re-hirement. Almost 20% planned to retire from one career and then take a less stressful job "for the benefits."
- Almost 30% planned to sell their home, move into far more modest accommodations, keep the old autos running, and change their lifestyle.
- Five percent were anticipating a windfall inheritance and believed that it would be sufficient to support their lifestyle through their retirement years.

Almost all of the interviewees expected to be more frugal, usually implying a major shift in consumption and spending.

## The Last Taboo

Compounding these real difficulties is a reticence to talk about them. Responding to questions about finances is not easy for most people. Money may be the last taboo topic in our society. Long after they confide in their therapists, rather unconventional sexual yearnings or behaviors, will clients keep their income or financial wherewithal secret. Both debt and largesse somehow are shameful to make public. Boomers, for all their competitiveness and comparisons of the cost of their real estate, remain guarded about the topic. Indeed, in our interviews, the most frequently unanswered queries were the ones about finances. Hopefully, in the privacy of your home there are some opportunities to consider openly your financial concerns, and how they may be addressed effectively.

## Okay, Bottom Line, How Much Do You Need?

Headlines of popular periodicals, unsolicited email, and daily surface mail carry dire predictions for the boomer generation, and even more for Gen Xers. Course offerings at local community centers, radio and television programs, a host of experts, websites, calculators, and programs offer an opportunity to determine "the number"—the amount needed to retire successfully, without worry. Sadly, these "experts" provide quite contrasting opinions. With all the media attention, sales pitches, "free" enticement dinners for annuity sales, numerical models, and scare tactics, most people are increasingly uncomfortable about their financial planning.

Is the problem real, and, if so, what can you do now? Can we just turn our finances over to experts and have them do what's necessary? Many did that and suffered tremendous losses in the infamous Bernie Madoff Ponzi scheme. Who can I trust? Is it already too late if you are in your 50s?

## Diminished Trust

Recent economic catastrophes in the United States and worldwide have roiled retirement savings, and even though the stock market has rebounded, the psychological anxiety, engendered by the exposure of massive fraud and theft by those who were supposed to have fiduciary responsibility, remains in our hearts and minds. For a large number of people in the 45- to 65-year age range, there is great mistrust of investment advisors, who may place their own interests ahead of their clients, or bankers who have done little to regain the trust dashed by the 2008 mortgage crisis, credit default swaps, and other arcane financial instruments with little or no underlying basis. Several of these may emulate pyramid schemes, shell games, and "last fool in" perspectives. Compounding this is that regulations put in place to protect against such practices have been largely decimated or eliminated by the Trump administration.

Developing strategies to reach your financial goals should involve a simple mathematics equation and a little discipline. Unfortunately, for many it is far more complicated. Whatever method is used to establish "the number" involves guesses, probabilities, and assumptions. Take any of the retirement calculators available on the internet, at the brokerage houses, or insurance companies. Inevitably, the future retiree will be asked to estimate long-term inflation rates, a speculation the Federal Reserve chairman is loath to make. Even more disconcerting is the bottom line that these computer programs yield; the vast majority of individuals cannot save enough or afford to retire.

## Estimating the Number

For the majority of Americans, retirement income will have to be pieced together from a variety of resources. Social Security benefits may provide only about 25% of your needs, meaning IRA accounts and other tax deferred accounts or savings have to make up the deficit.

As a quick rule of thumb, it takes a million dollars in savings to throw off $40,000 in after-tax income, assuming a small decrement in the principal over time. If your expenses are around a $100,000 a year, and Social Security yields for a married couple is about $40,000, that leaves a remainder of $60,000 to come from your retirement savings. That would require at least $1.4 million in savings. That level of savings is well beyond the average family. This means that strategies to both increase income and reduce expenses will be necessary.

## Sad Realities

Until the real estate bubble burst in 2007–2008, many Americans seemed to believe they could live beyond their means, as long as the values of their houses were rising. Meanwhile, half of the families without traditional corporate pension plans or 401(k) plans have saved less than $40,000, and fully a third of households have saved nothing for retirement.

## The Lucky Few

In fact, some modest number of the Boomer Generation and fewer Gen Xers will be spared any inconvenience because of an expected generational transfer of wealth through family estates,[3] trusts, or because of a careful, long-term, regular savings program. However, for a number of reasons, this great wealth will not be not equally distributed. Many boomers who grew up and thrived in times of open possibilities and a fantasy of few limits are going to have to face some other realities.

---

3  The estimated $70 trillion expected to be transferred in the first 3 decades of the 21st century has shrunk dramatically because of the longevity and financial needs of the current older generation and market downturns, despite the longest economic expansion in history. It seems at this point less clear what the actual wealth transfer will entail, but for the average middle-class person, $50,000 to $100,000 may be considered a substantial inheritance. The $11–22 million exclusion on taxes, enacted during the Trump administration will be a pipe dream for all but the wealthiest 1% of the population. (the current exclusion is scheduled to drop to $5–10 million in 2025).

# What Can You Do to Vouchsafe a Viable Retirement?

There are two phases of financial planning: accumulation and spending.

Most of the attention by financial advisors is at least initially on the accumulation phase. How much do you need to accrue to have a secure retirement? The retirement calculators and related questionnaires, available from brokerage houses, insurance companies, and organizations like AARP, provide some general perspective on what your fixed costs will be and how much principal you will need for the number of years you are likely to live.

The calculated number you need to reach will vary across calculators and assumptions, so they are best viewed as a general guideline. *Spoiler alert*: Most individuals who do complete the calculations suffer from some kind of sticker shock at the sheer numbers of dollars involved. The notion that a million dollars or more in savings may be necessary for the average family to maintain their lifestyle is quite daunting.

## Will I Outlive My Money?

That question has grown from a perplexing query, discreetly posed across the dinner table or by confidential financial advisors, to an almost unending threat that comes at the post-midlife crowd from a multitude of media.

Look at the headlines of popular periodicals. The issue of financial security is front page, from expected sources such as *Money* magazine, *Forbes*, and the *Wall Street Journal* to mainstream *Time*, daily newspapers, and even alternatives such as the *Utne Reader*, and to innumerable internet-based articles, inquiries, and sales pitches. What answers do we have to the question pondered on the late July 2009 cover of *Newsweek* are again center stage, "the recession is over; will you survive the Recovery?" Today, another economic downturn, has accompanied the pandemic crisis. This time, the discrepancy between the wealthy and others is more extreme. While the stock market has made up the March, 2020 losses and hit new highs in December of 2020, those who are not invested in securities have had to place their retirement planning on hold. With rises in unemployment, pressure to feed and shelter their families, greater medical costs, they are unable to put money away for the future.

For anyone worried about retirement, there are endless course offerings at the local community center. Listen to the radio or watch television programs and many of the dominant themes involve money, money management, financial issues, and retirement. Follow some of the web links or pop-ups whenever you do a Google or Yahoo search and once again there are computer estimators to provide "the (magic) number."

Although these media warnings are important in a world in which most of us will be funding our retirement life personally, they are frustrating for several reasons. For one, they ask you to provide some expertise that may be beyond your capability.

Here is a typical example from one of the internet-based services. The numbers represent the situation of Sal, a well-employed single person.

### BOX 10.1 Sal

| | |
|---|---|
| Your current age | 55 |
| Age at expected retirement | 65 |
| Annual income | $85,000 |
| Expected expenses in retirement | $70,000 |
| Social Security benefit | $24,000 |
| How much you currently save annually | $8,500 |
| Your estimate for rate of inflation for use in this calculation | 4% |
| Current value of your investments | $400,000 |
| Annual return on your investments, or what rates you expect to receive | 7.5% |
| Other sources of income you will have post-retirement (inheritance, pension, royalties, etc.)? | $24,000 |
| Rate of increase in income (i.e., raises) expected between now and retirement? | 3% |

According to the resultant calculation, the amount needed for retirement is over $2 million and Sal, the individual in this example, will have just under $1 million. Except for his Social Security benefits of $2,000 per month, his funds will completely run out 11 years after retirement, when he is 76.

By working 3 more years until age 68, the funds will last an additional 4 years—until age 80, still below the expected life span for men and women who reach age 65. By cutting his expenses in retirement to $60,000, he can add another 3 years.

Any changes in assumptions can have major impact. For example, an inflation rate of 3.5% instead of 4% will add 2 more years onto the time before money runs out and an 8% return on investment also adds 2 years. If Sal were married and his spouse also receives Social Security benefits, the age increases to 86.

The calculations are solely for planning purposes. Nobody can reliably foretell many of the crucial criteria. In addition, this particular example does not account for cost of living differences. Sal resides near Cincinnati, Ohio. A person living in San Francisco, Honolulu, or New York with identical resources would have a far bleaker picture.

> ### BOX 10.2 Bob and Alice
>
> Bob and Alice do live in one of those more expensive areas, a suburb west of Boston. They are a healthy, vibrant couple who until 2020 were on the brink of retirement.
>
> At ages 60 and 62, they've done it all right, saving 15% of their income for retirement and living within their means. Their vision of the "golden years" includes an active life with a moderate country club membership, increased time with children and grandchildren, and occasional travel.
>
> According to a summary provided by their financial planner at the end of 2019, "You are on track to fully and easily fund your vision." By April of 2020, their portfolio had lost 35% and their retirement vision seems so much more distant. To be sure, Bob and Alice will probably be okay, but they are now faced with a significant choice: Do they retire in 2 years as planned when Bob reaches 62 with a lower standard of retirement, or do they delay retirement to rebuild their savings and portfolio?

> ## BOX 10.3 Carla and Will
>
> At approximately the same age, Carla and Will face a more dire consideration. Unlike Bob and Alice, they do not have the "luxury" of a decision about working longer, cutting back on country club memberships, or travel. In 2018, they had made plans to wait 3 years until they were both 65 and then retire to their low mortgage rate home in upstate New York.
>
> Because they had some debt and began to save for retirement later in life, they had been more aggressive in their investment choices. It was working well for a few years and then they lost over 40% of their savings in the market downturn of 2008. Worried about continuing losses, they sold the remaining stocks and converted investment income to cash. Thus, they missed the lengthy bull-market rebound. They also suffered an unexpected escalation in their adjustable mortgage and had to take out a home equity line of credit for both repairs and living expenses. They did get some relief by refinancing their mortgage at a significantly lower interest rate.
>
> By April 2020, they were faced with a reassessment of plans and a realization that retirement would be put off a minimum of 5 years.

These couples are not unique. According to a July 2009 issue of *U.S. News & World Report* and confirmed by similar estimates, the 1-year loss in equities to "Main Street" portfolios was over $7 *trillion*, about 30% from retirement accounts. Naturally, the boomers were among the hardest hit. Gen Xers have suffered similar losses, and although they have more time to make up the difference between what they have and what they need, they are reportedly more stressed. In fact, one of the most common responses among those currently 45 to 55 is "My generation really got screwed between 2008 and 2020."

So what if we all have to work longer? After all, we also expect to live longer and healthier as well. Two factors play into this phenomenon: Jobs for 60-somethings are not always easy to get or keep; each job we do land in a contracting economy that has significant levels of unemployment means one job that will not go to a younger worker, one whose FICA deductions will presumably be funding their elders' Social Security and Medicare.

## Debt

Another complication for boomers and Gen Xers is debt. According the New York Federal Reserve and Experion, Gen Xers have on average around $40,000 remaining in student debt. Despite their greater time to repay student loans, boomers reportedly have just under $35,000 on average. Any debt impacts the value of one's assets and adds another expense.

Many people in Gen X are juggling several different financial obligations: paying down a home mortgage, credit card debt, raising children, education debt, and perhaps helping out their aging parents. This leaves them with shifting priorities and innumerable financial masters to serve at once.

It is always very difficult to deal with a discrepancy between what we expect and what we actually receive. This discrepancy may be psychologically both disorienting and quite distressing. If you expect that you will not be able to retire until you are 70 years old, new information that you will not be able to retire at age 67 may be stress free. However, if you expect to retire at age 65, that same "new" information may be quite disturbing. Thus, adjusting your expectations for retirement date and lifestyle may be particularly useful.

# Properly Sequencing the Closing of the Barn Door and the Horse's Potential Departure

For those with standard (defined benefit) pensions, the past may be prelude to the future, but the number of individuals who can count on company pensions and benefits is shrinking dramatically. Eric, a professor for 30 years at a private college, reported,

> On my last day at work, I expect my colleagues and the staff in my department to give me a small party.

> The administration will allow me to keep my e-mail
> account for at least a while, offer me some cartons to
> unpack my office and demand I surrender my keys to the
> building. There will be no pension, save my own 403b
> account, no health care until Medicare begins unless I
> pay for it myself through COBRA, and no gold watch!

He added, "When my father retired as a professor, he had a
pension, lifetime healthcare and use of the university facilities. He
didn't get a gold watch either."

At age 65, Eric will not be able to support himself and his wife
on their accumulated savings and Social Security benefits, unless
they decide to sell their home, move into much more modest accommodations, and live an even more modest lifestyle. What are his
options? One of the most likely for Eric and many like him will
be to stay on the job beyond age 65. As a professor, the physical
demands of his work will likely permit that. Another option is for
him to use his skills to find a new, different kind of part-time work
after he retires.

## So, What Can You Do?

Here are 10 considerations. Obviously, those who are closer to
retirement will likely have to take more aggressive measures to
reach the goal.

1. *Try to generally estimate your life expectancy.* Although
   none of us truly know our real life span and the timing and
   nature of our death, there are some guidelines based on
   statistics and general trends. Factors such as family history,
   education level, and health will help you make an educated
   assessment of your financial needs and more informed choices
   for income sources such as Social Security, IRAs, and pension
   plans. This will help you address any predictable shortfalls
   and plan to cover them in advance.

2. *Keep working.* One of the fastest growing segments of the
   workforce is the number of over 65-year-old employees and
   entrepreneurs. According to the U.S. Department of Labor,
   the number of workers over 65 was at record levels in 2012.
   Furthermore, as people extend their working years, even

on a part-time basis, they create opportunities to feather the nest egg. *Remember, each additional year of working counts threefold: more income and savings; increased time for saved assets to grow; and a year in which you are not spending down what you already have saved.*

3.  *Increase capital.* For a generation that has been marked by consuming, it's not always an easy transformation to saving. The easiest methods for increasing principal occur with the most time left for saving. Forty-five-year-old individuals have a much better chance of increasing their savings rate and getting compounding of their investments than a 60-year-old. Understand the importance of compounding and the rule of 72[4] in allowing money to work for you instead of the opposite. While you are working, get in an automatic savings program and stick to it. Maximize any matching contributions from an employer as early as possible. Self-employed individuals have recourse to some interesting options including defined benefit plans, SEP IRAs, individual 401k plans, and so on.

4.  *Review more carefully and alter and cut spending.* Discretionary spending often needs to be the central focus for reprioritizing. Sometimes, however, the fixed expenses also have to be addressed. In general, when individuals are asked about their fixed expenses, their estimates tend to be excessively high or low. A budget should provide guidance, not be a prison sentence. The question is, what could you give up without distress or suffering?

Mehgan and Walter are both in their mid-50s. Married for decades, with their children launched, they have to consider reducing their spending to increase their retirement savings. They both agreed that their customary morning lattes at local coffee shop were costing them about $30 per week, $1,500 per year. "Retail therapy," unnecessary purchases

---

4   The rule of 72 is an arithmetic method to calculate the time in which your investments will double. Simply divide the interest rate into the number 72 and the resultant sum will be the number of years for the investment to double. Thus, if you are receiving 6% on your investment of $10,000, in 12 years you will have $20,000. If your investments are yielding 8%, you will have the $20,000 in just 9 years. The rule also works in reverse in exploring debt and the time to half your principal.

at a local mall, was adding another $4,000 annually. They also had considerable credit card debt for which they were paying over 20% interest. They wisely resolved to begin by putting the saved money into eliminating the credit card debt. In addition, when they looked at fixed costs, an examination of their monthly bills indicated that they were paying over $150 per month on cable TV bills, yet they used only about 15 channels, and an additional $200 per month on a storage unit that mostly contained their children's belongings. Finally, they were paying a very high fee for their cell phones. By making adjustments to these and some additional unnecessary expenditures, they were able to save more than $5,000 per year in their investment accounts.

5. *Work with a good financial planner.* If your own savings plan for retirement needs is not clearly on target, get help. It's hard to talk about finances to a stranger, but your fiscal health may need some professional care just as your physical self does. A person over 50 during an annual physical check-up is exposed in a variety of ways to professionals, so it should be with your investments. In addition to managing current assets and plans, a financial planner will be able to assist in accounting for your extended longevity and the vagaries of inflation. There should also be a regular annual check-up and review.

6. *Teamwork as a couple.* If you are in a committed relationship, be sure to examine both visions of retirement and talk about these before setting a plan that will inevitably fail. If your vision and your spouse's are discrepant, talk it over. Sometimes a professional third party is invaluable in helping you align your retirement desires.

7. *Health care.* Be sure to provide for continuing health care after retirement. Many people are surprised that they will not be covered by a former employer. Find out about Medicare and other available programs well before your 65th birthday. You can apply for Medicare 3 months before that birthday. Recent (2017) estimates are that if your longevity will be average, your out-of-pocket lifetime costs for medical care will be over $300,000. That means saving an extra $10,000 for 20 years to cover that expense. These figures do not account for long-term care such as nursing homes; those costs can exceed $70,000 per year. Many investment

advisors recommend long-term care insurance, if necessary, as a substitute for life insurance.

8. *Make a will, or better yet, put a will in a trust.* Although most of us prefer denial to the reality of our personal demise, any financial plan must include considerations for our personal care and for our desires for our children. A living trust will handle a number of these issues and eliminate many of the hardships of probate.

9. *If you are not in a traditional long-term marriage, extra planning may be essential.* Blended, step, alternative, and cohabiting lifestyles demand a much more assiduous look at finances. When there are children from different marriages, their care needs to be well-planned and set forth in formal agreements. So too should inheritances be made clear. Managing existing assets and responsibilities may require knowledge of how your relationship is treated in the jurisdiction in which you reside.

10. *Talk with the adult children.* If there will be a need to get help from children during a lengthy retirement, talk with them in advance and work out details as best as possible. Again, a professional third party may be able to facilitate these conversations. This is especially true when there is a family business that may be passed on to another generation.

# Retirement Plans

One key to successfully creating a retirement nest egg is to use tax-advantaged methods to have your money grow before taxes need to be paid. Tax-advantaged retirement plans come in two general categories: defined benefit plans and defined contribution plans.

# Defined Benefit Plans

These plans focus on what you will *receive* as retirement benefits.

## Employer Plans

The traditional pension plans often enjoyed by employees of large corporations, especially those with union workers, and civil servants are both wonderful and rapidly disappearing. Very common in the middle and late 20th century, these are currently primarily found in government positions, including public schools, and in compensation packages for the highest-level corporate officers. As a benefit of employment, workers receive on retirement a fixed percentage of their earnings annually for life.

**Personal defined benefit plans** target a desired level of retirement income and allows for aggressive savings to reach the goal. Contribution amounts are adjusted each year to help you reach your goal. This could be the right choice for you if you're self-employed or a small business owner near retirement with no nonfamily employees, and you are able to contribute a significant amount of your income each year. These plans require special tax reporting and an actuary to compute the annual contribution. For that reason, they are more complex and tend to be more expensive. The primary advantage is for individuals who have fewer years until retirement and need to contribute a large amount in each year. Almost your entire income may be contributed for tax-deferred savings and investment.

## If You Are the Employer and Employee

It is important to note that if the employer does create such a plan it must be offered proportionally to every employee who works at least 50% time in the business. That is why it is particularly attractive for solo businesses.

## Defined Contribution Plans

Instead of determining the ultimate payout during retirement (defined benefits), these plans determine the monthly/annual contribution from one's paycheck, draw or profits. In these plans, the employer creates the plan and the employee contributes tax-deferred dollars as a deduction from income. Sometimes employers encourage these contributions with matching funds for some of the total. However, as we have seen, these benefits are not guaranteed. For example, several employers have opted to reduce or eliminate their participation/contributions during the COVID-19 pandemic. There is yet no information when, or whether, these will be reinstated.

Good examples of these tax-advantaged plans are the 401(k) plans offered by many employers, 403(b) plans offered by nonprofit organizations, and 457 plans, primarily available for governmental and specified nongovernmental employers. The employer provides the plan and the employee takes before-tax deductions from salaries. These deferred compensation plans place the pre-tax money into a retirement account that is managed by a money management company, such as insurance companies or large mutual fund investment firms like Vanguard or Fidelity. Choices of how the money is allocated are determined by the employee, usually from a certain list of qualified mutual fund investment choices, including annuities. Each of these plans has some differences, particularly around withdrawal penalties (prior to age 59.5). One advantage of these plans is that money in these accounts is not subject to taxable required minimal distributions after age 70 as long as the employee is still working.

Thus, Dr. Soto, a professor at a private university, is receiving her salary and doesn't need to tap her retirement funds while she still holds a position at her school. Unlike IRA or Keogh plans (described next), she is not required to take an IRS-determined distribution of her funds until her retirement. That election allows more of her retirement funds to continue growing and avoids her paying a maximum tax rate on the combined net income of salary plus distribution.

**Keogh plans** are tax-deferred retirement plans designed to help self-employed workers or individuals who earn self-employed income establish a retirement savings program. Keogh plans are for profit sharing (variable contributions based on income) or money purchase (mandatory percentage per annum). One advantage of Keogh plans is the opportunity to contribute a high maximum per year. Two disadvantages are the need for annual tax reporting (IRS Form 5500) and the mandatory contribution even in lean income years.

## Business 401(k)

If you're self-employed or have your own business, it is possible to create a small business retirement plan. These plans provide tax breaks for the business and savings for retirement and are competitive for recruiting. They are relatively easy to set up with professional help.

## Individual 401(k) Plans (Also Known as Simple K Plans)

If you or you and your spouse are the only employees in your business, it is possible to create a simplified 401 plan. These plans are usually administered through a stock brokerage house or through a specified number of mutual fund companies. They are easier to create and set up than larger 401 plans.

A **SEP-IRA** (simplified employee pension plan) is one of the easiest small business retirement plans to create and maintain. Tax filing isn't required, and it allows for a sizable retirement plan contribution for yourself and any eligible employees.

**IRA** (individual retirement accounts) are the most common and well known of all retirement plans. These are trust or custodial accounts that are designed for taxpayers (and their beneficiaries). They are funded with pre-tax dollars (thus reducing the taxable income) of up to $55,000 per person annually, more if you are over 50 years of age. Like all other tax-advantaged plans the amount in the account grows tax free until mandatory required distributions begin at the age of 70 and a half. These are designed for earners who are not covered by employer plans. Withdrawals are treated as ordinary income for tax purposes. They are available at banks, savings and loans, brokerage houses, and several other financial fiduciary institutions. They are very easy to set up.

A **Roth IRA** is similar in some ways to a traditional IRA, but contributions are in *after-tax dollars*. Thus, they do not reduce the current taxable income. However, all money in these accounts grows tax free and when withdrawn is not subject to additional taxes. For this reason, they may be passed on to heirs who also benefit from the tax-free withdrawal value. Both traditional and Roth IRAs may limit investments and presumably do not allow riskier investments.

# Investing for the Uninvolved Investor

Start: Don't be an ostrich! You don't have to become a seasoned investor, trade frequently, or be at your computer screen at 4:00 a.m. to check on the overseas markets, but it is wise to have a sense of what you have and how it is invested and most important that the investments reflect your retirement needs. For most of us, nobody will be as watchful of or careful about your finances as we are personally. However, being aware and involved with financial decisions is not for everyone. In fact, many feel like Stephen when he opines,

> I just want to not know about any of it. I can't pay
> attention to money and I wouldn't know a good stock

from a bad one anyhow. All I want is for someone to take it over and for me to see the balance going up from year-to-year.

Chanelle agreed with Stephan. Confronted with an array of choices for her company's 401(k) plan, she said, "Just tell me what fund to choose so I don't have to look at it again and I can take out the money when I need it."

When told by an older colleague that it doesn't work that way and she needs to check on it and talk with an advisor at least twice a year, she replied, "I know I won't do that, so what should I do?" He recommended a financial advisor and a balanced growth and income fund as a start.

In truth, the array of mutual funds, index funds, and exchange traded funds (ETFs) are expanding exponentially. In fact, there are far more mutual stock funds than there are stocks traded on the major exchanges. The proliferation of choices can be confusing even to an experienced investor.

It is always advisable to have a trusted person (fiduciary) with no personal proprietary interest in your financial state. A brief description of the available experts will follow. Clearly there is no right answer for everyone, but there is probably a right answer for each individual. For most of us, the KISS (keep it simple stupid) method is most effective and usually least expensive.

Some general guidelines:

1. If you don't understand an investment (i.e., commodity futures, private equity, hedge fund strategies, companies that engage in businesses you don't understand), stay away from it.

2. Recognize the good news/bad news truth that most professional market timers and stock pickers do not do better than index funds. In other words, over the long run an investment in the entire market or a large segment of it will do better than the experts, especially those with expensive television exposure or slick marketing materials.

3. Get the right kind of help. There are two types of advisors: fee based and commission based.

*Fee-based advisors* charge either by the hour or by a percentage of the portfolio that they manage—normally around 1% annually for moderate-sized estates. The disadvantage of these advisors is the annual fee even if trading is minimal. The advantage is that the advisor has no personal stake in buying or selling investments.

*Commission-based advisors* in most brokerage houses make their money by charging a fee for each trade you make, buying and selling. The advantage is that in a relatively inactive account (as are many retirement accounts) annual trading fees may be fairly minimal, although, particularly for smaller accounts, some brokerage houses also have a host of additional fees, even for inactive accounts. The disadvantage is that when a broker makes money on each trade, they are at least subconsciously prone to trade more often "for your benefit." The better brokers operate as true fiduciaries focusing on our personal needs and goals and will recommend rebalancing investments when the preferred allocations and diversification shifts out of the desired range. They may also help clients be more tax efficient with their gains. One note of caution, most brokers are far better at knowing when to purchase a stock than when to sell it.

Seasoned investors characteristically set a price to sell a stock when they buy it. Thus, if you purchase 100 shares of XYZ company at $25 a share, you may want to determine at that time that you will sell XYZ if it falls 20% to $20 per share or to sell it at $30 when it gains 20%. Of course, market fluctuations and a company's health may influence your decisions. In general, again, the most frequently successful strategy is to purchase Index funds and let the market buy and sell for you.

1. Shop around and don't be reticent to switch advisors when it's not working out the way you want or when your personal broker leaves and the firm reassigns you to another.

2. Tax efficiency is essential. At the moment, there are many tax-advantaged investments and ways of investing. You want to be aware of these and to maximize what you get to keep—not always how much you earn. Some tax-advantaged investments and methods maximize use of tax-deferred retirement plans. Remember, a penny earned may be less than a penny saved once taxes are paid. Allowing your money to compound in a tax-deferred or tax-free account will likely yield a far greater return. In addition to placing income-related vehicles in tax-deferred accounts, municipal bonds are often both state and federal tax free.

3. Asset allocation. Place your retirement building funds in a variety of markets. It is rare for all aspects of the economy to be down at the same time, although that did occur to some extent in the recession that began in 2008 and again in March of 2020. Percentage investments in large companies, small companies, foreign investments, real estate, and so on allow us to ride out the inevitable ups and downs in the economy. No single market segment is always the best or the worst investment. A plan in which one is properly diversified that rebalances investments on a semi-annual to annual basis is often a workable strategy.

Malcolm is an example of a person who had a good income, excellent retirement plans, and a shortsighted perspective. His 401(k) plan contained several thousand shares of his company's stock and little else. When the company hit rough times, the stock went down precipitously. In Malcolm's words, "My retirement tanked along with the company. ... I was a millionaire on paper, but by the time I could cash out, it wasn't worth very much at all." What was worse was that he was paying taxes on the stock when it was allocated as part of his regular income. Most advisors recommend that once stocks vest (are owned totally by the employee) it is wise under most circumstances to sell some of the company stock and diversify.

Unlike Malcolm, his colleague Andrea kept moving funds from the company stock to a portfolio that was 40% stock, 40% bonds and income vehicles, 10% real estate and 10% international. Each 6 months, she sat down with her financial advisor and they rebalanced the portfolio to meet their predetermined percentages. Thus, only 5% of her total stock holdings were in the company stock. When the stock portion of her portfolio went below 40% and the real estate climbed to almost 20%, she rebalanced, taking the excess real estate profits and putting them into more stock purchases.

Normally as we get closer to retirement, our portfolios become more income oriented and less subject to the vagaries of stock market trends. To paraphrase slightly the words of legendary investor Bernard Baruch, the return *on* investment starts to dwarf in importance the return *of* investment. As the years to retirement become closer, the number of years to make up a loss decreases. Had Malcolm suffered the loss of his stock's value at age 35 instead of age 55, he may have been better able to ride it out and recover.

# A Time to Reap

Until now, the focus has been on the accumulation of assets to fund retirement, but regardless of how much has been accumulated, a lot of problems can result in spending these funds inappropriately. There are several risks that have to be addressed in the process of planning, and many of these cannot be known in advance.

Common risks include the following:

- Our longevity
- Market volatility and the chance that the value of our investments will be down when we need them
- Inflation rates
- Health care costs
- Withdrawal rate

Many experts are now talking about sustainable systematic withdrawal strategies. These strategies for spending are dissimilar from the strategy for accumulation. One of the most widely used and supported strategies is the time-segmentation approach.

# The Time-Segmentation Approach

Resources are divided, typically into three categories: one for the first 5 years of retirement (cash and cash equivalents such as laddered CDs or short-term treasury instruments), a second for the next 10 years (fixed-income vehicles such as bonds) and finally one to meet expected needs after 15 years (stocks and more volatile investments).

The reasoning behind keeping the more volatile investments in the long-term category is to give them time to grow. No 15-year period in the overall stock market has resulted in a loss. So, investing for the long term is the best way to skew the odds in your favor. By contrast, market timing and day-trading strategies are far more risky and statistically far more likely to fall short.

Other strategies that have been favored by financial advisors are the 4% annual withdrawal rate and target date funds offered by many financial institutions. The distinct advantages and disadvantages of each of these approaches is far beyond the scope of this chapter and truly needs individual consultation with a trusted advisor. However, the general principles for withdrawal will generate a good discussion with your advisor and are psychologically more salient, especially if you are concerned that you will run out of money. Regardless of the approach, both fiscal and psychological security are always primary.

## Goals

As recommended by my Santa Clara University colleagues, behavioral economists Drs. Meir Statman and Hersh Shefrin, it is also advisable to target spending to specific goals for an additional sense of self-control. The first question one should have about even a small "estate" is how we want our money to be used. Is our goal to spend it down until there is only enough available for our funeral expenses? Do we want to leave as much as possible for our children, grandchildren, or to a charity? Do we want to spend now or provide something as a legacy?

Of course, for many of us, the only question is can we make it on what we have accumulated and not be dependent on our children? Generally speaking, if we have planned well during the 20 to 25 years prior to retirement, spending below our means and putting away what we can for retirement, there are likely to be sufficient funds for withdrawal to support a decent lifestyle for us and potentially some bequest to others. Reassessing these categories may need to be done over the lifetime.

# Other Considerations

As daunting as the financial considerations may seem, psychological, emotional, and personal realities may be far more salient. In fact, it is the influence of the psychology of finances that may overwhelm the influence of fiscal realities. These issues are addressed in Chapter 11.

# Exercise: Getting to Your Financial Retirement Number

A.  To best prepare financially for retirement, do an assessment of current and anticipated costs in retirement. This is best done by looking back for a year at your checkbook, charge cards and other receipts. If you do not have such records, start now for the current year. It may be useful to use a paper and pencil ledger or a convenient money management software program that will also break expenses into annual and monthly reports.

1. Examine your current fixed expenses such as rent/mortgage, property taxes, food, insurance, clothing, medical, utilities, transportation, debt payments, etc.

2. Examine your current discretionary spending including travel.

3. Consider which of these expenses will continue once you retire and which can be eliminated. For example, will your mortgage be paid in full by retirement? Will you have a reduction in costs of office/work clothing? Will your desired travel expenses increase? Will you be helping your children, grandchildren or other family members financially? If so, adjust the fixed and discretionary expense categories.

4. Take the sum of your monthly expenses, subtract your expected social security (available annually and mailed from the Social Security office) and other pension benefits. That sum will be the amount you will need to cover with your savings each month.

5. Consider how much in savings you will need to last your expected lifetimes.

6. Usually, it is best to add approximately 10% to 20% to that number each year to account for inflation and unanticipated expenses.

7. Recognize that this exercise is usually very difficult to do and very easy to put off. Working with a financial advisor can be very helpful.

B. Answer the following question. Keep at it until you get down to the most basic concerns.

What does money mean to you? Is it a scorecard? Does it represent security? Freedom? How do you understand the rational and unconscious beliefs you have about money?

# chapter eleven

# It's Not Your Father's Retirement

*Retire from work, not from life.*

—M.K. Soni

F inancial considerations may color the timing, the nature, and the very possibility of retirement, but they are not the only considerations. Many of the baby boom generation can expect to retire later than their customary 65th birthday, some for practical reasons and many from desire to keep going or to explore a second career. Although predicting 20 or more years into the future is chancy, it now appears that the actual retirement age for Generation Xers will be even later than the expected 67- to 68-year retirement age with full Social Security benefits.

Despite the optimistic, and illusory, promise of early retirement during the economic boom of the 1990s, most of us aged 45 to 65 will be working through our post-mid-life years and beyond. In fact, age 65 has already begun to diminish as a marker of retirement. To retire successfully, you'll need a considerable amount of planning. We are likely to encounter a host of psychological and financial issues in the years that follow our 65th birthdays. Here we are focused on some predictable hazards and some methods to plan for a personally satisfying retirement.

# When Can I Retire?

For most of human existence, retirement was a nonissue. Individuals worked in their communities until they died. The nature of the work shifted over time, but people didn't expect to have extended time off to enjoy the fruits of their labor.

## Disappearing Extended Family Support

Nathan immigrated to the United States when he was in his 30s. Like most first-generation Americans who come as adults, his English skills were limited, and he lived and worked with other immigrants from his native land. He toiled as a self-employed artisan his entire life to support his wife and five children. When he was in his mid-60s and could no longer ply his trade, he retired. His Social Security benefits, based on his relatively low income, were insufficient to cover the basics. Following Old World custom, he and his wife moved in with their oldest daughter and her family. Additional financial support came from the other children. Nathan and his wife both died within 5 years of the end of his work life.

Mei left China with her two youngest children during the Cultural Revolution, when the Mao Tse-Tung government sent her husband and parents to a reeducation camp. She lived with relatives in San Francisco and worked long hours in the family-owned restaurant. Although she was well educated in China, she took to manual labor and care of her relatives' children for many years. It was 10 years before she saw her husband and oldest son again. Because of their experiences in the camps and their lack of English-speaking ability, she supported them also. When her husband died in 2014, she left work (at age 68) and moved in with her oldest daughter's family. All parties expect that she will live out her days with them. Because they come from a collective culture and are first generation, this retirement plan is both appropriate and natural for them.

Not everyone is so fortunate. For both Nathan and Mei, retirement was guaranteed as part of being an elder in a traditional subculture. In the more individualistic culture of current American generations, self-reliance has replaced counting on family members.

Linda, a single woman who built a solid business in New England, had no anticipation of hands-on extended family support for her aging parents. She and her two sisters offered to contribute financially to support their relocation and some costs at a retirement community in South Florida. When her father passed away, Linda spent a few weeks with her mother to help her move into a progressive retirement center. Neither Linda, now 55, nor her two married sisters, aged 49 and 52, had a thought of moving their mother in with their families, nor did their mother have any desire to relocate. In the individual-oriented model of their culture, family-based elder care consists primarily of phone calls, annual visits, and potentially, some financial assistance.

So it is for many in the boomer and Xer generations as they prepare for their own retirement years. It is unlikely that they will be able to count on much financial help from their children. For generations that stressed self-sufficiency those are both the benefits and price of that lifestyle.

Those who have passed midlife today will more likely have to prepare for their own retirement needs. As Linda reports, "I can help out my mother, but there are no kids to help me when I can't work anymore. My sisters have families and they can't support me, and I doubt at this point that any man will want to marry and support me as a retired person."

At the time of the interview, Linda had been living with a fellow for 6 years. "We share a home and a bed, but our finances are all separate and we don't talk about being together forever, or of separating."

Darlene just turned 60. Thrice divorced, she is currently living with her "boyfriend" and his daughter. Her "two sons have their hands full with their own families, and I can't expect them to lay out the kind of money Rick and I will need in retirement." She says that she has no interest in remarrying, nor does she expect Rick to provide financial support for her aside from sharing living expenses. Darlene has some minimal savings, a few IRA accounts, and an expectation of about $1,100 a month in Social Security benefits. The aggregate of those will not approximate her current basic expenses of close to $4,000 per month. With no mandatory retirement age in her current position, she simply plans to keep working until she is no longer physically able, "and then I hope I die before I'm out on the street."

Career counselors, financial planners, and social science professionals conclude that only a minority of people reaching their mid-60s are well prepared financially for retirement. Though you may expect to retire at age 65, statistics show you can also expect to live into your 80s, or one-fifth of your life. What will you do during those years? How will you find a way to thrive? What are the psychological considerations of a successful retirement? Are there options other than the kind of retirement your parents experienced? Whatever your answers, preparation and planning during these years are essential. When Darlene asked the big financial question, "Will I outlive my money?" she spoke for her entire generation. Yet she omitted another big question, "Once I am no longer defined by my work, who am I, really?"

## The Numbers Game, Redux

As described in the previous chapter, looking at current expenditures, anticipated expenses after the paychecks stop, and available assets is a valuable enterprise for individuals and couples. What will pensions and Social Security offer? What can you expect from savings and investments? What about healthcare costs, especially before you qualify for Medicare? The answers to these questions may make the decision to retire somewhat moot. Most of us will have to consider continuing working at the current position if there is not a mandatory requirement age, change our lifestyles, relocate to an area with a lower cost of living or find a new income-producing position. Advance knowledge of these factors can facilitate better decision making while still between the ages of 45 and 65. It is of primary importance to be on the same page as your partner. What is essential here is that preparation can head off unpleasant surprises when it is too late to properly adjust.

Arthur at 47 is a good example of early planning. He and his partner, Ronny (48), had not been able to save much for their future financial needs. Since they are both in the construction trade, they are aware that their ability to continue in physically demanding labor cannot go on for very long. Arthur is also very aware that he got into construction primarily for money, but his personal passions lie elsewhere. After reviewing his anticipated needs, he decided to complete his college education and become a teacher. Ronny, inspired by Arthur's move followed in kind, taking business classes and studying to be a general contractor. As he described it, "I love construction, but maybe I am now better suited to getting younger guys to do all the heavy lifting." Three years into their transformation, they both described their current lives as better, with major hopes for the future.

Although it was not easy for them to confront the impact of aging and finances, Arthur and Ronny stopped avoiding those discussions and with the help of a couples therapist began also discussing their hopes for the future.

## The Last Taboo

Arthur and Ronny may be a little atypical. Compounding the issues of retirement planning is a reticence to talk about them. Linda, the New England executive, and her boyfriend are not unique in avoiding discussion of their future, or present, financial issues. Responding to questions about finances isn't easy for most people. Money might be the last taboo topic in our society. Long after they confide unconventional sexual yearnings and behaviors to their therapists, clients keep their income and financial wherewithal secret.

Both debt and largesse are somehow embarrassing or even shameful to make public. Boomers, for all their competitiveness and comparisons of the cost of their real estate or other new possessions, remain guarded about the topic. Indeed, in our interviews, the most frequently unanswered queries were the ones about finances. Rafael, a 60-year-old executive, exemplified this reticence by responding to each question about finances with the retort, "Next question!" This was not a topic he was willing to address, at least in our interviews.

## Money Secrets

There are deeper, more psychological reasons we are uncomfortable with financial matters. Financial experts look at two emotions that drive the economic world: greed and fear. As compelling as their analysis of what drives motivations around finances, it may be limiting when exploring any individual's or couple's relationship to money. Exploring psychological reactions and willingness to share information in this realm are often more complex and nuanced than these two contrasting emotions. Financial vulnerability often also involves core feelings about freedom and security.

## Secrets Within Relationships

It can get complicated when people who marry have divergent financial perspectives. Often a person who grew up with a personal guideline of "a penny saved is a penny earned" or "money doesn't grow on trees" will be attracted to and marry someone whose childhood guideline about money was "eat, drink, and be merry, for tomorrow we die." This can lead to long-term conflicts and secrets. In fact, money secrets are among the most common that married people keep from their partners.

When married couples withhold financial information, or even lie to their partners about finances, it is most likely to be about personal spending, credit card debt, gifts and loans to children and other family members, and income. Fifty-year-old Caitlin describes this expectation: "If he knew how much I made or spent, he'd be very angry with me. So I just keep these little secrets to myself. ... I learned it from my mother. She used to tell my dad that she spent more on groceries than she did and pocketed the rest in her 'all saints kitty' jar in the pantry. Then she would treat us kids to something special. When I got married the only advice she gave me was 'Always hold out some money for yourself that he doesn't know about.'" That maternal advice may have made sense for someone who had no income of her own and was financially fully dependent on her husband. Yet even today, some couples with two incomes do the same thing.

Fears of rejection or being out of control often play into individuals' surreptitious beliefs and behaviors about money. These emotionally-laden aspects of fiscal matters complicate the estimations of what we need in retirement. Psychotherapists, family counselors, and certified financial planners who are comfortable talking about money, family history, and emotions can help bridge the relatively unconscious drivers blocking honest discussions about monetary issues.

# The Psychology of Money and Retirement Planning

Disquieting though the financial numbers may be, our psychological concerns can be just as daunting, because they speak to the core of life's meaning and lifestyle. It's important to be able to support ourselves after we're no longer working for income, but that's only the beginning. More salient is how we live and what we feel, think, and do as a retiree. Plans for these lifestyle choices are best made earlier, during the stretch years.

Much of the adjustment involves facing and dealing with certain predictable losses. Do you really want an endless vacation? Not everybody does. Gary, a 64-year-old insurance broker, relates, "I'm not ready for three days a week tee times in funny pants, cocktail hours, and early bird specials. I need something productive to do or I'll go crazy." His wife, a soon to be retired schoolteacher, took that moment to join in the conversation: "Worse still, he'd drive me crazy if he were around the house all day."

For most of us, three forces make the transition to retirement more difficult:

1. **Not dressed up and nowhere to go.** The loss of the workplace can be daunting unless we can find a way to replace our needs for a place to go, self-esteem from work accomplishments, rewards in the form of a paycheck, and collegiality. The shelter-in-place and seclusion that was brought on by the COVID-19 pandemic, provided many with a peek into what it was like to not go into the office. Whether working remotely or unemployed, respondents described a life of online meetings wearing shorts, PJs, or sweats. Many reported that the novelty of the first few online meetings or remote cocktail hours "got old quickly." They also commented on how video meetings had to be much shorter in duration, "being much more work than leisure."

2. **Dead person walking.** During retirement, social norms and subtle pressures enhance feelings of our being "finished" and psychologically closer to decline and death. Stress from inactivity and a not uncommon post-work depression can lead to actual physical deterioration.

3. **Facing the primary relationship without buffers.** Marital difficulties that were less pressing can grow quickly in the crucible of 24/7 togetherness. Unresolved conflicts, poor communication, and inadequate sharing of dreams and visions can exacerbate these difficulties dramatically.

# Different Strokes: A Tale of Two Friends

Alfred and Brad grew up together in one of Boston's ethnic neighborhoods. They went to the same high school, and both went to colleges in New England. They were married about a year apart, both to women who also grew up in their community. From there their life paths diverged considerably.

Soon after college, Brad enlisted to avoid being drafted and served two terms in Vietnam, returning with an artificial limb and post-traumatic stress disorder. Within a year of his return, he and his wife divorced, and after a while, he used his veterans' benefits to move to California and attend graduate school.

Meanwhile, Alfred took a job at a local corporation and began to move slowly but surely up the ranks of management. Like Brad, he divorced after a short marriage. He remarried within a year to a woman he met at work, and they had three children in 5 years.

Brad was married three times "before I sobered up and got it right." Recently, he and his wife celebrated their 25th wedding anniversary with a trip back to "The Cape" and the old neighborhood. It was during that trip that the two old friends spent face-to-face time together for the first time in decades.

Alfred and his wife had put their three children through college and were enjoying regular trips to Washington and New York to see their first two grandchildren. Relocation was not possible for them because they were the sole support of both of their mothers.

By contrast, Brad's two children were still in the launching stage of life; Brad was in no hurry to see them leave home.

Alfred and Brad took an afternoon walk through the family cemetery and caught up on their accumulated aches and pains (the characteristic "organ recital" of folks in their 50s and beyond), friends lost, and hopes for the future. Brad talked about how he and Julia were becoming more active in their church, and Alfred replied, "I left religion after Vietnam and don't have any use for it now—too much useless killing. I just don't believe anymore. Besides Sachiko is a Buddhist, if she's anything." Chuckling, he added, "How'd you think that'd go over in the old neighborhood?"

As they looked into the future, Alfred said, "Five more years. Then I pack it in, and me and Julia spend more time at the cabin up by the lake. I also thought about going in with a few guys at work and getting season tickets to Fenway. That'd be like when we were kids and used to sit in the bleachers for a buck." He added, "For me, being retired and out of my suit and tie is the ultimate freedom."

Brad was of a very different mind-set. He didn't ever plan to retire, because his work was so fulfilling, his friends all came from work, and his wife worked out of their home. "If I were around all the time, she'd just turn me into her assistant—not exactly my first choice. I guess for me, full retirement would be like an early death."

As the afternoon wore on, they made a plan to have a reunion in San Francisco.

They did meet a year later. In the interim, Alfred had retired and Brad was enjoying his family, their friendship spanning decades still intact.

Their divergent paths are a strong indicator that for any of us contemplating retirement, there is no one size that fits all. We each need to discern direction based on who we are, what is most appealing to each of us, and where we are going.

## The Meaning of Retirement

These boyhood buddies took different paths and each found a way to pursue what was best for the upcoming era of his life. Alfred got out of his suit and tie, traveled, and spent time at his cabin. Brad learned to work smarter and to enjoy all that his job and family could offer.

Some people's thoughts about what's most important in life evolve over years. Others' insights seem to come more as a sudden realization. When she turned 59, Donna decided to divorce. She and her husband of many years had grown distant, and their three children were out of the home and lived far away. After the divorce, her husband became closer to the children through internet contact and upon retirement moved close to their daughter and youngest son.

Donna was more interested in following her personal interests. About a month after entering individual psychotherapy, Donna began exploring her pursuit of a high-level position in a new field and her sexual orientation, something she "hadn't thought about since I was a teenager. I want to know who I've been, what I want to be, and what it would take to get there."

Donna was almost 60 when she began to take her personal inventory, although it could be surmised that her decision was brewing in her subconscious mind for some time before it came to fruition.

Where are you along your life's developmental trajectory? One part of planning for a successful retirement is to ponder some of the larger questions well before retirement is looming.

## Retirement Means Not Having to Earn a Living. It Doesn't Mean We Are at Death's Door.

Studies on individuals during their preretirement and retirement years indicate that an active lifestyle is a great antidote to deterioration from "sitting."

Joseph, sardonically describing his late father's life, said,

> He left the postal service with his double pension and just sat down in front of the TV. He had a heart attack within a year and died. I don't know whether he just wanted to get away from his harpy of a second wife or it was inactivity that took him ... or maybe he was always depressed and work was an eight-hour respite in his day when he couldn't think about his miseries.

Joseph, who was 55 when he described his father's fate, affirmed that he would not succumb in that way. He was taking care of his health, was in a favorable second marriage, and was devoted to their combined nine children and 14 grandchildren. He had arranged to get involved in community service by using his skills as a software engineer to upgrade the computer systems of nonprofit groups.

Some of us take a little time to find our active lifestyle. Antoine retired at age 65 after many years in corporate life. Early on, he enjoyed "just doing nothing. I must have spent four, five months watching TV and reading a bit. The big event of the day was going to the mailbox or the supermarket. I was going to see too many doctors for too many ailments, when I realized that by being inactive, I was just waiting to die. Besides, my wife was all over me to get my fat ass up and do something useful."

Antoine began slowly meeting friends for coffee at a local restaurant. Later, he joined the local library board and was involved in a bookmobile project that went to schools, assisted living facilities, and neighborhoods. A year into his new activity, he said, "So if you came to me to ask the meaning of life, I can tell you it's keeping busy. It doesn't matter what you do, but if you stop moving, the grim reaper is gonna catch up with you real quick."

Many have echoed Antoine's insights. Not only is it useful to be active and involved in something, but it's good to have some ideas of what kinds of activities are most personally suitable.

## Common Dangers in Retirement

A common complaint of retirees is the loss of a place in the world that work provided. When Harvey was 58, his position was eliminated in a corporate merger. Harvey accepted a retirement package rather than a lower-level job in the new company.

After a year of searching for a new position "and far too much drinking at night," he took the only offer that came along, a CEO position at a family-owned business that was about an hour's commute from his home. Two years later, the family fired Harvey and installed their oldest son in the position. Although it was the son who made some unwise decisions that caused the company a lot of red ink, the family blamed Harvey.

At 62, Harvey was again out of work, in a tougher market with a failure on his record, and convinced that he was no longer hirable. He and his wife, accustomed to a high lifestyle, burned through their funds recklessly and Harvey again began drinking heavily. He became increasingly depressed and subsequently was hospitalized after a serious suicide attempt.

When he came into treatment, Harvey could only talk about how useless he was and how, "my whole life is a sham. It's over." He added, "Nothing left to look forward to but a big wake!" With weekly psychotherapy, he partially recovered, stopped using alcohol to self-medicate, and when he was 65 was able to take a few lower-level positions with some former colleagues from the original firm. However, his sense of uselessness lingered and his depression about being a failure as "the top guy," dominated his later years.

Harvey experienced a number of losses common in a generally unchosen retirement. Often our self-esteem is connected to work. When meeting someone new, one of the first questions we ask is "What do you do?" It's a question we can usually answer readily and proudly. It doesn't have the same cache to say, "I'm a former teacher, CEO, or restaurant owner." Everyone approaching retirement should consider the potential loss of identity, a significant part of our self-esteem.

Many are concerned about what life would be like without a place to go and call "mine." The loss of that workplace is no small matter to most. The job is a place where we can be successful, feel good about what we accomplish, be with like-minded others, and get appropriate rewards. Traditional retirement does not offer the same perks. MaryLou spoke for many when she described feeling lost when she cleared out her office. "It was like a personal turf with my books, [artifacts] and desk where I knew where everything was." After my two sons and husband helped me move all my personal stuff and it was over, I got really sad. I was ready to stop working, but not so much ready to lose that little second mini-home."

Because the traditional expectations in our culture have been on men to be the breadwinners, the loss of a position may be more devastating to male egos. Men who are out of work involuntarily or receive a lower paycheck often experience it as a comment on their self-worth, rather than just on the position or finances. This remains true in our culture despite recent data showing that in almost 40% of heterosexual households, the woman is the higher wage earner. In a 2011 *Newsweek* article Rick Marin coined the phrase "bread loser," describing in particular White males who are unemployed without immediate prospects.[1] In fact, divorce rates are particularly high when the man is unemployed.

## Preparing for a Positive Retirement

To plan a successful retirement, ponder these eight sets of questions that we explored in our interviews:

1.  Do you plan to retire at a given age? What is important about that age? At what age did your parents retire, if at all? Are there older family members or friends in your generation who have retired at a certain age?

---

1   https://www.newsweek.com/can-manhood-survive-recession-66607

2.  How would you like to spend your time upon retirement? Do you have images of frequent travel? Will you become more involved with friends and family? Do you want to be more involved with your grandchildren? Do you have hobbies or activities that you wish to pursue? Will you continue working part time or commence a new career?

3.  Do you have particular goals? Do you have ideas about serving or improving your community? Do you want to live a different lifestyle? Is there something that you have long desired to accomplish but until retirement didn't have the time?

4.  Do you have "a bucket list?" Did you always want to pursue some creative possibility? Are there secret desires to fulfill? What might you have attempted if not for family or job responsibilities?

5.  What activities did you give up to live an adult life that you'd like to reclaim? Before you became a responsible adult, were there skills that you enjoyed that you'd like to recapture? Were you a musician? An artist? A gardener? Did you always want to have a small business and be your own boss?

6.  What do you enjoy doing when you don't have to worry about income? Do you have an avocation, a hobby, or a pastime that engages you? What did you always claim you were putting off until later?

7.  What spiritual quests will be possible and desirable? Are their inner pursuits that are important? Would you like to look at the greater questions in life? Do you crave knowledge of something "more" in life? Have you lost your spirituality in the workaday world? Do you find something resonating in religious services, in meditation, in the mountains, by the ocean, or with other people? How could you pursue these?

8.  What kind of relationships will you desire with your partner and friends when you are available full time? Do you want to pursue your intimate relationships more? Do you want to connect in new or old ways with your partner? Are you interested in exploring a different lifestyle?

# Successful Resolutions

Two of the answers to these questions involved participation in music. Marco began playing guitar in his 50s to prepare for the next phase of his life, and Maricel recently retired, joined her church choir, and took singing lessons. Both also took up community volunteer positions; in Maricel's words, "That made me feel like I can really help others."

Others, like Marge and Ed, pursued their love of travel and photography by volunteering to teach classes on a cruise line. Their retirement coexists with working for some time, because their financial strategies have been less well-planned.

After stepping down "semi-voluntarily" from a full-time executive position, Andy took several positions as a consultant. He currently offers his skills as a short-term troubleshooter. He reports, "It's the same kind of work that I used to do, except now I'm in and out. I do my job and turn the company back to the CEO. I love it—no annual reports, no "squawk box," no quarterly reports to the board. I'm just the temp, and in one case, a board member."

Finally, Renee, a teacher who has used her summers to engage in a meditation practice, plans to go on an extended spiritual retreat when she retires. Fifty-two now, she said, "I'm single and able to do this. I'm not worried about anyone else at this point. I'm just dedicated to getting to know me better and see where it takes me. At the very least, it will make me a better teacher."

## Practical Considerations: What to Expect and What to Do

We decided to learn about what people did best and what mistakes they made by consulting several current retirees. One of the most dominant findings echoed other such studies.[2] Retirees frequently described retirement as the happiest time in their lives. Where there were deviations from that picture, there was a corresponding discrepancy between expectations and reality. When the gap between them was small, there were greater expressions of satisfaction and happiness. When what individuals expected was significantly different from how they experienced their day-to-day lives, there was a lot more unhappiness.

---

2   See for example, Dychtwald, K., & Morison, R. (2020). *What retirees want: A holistic view of life's third age*. Wiley.

## Expectation and Reality: The Gap

A great deal of what troubles us has to do with the difference between what we expected to happen and our perceptions of what is occurring in our lives. Many retirees described becoming aware of the importance of many aspects of work—status, social contact, achievement, feelings of self-esteem and competence, and the pay-check—only after they stopped working. They had so anticipated the break from the daily grind that they paid less attention to the positives of work.

Anna, who spent years on a sales floor, described her first 2 years of retirement: "I couldn't wait to get out of that job and off my aching feet. I just wanted to sleep in, hang around the house with my hubby and the dogs, and stay in my old housecoat until noon if I wanted to." A few weeks after she retired, her husband returned to work. She recalled, "The house got very quiet, and I never seemed to have the energy for the projects I swore I was going to do. I called friends from the office, but lunches with them were not very inter-esting. They mostly complained or gossiped, and I wasn't feeling it anymore. I didn't have to deal with a mean boss, and they were so jealous of me that I felt uneasy. I know I should've expected it, but I was so focused on what the job prevented me from doing, I didn't think much about how much I liked working."

Chet had a similar reaction, "I never thought about it, but all my friends were at work. When I retired and left the job, it got real lonely fast. Nobody called anymore, and I didn't think they'd want to talk with me so I didn't call either. I do like not having to set the alarm for six every morning and fighting the rush hour over the Sunol Grade, but I'm surprised that I miss the morning news in the car." Later, he added with some embarrassment, "I know it's crass, but I miss the biweekly paycheck. I don't really need the money, but it's just that it feels good to get that acknowledgment twice a month. You know, someone knows I'm alive and useful and worth something."

Both Anna and Chet had expected the reduction of stress and the inconvenience of a full-time work life, but those gains didn't fully compensate for the loss of work-related rewards like pay and camaraderie.

## Managing Expectations in Retirement

Because the discrepancy between what is expected and what is real has such potential for disappointment, we have to make adjustments in either the expected or the real. The former is typically far easier to alter.

There are two steps in managing our expectations: knowing them and exploring alternatives.

Gaining a realistic perspective involves information gathering (such as from current retirees). It involves understanding our own fantasies about retirement and considering what "retirement" means for us. If you are part of a couple or live in a family environment, it would be wise to discuss your retirement plans carefully with your significant others, especially in terms of your day-to-day plans.

Once the information gathering is underway, you can explore and try alternatives, at least in mental experiments. These "what-ifs" are often both sobering and creativity evoking.

Considering and adjusting our retirement fantasies to financial, psychological, and social realities will go a long way toward finding the sweet spot of our personal retirement living.

## Managing Time: Keeping an Active Calendar

Arjun, now 82 and retired for almost 20 years had some advice for all those "half my age":

> You've got to plan for retirement. It doesn't matter so much what you do, but you have to do something. I think the most destabilizing thing that occurs is the loss of a schedule. If you don't have to be somewhere at a particular time, you won't be motivated to go anywhere or you'll put it off till tomorrow. I've seen a lot of my friends just lose their zest for life when they didn't have somewhere to be at a certain time ... and I don't mean doctors' appointments.

Arjun's words resonated with almost all the retired people and many of those who were semi-retired. The need for structure came up as a most significant concern. Nearly all of them said that they welcomed the end of a fixed schedule when they first left work, but after a few months, they really missed a routine or schedule. As Marni described it, "You just got to get your butt off the recliner."

What kind of a schedule would you like to consider during the winding down from work and thereafter? Is it possible to phase into retirement with a reduced workload and part-time schedule? University professor Marcia taught fewer classes and kept her benefits, albeit at a reduced salary, for 5 years. She said, "My three days a week class schedule makes me get up, prepare, teach, and grade. The good part is that I still have four days to myself."

Jeff, a commercial pilot who retired in his mid-50s, agreed on the importance of set events on his calendar: "I used to hate that monthly draw to figure out when I was working and where I'd be, but now I miss someone else putting those flight plans on my calendar. I have to set up something myself, because if I don't, I'll get old before my time."

Where did the time go? One curious factor related to scheduling is how unscheduled time seems to disappear. Many retirees commented on how busy they were just doing daily tasks. A popular refrain was "How did I manage my life and work together? My time is full just keeping up with errands, repairs, and meals."

## Retirement and Marriage

Unlike most members of prior generations, modern couples approaching retirement can expect to live together for another 15 years or more. That's a long time to go without some real planning. Members of a couple must consider both personal and couple expectations. They must share and discuss in some depth those expectations with each other.

All of us have a certain preferred balance of alone time and together time. Frequently we evolve that over many years. Retirement should allow for some adjustments in the balance, but you should be aware that both you and your partner might be reticent to change it much. There are a host of psychological needs, often formed in childhood or basic to inherited aspects of our personalities, that are reflected in the overall equilibrium of time together and time apart.

## Does Retirement Lead to Marital Distress?

Is your relationship at risk when you or your partner retires? This question is often asked when there is no planning for post-retirement life. Any period that involves a significant shift in behavior and major adjustments for one or both persons can create relationship instability.

Is there such a phenomenon as "gray divorce?" It seems that every-body knows of an apparently solid long-term relationship that didn't survive the husband's retirement from work and return to being home full time. There have also been some very well-publicized, high-profile divorces of couples after long marriages.

In 2010, for example, Al and Tipper Gore famously divorced after 40 years. In the same year, another high-profile divorce of Los Angeles Dodgers owner Frank and Jamie McCourt was so expensive that they had to sell the team. In 2020 there was a reported divorce of Ellen DeGeneres and Portia DeRossi, over the latter's desire to retire, and in 2019, the highly publicized divorce of Jeff and MacKenzie Bezos (Amazon.com) set records with a reported $38 billion settlement.

In recent years, there seems to be an increase in reports of marriages ending when the couple is in their 60s. In fact, the divorce rate for couples approaching or in retirement has doubled since 1990 with the boomer generation. However, it is important to note that although such "gray divorces" come as a surprise to others; the divorce rate of people over 50 is still less than half the rate for those under 50.

The most common reasons given for later-in-life divorces is that they grew apart, that they were waiting for the children to be launched, boredom, and finances. Women are more likely to insti-gate these divorces.

## Familiar Stories

When Jeremy retired from his job as a plant supervisor, he went from 50 to 60 hours per week on the job to full-time home person. For a while, he played tennis and watched television. After a few months, he was ready for something different and wanted to be more involved with Bonnie's life. This was not the retirement she had envisioned, "with him underfoot all the time." Bonnie's notion was that when he stopped working outside the home, he'd pick up the lion's share of work in the home, under her supervision. When they came into marriage counseling, they were close to ending their 30-year marriage.

How did Bonnie and Jeremy pull it together? Their counsel-ing involved reconciling three separate visions: his, her, and their mutual expectations. Other couples face similar disenchantments.

For Franklin, retirement was all about travel; for his wife Eve, retirement meant gardening.

What happens to a relationship when one member likes things the way they have been and the other wants to live a different lifestyle? What does it mean when one or both go back to school? What happens when one person wants to move closer to grandchildren and the other wants to stay close to lifelong friends and community?

Finally, long-time expectations can run amok when one person retires and the other doesn't, particularly when it's the man who retires. After 30 years at a publishing firm, Ellis decided that he wanted to slow down, retire, and enjoy his life. At roughly the same time, his wife Georgia was finishing her training as a real estate broker and was the new person in an established office. Not only was her work demanding, but it also involved a lot of weekend showings.

Ellis expected that he and Georgia would have a lot more time together, especially long weekends away, and that she would be a support, an "on-call comfort," to him. Georgia expected that while she was working and he was home, he'd be responsible for keeping the home running, become the social secretary, and prepare meals most nights.

Couples like this need a lot of conversation about expectations, desires, and each other's limited capacity for mind-reading. Often significant renegotiation and compromise is obligatory. Many couples find that a professional third party, such as a marriage and family therapist, is indispensable for these often difficult conversations.

## A Stitch in Time

The time to deal with all this isn't after retirement. It's years before.

Successful couples explore together both the big picture and the details of what they expect when one or both retire. What hopes, dreams, and big plans span time periods? These need to be shared, and if discrepant they need to be worked out, often with an uninvolved third party. However, the devil is often in its usual place: the details. How will each spend the hour-by-hour days? What tasks need to be done and how will they decide how to do them, who will do them, and when they will be done?

Javon and Desiree had been married for 40 years when she decided that she wanted to retire at age 63. Javon was comfortable with the idea of her retiring after they consulted together their financial advisor, who assured them that their combined savings and Javon's continuing salary until he was 70 would be sufficient.

Although they had faced the financial issues, they hadn't discussed in any detail how each one would spend their days. There was no problem for him when Desiree spent days with her group of friends and even had a few weekend camping trips with a group of retirees she met at a community center class. The problems arose when it became clear that she envisioned spending her retirement being with friends and doing multiple projects in their home and in their small beach cabin. That came with an expectation that Javon would spend all his off-work time engaged in the projects under her aegis. He was not inclined to either have his schedule filled in this way or to have another demanding boss away from his worksite. Desiree saw his resistance to her ideas as his not wanting to spend time with her.

When they began to argue, they sought help from a therapist. It took a few months, but once each one could listen to the other, they were able to negotiate and compromise on what was real in their relationship, rather than being disappointed at unfulfilled, and unspoken, expectations for their partner's behavior.

## Rebalancing: The Better Alternative

Retirement may conjure up days of leisure or travel for many, but the reality of a happy, healthy retirement is more about realigning priorities and setting new equilibria than about retreating into a solo activity. Most retirees are happier with a reallocation of time than a revolution in life. They want to keep active. They want to be productive. They want to make a difference. They also want time to relax and, in the vernacular of their grandchildren, "chillax and hang out."

How can we progress into our retirement years, pursuing our avocations and maintaining our active involvement? What losses can we anticipate and address? What new opportunities will emerge? How can we find new balance in our lives?

Rebalancing is essential for a generation who will live longer as retirees than our predecessors. As a person approaching retirement, you may well feel younger, more vigorous, and less constrained by tradition than your parents did a generation ago. A very small minority of those interviewed assumed that they would enter a period of slow decline leading inexorably to death. Most perceived this transition as a challenge and a new opportunity for growth and personal discovery.

What makes for a retirement that provides the kind of exciting opportunity for learning that you seek? Many of us find the answers in different directions than those in our previous life stages. How can we find previously unchosen paths and opportunities to live unfulfilled dreams and use hidden talents—things that were necessarily set aside to fulfill the responsibilities of adulthood?

*Focus inward.* Pay attention to that inner voice. Consider your personal values. To successfully navigate this preparatory stage, we need to seriously consider questions such as "Who am I?" "Now that I'm all grown up, who do I really want to be?" "What are my underdeveloped talents and how can I use them productively?" "What do I really believe?"

*Dream about the things you always wanted to do.* Perhaps it involves relocating, living simpler, buying that long-desired vacation home by the lake, learning a musical instrument, or taking classes in an academic field of interest. Perhaps it even involves "re-hirement," returning to work in a new business or in a low-stress position.

*Rebalance your life.* Break down and explore individually the major components of your life and time expenditures to date. Look separately at family, finances, friendships, health, career, intellectual stimulation, personal values, spirituality, community, and other support systems. Carefully list your prior successes and try to see where you can apply your existing strengths to new challenges. Which areas are challenges? Where would you like to improve?

*Set tentative action goals for growth.* Make commitments to yourself. Then make it easier to stay on track by also informing a few trusted companions. It seems counter-intuitive, but without measurable goals, other "demands du jour" can get in the way of following your bliss. Work will always expand to fill the allotted time frame. Many recent retirees become loaded down with the deferred maintenance and other "stuff" that has accumulated over the years and seems to cry out for their attention, so much so that the thought of dealing with it all may just seem overwhelming. Although getting to those things that you've put off for years might be of value, there might be good reasons you've deferred them for so long. I have often told clients that questions such as "When will I reorganize the pictures from the trip we took in 1976?" "When will I empty that catch-all drawer in the kitchen?" and "When will I replace the paper on the top shelf of the closets (and don't get me started on what to do with the things in the attic)?" will be irrelevant 7 years after they are dead. Bottom line: The goals for now may have precedence over those ancient items at the bottom of the to-do list.

*Keep your calendar current.* After working and having lives determined by smart phones, day-timers, and work logs, many people are very happy to dispense with them permanently. This can create a vacuum in which priorities are lost in the lack of appointed scheduling. We want to be master of our own ship's clock and compass. Rather than letting the tides carry us, we want to explore and discover where and when we will alight.

*Recognize and face your fears of the unknown.* Anxiety accompanies change. For the most part that anxiety is healthy and normal, but there is also neurotic anxiety that can have deep personal roots and engender immobility. It's important to recognize the difference and be especially wary of any inner voice that automatically discourages you from trying something. Statements like "Nobody will hire or date someone of my age"; "Everyone wants experienced people"; "I don't understand this new technology"; "There's no way that my spouse will let me ..."; or "What if I take that class and don't do well?" often reflect the avoidance of facing new fears and slipping toward stagnation. I have often reminded clients that grades don't matter in adult education classes. The only criterion is if they learn something new. Positive psychology focuses on "The Little Engine That Could" philosophy: "I think I can" beats "I think I can't."

*Take care of your health.* You can defer maintenance on your property and keep having to "jimmy" the key in the lock a certain special way because it's too much of a hassle to get it fixed, but it's a bad bet to do that with your body. Get regular physicals, and follow through with good maintenance regimens. All the dreams in the world can be dashed by physical failure.

*Try to avoid repetitive conversations about others' infirmities or deaths.* It's amazing how fast retirees can fall into depressing conversations that begin with statements like "So, Murray, are you regular?" or "You'll never guess who I saw in the obits yesterday." It is commonplace to begin conversations with friends we haven't seen in a while with an "organ recital." It's fine to share and to talk realistically and transparently with others, especially if it normalizes one's own feelings. It just doesn't make sense to dwell on one's alimentary canal or colonic content and output if the goals are to be far more lofty, and exciting.

*Consider the spiritual sides of life.* During preretirement and in retirement, it's common for some of the bigger questions to emerge naturally or surface in a new, more poignant manner: "What is my role in the greater scheme of things?" "What does my life mean?" "To what extent, am I a part of something larger than my own life?" "Is there something beyond my conscious senses, something more eternal?" "Is there a life after death, and if so, does this life govern that one?" Questioning the more ethereal questions is an opportunity for growth, peace, and new understandings.

*Focus on your sexuality.* There is a natural shift in sexuality over the years as hormones diminish and biological reproduction becomes less central to life. Yet, desire for sexual connection, albeit in modified (possibly less acrobatic or rigorous) form is often important in keeping relationships and individuals alive. Sexuality represents an important means of communication and connection to your body and to your partner. If either of your sexual desires is waning, it's important to talk honestly about it and to devise means for you both to find physical satisfaction. Friendly, desired physical touch is stress reducing, healing, centering, and interactive. Milt described one of the most isolative problems for widows and widowers: "The worst part about being alone is that there's no warm body in the bed to cuddle."

*Tune in to shifting family relationships.* Among the most important relationships that often get redefined at this age are those with children and elderly living parents. Do you want to move to be close to your adult children? To what extent can you let go of your parenting responsibilities with your adult children? Do you have continuing caretaking relationships with elderly parents, minor children, or grandchildren? What plans need to be made for their care?

*Consider your legacy.* Retirement offers an opportunity to consider what you want to do for others, before or after you are gone. What is the current and potential nature and size of your current estate? Do you want to follow the dictate of that cynical bumper sticker and spend your children's inheritance, or do you want something specific to happen to your estate? How do you want to be remembered? Will you support particular charities or your community? Which gifts would honor your values and continue your beliefs and how you want to be remembered? Is education one of your core values? Perhaps investing in a 529 savings plan for your grandchildren' schooling for example, is a way to express that.

*Consider whether you will relocate after retirement.* Many opt for Sunbelt climates or proximity to family, but such moves need to be considered carefully. Moving might offer a more favorable climate, but leaving a social comfort zone means needing to make new friends and other adjustments. Do you plan to downsize or move into a senior community? While the advantages of streamlining and being less "owned" by your accumulated possessions are obvious, there may be a sense of loss of nostalgia, comfort, and the community you have lived in. For those who have relocated periodically, such as military families, another move at retirement seems only one natural step in the progression, but what if you have lived within a 4-mile radius in Brooklyn your whole life? Will you or your partner need assisted living? When might that occur? What plans will you make now to ease those transitions?

*Practice self-forgiveness.* It is about time when your guilt about things you did or said years ago can be let go. All of us reviewing our histories have things we regret from years, maybe even decades ago. If amends are in order and feasible, make them, but if you are torturing yourself for things that cannot be changed, it is time that you let them diminish in importance. The best way to atone for these is to live the way you think is best now.

Randall (now 63) described an incident of being unfaithful to his first wife, over 40 years ago. After they divorced, he apologized to her and he has been true to his second wife of 35 years. It was still troubling him when he came to therapy. At one point, he said, "I think I can recall every mistake I have ever made throughout my life, and almost none of the successes." With something that almost seemed like pride, he confessed, "I have been the king of guilt since I was around seven." In therapy we worked on how he could forgive himself and continue to live an honorable life in the present and future.

# The Transition to Retirement

All transitions in life can be difficult. The rebalancing in retirement is a large one because the shift is away from a decades-long pattern.

Because this is such a big shift for most people, it is good to make early and consistent preparation for life after work. Among the important questions are "Who am I if I am not a manager, a postal worker, a physician, or a police officer?" "Am I more than an ex-worker and, if so, what?" "How do I want to view myself or others to see me? What is the best way to use my time?"

The earlier we begin the better the retirement we can anticipate, from both fiscal and psychological perspectives. Seriously consider working with a competent counselor or psychotherapist who can help smooth the way and provide help in confronting denial and the outdated personal patterns that are likely to trip up retirement.

# Exercise

One way to look into these core areas and prepare for retirement is to take a personal inventory. It's beneficial to begin well in advance of retirement and to repeat the exercise every year or two. Each repetition should increase your awareness and the opportunity for more comprehensive retirement planning.

Write down or enter into your computer the answers to the following. It's best to keep your answers dated and available for comparison with later iterations to explore trends.

- What does retirement mean to you?
- What are your passions?
- What would you do if money was no object or you won the lottery?
- What were the happiest times in your life? What elements stand out?
- How can you approach those?
- What is your purpose in life?
- What can you do to stay sharp and replace the stimulation of work?
- What is the nature of your social network? In what ways would you like to enhance or change it?
- What do you need in your life and how can you find it?
- What is your preferred new role in the home, in the community, with your children, grandchildren, and so on?

As you ponder these and related questions, consider the results of a longitudinal study by Yujie Zhan and her colleagues.[3] Their results confirmed what many experts in retirement and gerontology have indicated: Working at least part time after retirement is related to fewer diseases, fewer functional limitations, and better mental health than quitting completely. Part of this is due to the greater level of physical and mental activity. The authors reported a 17% lower likelihood of diagnoses such as hypertension, diabetes, cancer, lung disease, heart disease, stroke, and arthritis. Other studies show a similar reduction in diagnoses of depression.

Furthermore, postretirement work related to prior occupational skill sets was found to be particularly helpful, as was part-time work, volunteering, and creative endeavors as a bridge from work to full retirement. A related study indicated that retirees over 65 who continued work as volunteers had half the risk of death. This information isn't lost on our peers. A 2008 *AARP Report* indicated that fully 70% of workers in the stretch years were planning to continue working for some time during their retired years.[4] In a 2019 AARP study, over 20% of those between 65 and 69 were reportedly working full time.[5]

3   Zhan, Y., Wang, M., Liu, S., & Shultz, K. S. (2009). Bridge employment and retirees' health: A longitudinal investigation. *Journal of Occupational Health Psychology*, 14(4), 374–389.

4   Koppen, J., & Anderson, G., (2008). Retired spouses: A national survey of adults. 55–75. *AARP Report*, November. https://www.aarp.org/research/topics/life/info-2014/retired_spouses. html

5   Edelson, H. (2019) More Americans working past 65. *AARP Magazine*, April 22. https://www.aarp.org/work/employers/info-2019/americans-working-past-65.html

chapter twelve

# Recreation or
# Re-Creation

*People who cannot find time for recreation are obliged
sooner or later to find time for illness.*

—John Wanamaker

W hen do I get the time to do what I want?
Most people do not have the time to pursue
their recreational desires fully while they are
still working full time. The most prevalent fantasy about
retirement is "Finally! I have time for myself."

When Luke retired from his lucrative development business at age 62, he figured that he finally had time to pursue
his lifelong love of golf on a full-time basis. Divorced for
almost 4 years and with his children grown, he was able to
easily relocate from the Northeast to South Carolina.

At first, he was blissfully happy. He loved the game and
enjoyed the other people who were serious golfers at the
upscale country club community where he lived and played.
In a journal entry he shared, he wrote, "I never thought
it would be this way. This is truly the good life." He was
in good shape and health and living comfortably. He met
and married a woman who was also a golf aficionado, and
together they traveled, played golf, and lived their dream
life. When the initial rush of full-time golfing wore off,

Luke became increasingly involved with his community. He joined a men's group that actively performed community service, which he found most gratifying.

Isn't this the form of retirement we were all promised? Whether it was golf, contract bridge, travel, photography, music, hiking, spending time with friends or grandchildren, ceramics, or philately, we thought we would have time to do what we always wanted to do—live off the fruits of our labors. For some like Luke, retirement is precisely that—a time filled with recreation.

Luke's transition didn't require much preparation or ambivalence. Having eliminated the time demands of work, he increased time with his avocation and social life. He knew how he wanted to spend his leisure time. Once he could afford to do it, he did.

It might not be that easy for you. In addition to financial health and family considerations, there might be questions about exactly what form of recreation is right. When we have spent most of our adult lives dealing with responsibilities, it can be difficult to cultivate new ways to spend our time at retirement age.

## Do It Now!

After retirement there are numerous decisions and some time to consider the nature and time commitments to recreation, but what about while we are preparing to retire? These stretch years provide a host of possibilities to rebalance our time allocation to pay increased attention to our personal enjoyment.

For most of us, the time for recreation and laying the groundwork for future play and avocation occurs long before actual retirement. Orlando (aged 49) said in an interview, "I don't want to wait until I have the time, but not the energy or will. I don't know how much time I have, and I need to mix in some fun with all the work now." Orlando's plan was to re-create himself from a competitor to a mentor at work and to become more involved with the local youth soccer league as a referee, something his work commitments prevented him from doing when his children were playing for youth teams. He claimed that as a result, both his work and home life had improved substantially.

At 54, Kim was experiencing greater success at work than ever before, but she was feeling a contrasting emptiness in the rest of her life. Her single-minded work focus that had served her so well for many years left her feeling lonely on weekends unless she went into the office on her days off. She confessed, "I look forward to Mondays!" After consulting with a therapist for a few months, Kim decided to concentrate some of her energy on friendships and a social life. Although early attempts were unsuccessful, she did develop a gratifying network of friends and, for the first time in more than a decade, a romantic relationship.

# What Is Recreation and Why Do We Need It?

That term "recreation" itself is interesting. In a sense, we re-create our lives and activities and dedicate our time to pursuing those callings and desires. To function well at work and live a full life, we need some regular downtime to replenish and refresh ourselves. We are well advised to experiment well before retirement with activities and time expenditure that we might take up once we no longer have to work to make money.

Just as our body needs sleep to function during our awake state, our bodies and psyches need to lay aside the pressures of the workplace and focus on renewing activities. Some of these are active, and others more restful; but regardless of the nature of the break in our work schedule, re-creation is a necessary component of growth.

It is important that recreation be regular and frequent. Big, dramatic annual vacation trips to exotic locales may be wonderful and exciting, but they are often insufficient to replenish the body, mind, and soul on a day-to-day or week-to-week basis.

## After Midlife

From the time we leave school until we reach midlife, the majority of us prioritize our life focus on building a career and raising families. By setting reachable goals, we approximate the life we desire. The dedication and sacrifice required often leads us to set aside leisure activities. Once we begin to leave the midlife years, we need to recapture or develop anew those recreational aspects. Aging bodies need more rest and recuperation, and it is wise for each of us to focus on the full meaning of our lives. The goal is to rebalance our lives—an endeavor that will serve us before and after retirement.

## Rebalancing as a Prologue to Retirement

In the late 1940s, a popular song—"Lucky, Lucky Me"—had a refrain that included the line, "I work eight hours, I sleep eight hours, and have eight hours for fun." Among those we interviewed for this project in the first 2 decades of the 21st century, the idea of a 40-hour work week and a corresponding 40 hours of fun was laughable. The work week (including work in and out of the house) was reportedly closer to 60 to 65 hours. Daily time for sleep was an hour less on average. Fun was something that happened if there was time left over. If that time did materialize, the recreation was not optimal. Most interviewees reported that they were more tired and stressed than they wished.

Ichiro reported, "I work about a twelve-hour day counting commute. Then when I get home there are kids with activities and homework, dinner and dishes and chores to help out my wife, and then it's about six and a half hours of sleep before I am up and off in the car again. Sometimes I play racquetball at lunchtime, but it's only maybe twice a week."

Ichiro is in the majority. In her 1992 book *The Overworked American: The Unexpected Decline of Leisure,*[1] Harvard economist Juliet Schor reported that free time had fallen nearly 40% since the early 1970s. Since 1992, that imbalance has accelerated. Both boomers' and X'ers world of work has generally expanded at the expense of playtime. Not only is the 8-hour workday uncommon, but typically there are two adults in each family employed for those longer hours. Such a work-oriented ambiance over a long time period without a recreational break is stress inducing. American culture is somewhat unique in the West in this way. We do not have the lengthy vacations, paid holidays, and leaves common in Europe. In fact, the United States has been called "the vacationless society."

---

1   Schor, J. (1992). *The overworked American: The unexpected decline of leisure*. Basic Books.

The guiding theme for the 2020 American Psychological Association (APA) annual meeting was "stress in America." A combination of increasing workloads, COVID-19 and the failure of an effective government response, the murder of George Floyd, and the more general uncovering of structural racial prejudice had made 2020 a high point in reported stress.

The tragic events of 2020 contributed to, but did not create Americans' high stress lives. A major contributor to this is the shift from a manufacturing to a service economy. As the number of white-collar jobs has expanded, the expectation of being "on call" has also crept up. The saturation of our culture with ubiquitous access through wireless mobile devices (electronic leashes) makes us available to managers, coworkers, and clients long after we've left the office. In addition, downsizing has increased our workloads and globalization can create a need to be in contact with colleagues in far different time zones. In short, work is far more likely to follow us home than a wayward puppy.

Karen (aged 56) is a marketing specialist with a high-tech firm that has manufacturing plants in China and Ireland. At least twice a week her collaborative work occurs during the wee hours of the morning to accommodate corporate needs. In the past 3 years, her workload has increased dramatically as others in her division have been laid off without replacement hires. She said, "I love my job and the money, but my husband and I pass in the night and we can go days without seeing each other or really talking. At best we text each other during lunch or working dinners."

When my children were younger, I coached their Little League and soccer teams. I was always impressed with the number of white-collar parents who could get away from their offices for mid-week late afternoon games. It was equally notable that many of them were on their cellphones connected to work during the games, and almost all went back to the office for several hours when the games were over.

## Do It Yourself

In a world where the pressure of (often two) workplaces dominate couples' lives, it falls to individuals to craft personally replenishing recreation. Work won't help us find new balance; if anything, the work dragon has an almost insatiable appetite for more hours, and the threat of being laid off or falling behind competitively keeps us anxious enough to always push the limits of our endurance. If for no other reason than to be effective at work, we need to create a good work-life balance.

A psychiatrist friend once described to me how he had "burned out" and had to stop seeing patients for almost 2 years. When he returned, he developed a new form of practice. He saw patients from 9:00 a.m. until noon then had lunch with friends, a short nap, and some form of physical activity before returning to work from 3:00–6:00 p.m. He taught one evening a week and had the other six to be with his family. After doing this for 3 years, he reported that he was happier, healthier, and closer to his sons and wife than ever before. He also asserted, "I think the therapy I do now is far better than the production work I was doing when I had 35, 40 hours a week of contact time." With his new schedule, he was able to work comfortably, part time, well into his 70s.

## How Can We Increase Enjoyment Now and in the Future?

The answers will be personal, but several themes emerged from those who had already retired and the much larger number who were planning to retire in the next decade. Among the most powerful callings were play, escape, increased time with family and friends, mentor, teach, pursue spirituality, give back, and engage in philanthropy.

Chuck and Jill were blessed with great wealth from Jill's ancestors. They began a charity while they were working in their family business. They talked avidly about what they would do when they retired from the business. Their plan was to turn daily operations of the business over to their adult children, put their full effort into their philanthropy, and involve their children in decisions about giving to the community and assisting others. By making it a family activity, they also guaranteed more time with their children away from the business and an enhancement to their legacy.

Few have such grand plans or resources. Many reported a desire to spend more time with children and grandchildren, others to join a book club and read all that literature they previously put off for later. Some described a desire to take square dance lessons, join a bowling league, take up ceramics, or take college classes.

Of course, you might be like Kevin who reported proudly, "Work is my recreation and my profession. I figure I'll never retire. I just like doing what I'm doing." Among those who also feel this way are many who have become aware that they simply cannot afford to retire fully; they will engage in pastimes and service part time. Finally, a third group of retirees became "rehires." They found some part-time low-stress work for income, benefits, and time management. After years of owning and running his self-employed business and a year "on holiday," Mike joyfully took a few classes on tax accounting and then worked for a large tax preparation company from January through April.

What are your callings, desires, and opportunities to be generative during the latter years of labor? Will you go "back to the future," rediscovering skills, passions, and lost enchantments, or will you explore previously unplanned and unimagined adventures? Perhaps, you will perceive yourself not as "old wine in new bottles" but as well-aged wine with character that delights the palate.

The bottom line is that in the years after midlife, we are well served by attending to recreation and reallocating our time and life's pursuits. For the many boomers who espoused a "use it or lose it" mantra in their earlier days, recreation is a preventative to illness and decline.

## Benefits of Recreation During the Stretch Years

Leisure activities replenish body and mind. Whether the rejuvenation comes from passive enjoyment, such as sleep or sedentary entertainment, or from active pursuits, the need for recreation increases through the post-midlife years. Do you need an afternoon siesta at the office? Would a morning workout or walk make the workday more enjoyable and productive?

It's clear that recreation may be stress reducing, and lower stress is related to general life satisfaction, better physical and mental health, overall happiness in other realms of life, and the reduction of disability owing to chronic illness or pain. Stress affects almost every body system, and long-term stress can produce significant problems with digestion, heart beat, respiration, blood pressure, sexuality, skin, concentration, muscles, and the immune system.

When we perceive danger, our bodies activate our sympathetic nervous system, which is designed for fight-or-flight emergencies.

When stress—such as job pressures and long work hours—persists, bodily resources are marshaled to fight off danger by shifting resources from other systems. Although this system defends us well against imminent danger and recovery is relatively quick, it is designed for short-term bursts of protection; chronic stress eats away at precious body resources.

It's estimated that stress is a major factor in about three quarters of physician visits and is one of the leading causes of death in the United States. Any break from the stress allows the body time to replenish, rest the sympathetic nervous system, and recuperate from the emergency response. This is one reason recreation, involving both rest and play, is so valuable to the body.

## Returning to a More Natural Sleep-Waking Rhythm

Over millions of years of evolution, human beings have adapted to a host of environments. Our bodies are geared to be asleep when it is dark and awake during the light. Of course, this was more mandatory before the advent of artificial lighting. Yet regardless of technology, our physical selves need a significant period of rest throughout the day. Although the amount individuals need varies, the average need is 8 hours. Brief naps during the afternoon are fairly common for many over 50. In America today, it is commonplace for boomers and Xers to put in long hours on the job, add nightshifts, and work on the home computer or smartphone until they retire for the night. This both leads to, and is a result of, too much caffeine, nicotine, and alcohol.

Getting less sleep than we personally require leads to a host of problems, including diminished work performance, relationship problems, and mood problems like anger and depression. At least one study reports that drowsiness played a role in the disasters of Exxon Valdez, Three-Mile Island, and Chernobyl, and there are countless accidents caused by drowsy drivers, overworked medical residents, and sleepy air traffic controllers. In addition, chronic sleep loss is linked to health risks such as heart disease and diabetes.

Sleep deprivation or pervasive daytime sleepiness, insomnia, and sleep apnea are increasing dramatically for today's baby boomers and Generation Xers. Most sleep experts suggest that we are getting about 20% less sleep than our ancestors and that the reduced sleep plays a role in obesity, perhaps because of the unmet physical needs and the snacking we do to keep ourselves awake. The prescription of sleep apnea machines like CPAP and BIPAP has increased dramatically for the boomer population and is now rising for those in Generation X. The vast majority of users reportedly discard the apparatus after a short time. Does recreation provide a more lasting answer?

How does recreation help with sleep? Isn't it possible that recreation is just another chore to keep us up and going? There could be such a risk if we approach recreation the way we face work challenges, but for the most part, recreational pursuits allow us to ramp down and relax into a better night's sleep.

Recreation may do more than provide physical and mental restoration. It can also help us develop new skills and grow psychologically.

## Opportunity for Improving Self-Esteem

Although work provides us opportunities for success and acknowledgment, recreation does also. We experience teamwork and challenges in athletic and community activities. We also have opportunities to do something novel. Errors at work can have damaging consequences, but mistakes during a pickup game are typically less hazardous. Because of that, attempts to do something outside our safe range may be easier. As Florence described her Sweet Adelines acapella singing group, "We were in the middle of this song, and I just thought I'd try to hit the high note instead of my usual dropping to a lower octave. So, I tried and missed the note completely. The whole group got a laugh out of that. I think we actually had more fun because of the mistake than we would have if I'd played it safe."

## Ten Additional Benefits of Recreation

Based on our research, 10 characteristics of re-creation are valued:

1. Opportunities to plan and organize
2. Chances to experiment with adventure, change, and independence without having to abide by a host of rules others have set

3. Enjoyment of one or more of the arts and indulging in aesthetics and sensory pleasures without having to be a professional artist
4. Opportunities for reflection, thinking, analyzing, and asking important questions about scientific and philosophical truths and an understanding of life
5. Chances to tackle difficult tasks and achieve high standards in different venues for recognition of accomplishments
6. Chances to meet new people, cooperate on common goals, and be an integral part of a team
7. Opportunities to form and further relationships, attract others, make new friends, flirt, and experience new love
8. Experiences of altruism, including helping those who are in need and protecting and supporting children and animals
9. Chances to be on the go and replace boredom with action, distraction, and absorption in novel activities
10. A sense of being "in the zone," bringing joy, better mental health, and lower rates of depression.

# Common Forms of Leisure and Recreation Between 45 and 65

Over the past 4 decades, researchers have tried to categorize a broad array of recreational activities. George McKechnie's Leisure Activities Blank[2] generated some of the early work in the 1970s. Researchers and experts in career counseling have refined this and adapted it to new cultures over the years. The activities our own interviewees preferred fit well into 10 groupings:

1. Traditionally female pastimes (arts and crafts)
2. Traditionally male behaviors and trades (repairs, model building, electronics)
3. Home-oriented activities (socializing, media, shopping, social networking, reading, listening to music, streaming movies and TV series)

---

2 McKechnie, G. (1974). The psychological structure of leisure. *Journal of Leisure Research*, 9(4), 27–45.

4. Outdoor sporting activities (backpacking, hiking, camping, sailing, hunting and fishing, team sports)
5. Indoor sports (board and table games, dance, yoga, exercise DVDs)
6. Social groups (card playing, fraternal organizations, book clubs)
7. Travel and travel planning (photography, novel cuisines and cultures)
8. Artistic pursuits (painting and drawing, ceramics, photography)
9. Spirituality and religious pursuits (retreats, studying new religions, meditation, evangelism, prayer)
10. Other social pursuits (meeting new people, dating or online social networks, genealogy, reconnecting with lost friends).

# Starting a New Job or Career

Many of our interviewees described the pleasure of turning their recreation into moneymaking activities. Some began new businesses; others, like Mike in the previous example, found pleasure in a non-demanding job "that you could leave when you went home." Some sold their new creations or offered skills as consultants. In the early days of the COVID-19 pandemic, many used their sewing skills to produce necessary protective masks. Jonathan Clements of the *Wall Street Journal*, focusing on the potential financial implications of recreation, noted that a part-time job will bring in extra cash and that even volunteer work that keeps you busy will keep you away from the shopping mall.

# Work-Life Balance

It's unwise to overwork now to save for the golden years. For one thing, we miss out on many pleasures of being with our growing children, and we might never have a chance to collect. One of my former clients died at age 47. He would frequently talk with pride that he hadn't missed a day of work in 10 years. In fact, he had more than 2 years of accrued vacation and sick leave when he had a fatal heart attack. Indeed, the major beneficiary of his hard work was his widow's unemployed second husband.

One of my college classmates responding to a query on the occasion of our reaching 60 included the following in her list of things she'd like to do: "Be artistic more frequently; write a book; spend more time with friends and people I love; spend more time being and less time doing; travel; appreciate more; work to save wildlife and the environment; walk more frequently; learn how to sail; learn a language; take more photos of nature and those close to me; look at the stars and clouds as I did as a girl; and light more candles." She acknowledged, however, that she could not do all of those things and continue in a full-time job.

Having a balanced life before retirement could put retirement off for a few years, but they can be years of far richer life experience.

## Advice for Re-Creators

Wilma, a 60-year-old partner in a Silicon Valley law firm, was recently talking to a group of law school students when she answered a question with the following statement: "You can do a forty-five-, fifty-hour workweek, but if you really want to get ahead, the standard for serious billable hours is more like a seventy-hour workweek." Wilma was quick to admit that she had little life outside of the law practice: "I have three ex-husbands [one of them twice] and three grown kids who go to their father's house for Christmas. There just isn't much time left over for anything but sleep, my opera tickets, and an occasional social event." Particularly curious was that none of the final-year law students showed any surprise at her assertion. In fact, afterward two of them went up to Wilma expressing great praise for her work ethic. Wilma's life is emblematic of the "live to work" ambiance of this century.

Perhaps this is the kind of life you always wanted or maybe you are more like Kate, who discovered "a stealthy inflation in the number of work hours to the exclusion of almost everything else in my life. I was at my best friend's fifty-fifth birthday party when I realized that I'd almost given up time with my friends, didn't even know the people who lived next door to me, and had given up any activities that nurtured my soul." Whichever you prefer, "work to live" or "live to work" the recommended reassessment will provide some reassurance and an opportunity to rebalance.

Kate's use of the term "stealthy" is important. One reality of time management is that if we leave an activity to the time remaining after we do everything else, we won't ever have time for it. If we want more leisure in our lives, it has to get a priority-assigned timeslot on our e-calendars.

## Just One More Big Score

Responding to increasing financial fears that emerged after the severe stock market downturns of 2008, Clark took on a potentially lucrative project as a second job. Much to the consternation of his wife Jackie, he was at work roughly 17 hours a day, 6 days a week. When they came into couple therapy, she was threatening divorce if he didn't return to "a sane balance of work and home life." "He is like a man possessed," she reported. Jackie was willing to agree to wait for a deadline in 4 months when Clark claimed that the project would either "sink or swim." When the deadline slipped 2 months, her upset increased along with her belief that this would be a permanent lifestyle. Clark's position was that he'd "kill myself for seven months and then we'd be set for life if it works out. Either way, come December, 1, I'll walk away."

During this 7-month period, both Clark and Jackie suffered from stress-related physical ailments and were growing distant from each other. His blood pressure required daily medicine, and he had two small fender-benders with his car. He also lost his libido.

Was it worth it? Would it be for you? As it turned out, Clark did get his big payday and did walk away from the next deal on December 1, just as he promised. It also took almost 5 months before his blood pressure came down and his libido returned.

Clark was willing to give up a year of his life to overcome the financial insecurity he said he feared more than anything. Having grown up in abject poverty, the fear was not theoretical for him. His health suffered and he came close to losing his marriage as the price for assuaging that fear.

Fears of losing security can affect us all. We need to maintain a vibrant balance between security and freedom to engage in the unknown. Too much security can lead to stagnation, and too much freedom to fears of the unknown. In all our explorations, we must respect both needs.

### I Don't Know What Else to Do

Sometimes we cannot walk away because we haven't envisioned options. Warren Spahn, one of the best left-handed pitchers in major league baseball from the late 1940s through the mid-1960s, provides an example. During his career, he was an all-star 13 times, and when he retired, he was the sixth-winningest pitcher in history and one of my personal heroes. A few years after he retired, he coached, managed, and pitched for minor league teams. I was at a game at the old Honolulu stadium when he took the mound against the triple-A Hawaii Islanders. It was sad to see players who would never reach the major leagues hit his pitches and force him from the game in the third inning.

## Leisure Doesn't Mean an Added Challenge

In *The Overworked American*, Professor Juliet Schor, recommends that the first thing today's Americans do is cut back their work time. However, she warns us to beware of simply transferring the work frenzy into extracurricular obsessions. The joy of running, swimming, cycling, or competing need not turn into a struggle to become a superior triathlete. In short, just like work, any recreational activity can be a means to avoid those underdeveloped (shadow) sides of ourselves.

Researchers in the area of work-life balance would add a prescription for more sleep as a first priority and more play as a second. Perhaps that song with the haunting lyrics from the 1940s was right: Work 8 hours, sleep 8 hours, and have 8 hours for fun.

## Exercises

## A. Spending Leisure

- Set aside an hour a week in a place where you are free to contemplate. Write down your musings, even if they seem disjointed.

- During this time, revisit and evaluate your dreams. Are there things you really wish to include in your life? Are there spiritual quests that you have always wanted to pursue but haven't yet had the time or maturity for?
- Focus clearly on your "wants" and separate them from your "shoulds."
- Reassess how you spend time and reconsider how that time allocation reflects your current priorities.
- Consider what price (especially in time) you are willing to pay to pursue your bliss. What personal deals are you willing to make?
- Carefully examine how you are seduced back to the status quo and think of what you can do to reach out more to face your personal unknowns.

# B. Buying Time

- Create a time chart of your current life on your calendar. It's best to list what you are doing in 15- or 30-minute blocks. *Do not trust this to memory.*
- Make note of the most and least enjoyable parts of the schedule.
- Consider what you could do to minimize the less enjoyable nonmandatory tasks. Include figuring out what you could do to get someone else to do these and what it would cost you in time, money, or status.
- Set up a separate time chart that begins with what you most enjoy and create an ideal ongoing week. If this is the same as what you already have, consider yourself most fortunate and stop here.
- Redo the schedule with a sacrosanct free hour each day. What would you do with the time? Would you fill it with more work? Would you include recreation or leisure? Would you nap, contemplate, go for a walk or run, listen to music or watch sports?
- Consider your retirement plans and set up two retirement schedules: The first, a timeline to full or partial retirement, and the second, a time chart of your expected weekly schedule after retirement.
- Consider carefully whether the extra money is worth the extra effort and the corresponding loss of time for other things.

- If the discrepancy is large between what you are doing and what you'd like to be doing, seek help from a professional who can help you face your pull toward the status quo and your presumption of security.

# Part

**Realities and Opportunities**

# chapter thirteen

# Health and the Aging Body

*Aging is not for the faint of heart.*

— Bette Davis

Although individuals rarely notice their physical aging on a daily, monthly, or even annual basis, there is definitely an evident change over time that occurs primarily in the functional areas of life. The aching joints, slower reactions, memory loss (particularly for proper nouns), diminishing vision and hearing, slow healing, loss of skin elasticity (resulting in wrinkles and lines), reduced sexual responsiveness, drop in hormone levels, enlarging prostates, and influence of gravity are reminders that we are subject to the aging process.

For most of us, these factors—along with a creeping awareness of a diminishing amount of flirtation directed toward us—make us feel that birthdays, especially the decade ones (for example, 50 and 60) are markers of accelerating decline. Ahmed recalled, "I sailed through fifty, hardly knew it was my birthday. Now that sixty is looming in only six months, two weeks and three days (who's counting?), it seems like I have suddenly joined the aged set." His wife, Amal, reported, "I refused to celebrate my fiftieth and with sixty only five years away, I plan to deny that one also."

That reflection in the mirror may not perceptively age from one shave to the next, but while I experience myself and my visage as remaining young, my contemporaries seem to get noticeably older each time we meet.

Cindy returned recently from her 40th high school reunion. It was the first one she'd gone to since the 10th, and she found it disconcerting:

> I couldn't get my mind around being at the high school with all these "old" people. I also couldn't help but notice how time was not an equal opportunity factor. Some of my old friends were very old. They dressed old, acted old, and thought old. Others were joking about the big six-oh approaching and planning to redo their graduation bashes. My first boyfriend was among them, fully looking almost sixty and acting twenty. A few looked exactly as I remembered them—maybe not eighteen anymore, but certainly not more than twenty-five. It wasn't until I got home and saw my husband that I realized I was not just an observer of that group; I was one of them.

We don't all experience life with equal ease or difficulty, nor do we share the same history or genetic makeup. Some of us have done hard labor all of our adult lives. Some have suffered serious illness, injury, or psychological trauma. Others have chronic conditions. Some of us have let our physical selves go in a single-minded effort to make a living or because of the obsolete feelings of invincibility we had as adolescents. Some of us are blessed with longevity from our ancestors.

Others, like Amanda, wrote, "I am fifty-eight and have now outlived everyone back two generations in my family: my mom and dad died in their early fifties; so did my grandparents on both sides—all, from one sort of cancer or another."

## So Murray, Are You Regular?

Regardless of our genes or life experiences, it is clear that from cradle to grave, we are aging. After midlife, as the subjective experience of time accelerates, we become increasingly aware of bodily changes and of escalating frailties. For most of us, many of these changes are quite unpleasant.

"When I was twenty-five," Chester recalls, "I could pull a muscle and be back in a day or two, tops. Now it can be weeks before the pains subside." Similarly, Dan was shocked when he discovered that "I found myself making my father's 'oof' sound when I sat down."

Almost everyone we interviewed talked about the difficulty of losing weight. Lisette, a notable athlete in her 20s and 30s, reported that getting and staying in shape was far more problematic now. As she mournfully joked, "Surely, I am the same person today as I was when I played volleyball in college, except I spend more time icing and resting than I do digging and spiking."

When asked about their general health, our interviewees generally reported that they were in good or very good health. This was consistent with the results reported in the MIDMAC study.[1] Yet, having evaluated their health in a generally positive light, they began almost immediately describing a litany of recent and current ailments. Among these were aches and pains, surgeries, chronic conditions, deteriorating capacities, and weight gain.

It was a little surprising that many described these physical problems vividly, often accompanied with a nervous laugh or with a summary comment about aging. Myra, for example, kept punctuating her complaints with "Whachagonnado? I'm an old broad now." It seemed there was almost a kind of strange pleasure in detailing the physical problems.

Some of the physical ailments were far more serious than others. Certain interviewees acknowledged having life-threatening illnesses such as HIV/AIDS, lupus, multiple sclerosis, Parkinson's, ALS, heart disease, cancer, and Chronic Obstructive Pulmonary Disease (COPD). Others described being treated for chronic conditions that were disabling but generally not seen as life threatening. Among

---

1    Brim, O. G., Ryff, C. D., & Kessler, R. C. (Eds.). (2004). *How healthy are we? A national study of well-being at midlife.* University of Chicago Press. Based on the MIDUS report of the MIDMAC study, this is the most comprehensive study of middle age. Because the age of the respondents was 40 to 60, it maps fairly well with the stretch years (45 to 65).

these were hypertension; high cholesterol; sleep disorders, such as apnea; digestion issues, including constipation, acid reflux, and pain after eating; migraine headaches; urinary problems; enlarged prostates; arthritis; allergies; and asthma and other respiratory problems.

## Ubiquitous Aliments: Differential Disability

Indeed, it seemed that everyone we interviewed reported some injury, ongoing ailment, or loss of function; but the way each responded to the extra burden was quite different. With regard to quality of life, the illness or ailment per se seemed less crucial than the person's reaction to it. Some took a physical setback as just another hurdle to jump in living their lives as fully as possible.

Harold was suffering from emphysema when I spoke to him. Although he was a little out of breath even during the interview, he was jovial and focused on a new project at work and his granddaughter's 1st birthday: "I hope she can blow out the candles herself," he pronounced, adding with a laugh (and a cough), "I won't be able to help her." Although Harold's illness is both disabling and life-threatening, he was living his life as fully as he could.

By contrast, Leona had a suspicious tumor removed from her breast. Although it turned out to be benign, she had a hard time believing that she would not soon face a mastectomy and die from cancer. She retreated to her bed, cut off contact with her colleagues at work, and maintained limited communication with many of her family members "who just don't understand how bad this is."

Gina took another approach; when she developed a series of headaches during menopause, she refocused her life on finding a cure. She insisted on having all possible medical tests including CT scans and a MRI. When all of them were negative, she turned to alternative medicines, exploring acupuncture and herbal remedies. She became an avid user of medical and healing sites on the internet. At the time of her interview, she admitted to taking almost 30 pills and supplements daily and was entirely focused on her illness and its eventual cure.

Finally, Hank provided a good example of acting as if there were no physical issues in his life. He hadn't had a physical exam or been to a dentist for "5 to 7 years" at the time of our first appointment. He walked with a slight limp that he explained away: "I hurt it last winter skiing, but it'll go away." Hank also marked eight or nine other items on our symptom checklist. When asked about them he replied, "It's nothing; they'll go away in time. I just figure that if I don't worry about these things, they'll heal on their own."

The salient issue is that we will all develop some form of debilitation, illness, and physical hurts. How we adapt to them and what meaning we give them becomes the most significant factor in living life as well as possible. Is a scare and lumpectomy a sign of imminent demise as it was for Leona, or is shortness of breath and the likelihood of a portable oxygen tank just another impediment on the way to happiness as it was for Harold?

We have some choices in how we face various physical disabilities. We can determine the meaning we take from them. In short, they may become a new focal point in our lives or something that must be incorporated into the total picture of how we experience ourselves. Of course, we can, like Hank, give any physical downturn no significance at all, simply ignoring their existence.

## The Organ Recital: Social Connection Through Shared Complaints

Although awareness and reasonable intervention are probably the wisest approach for most, there is a phenomenon of "kvetching" (artful complaining) that becomes more dominant as we age. The discussions of such ailments and their specific details can be so ubiquitous in aging groups that they start to dominate most conversations.

Myrna and Philip described a recent dinner conversation with good friends they hadn't seen for a year after relocating to the Sunbelt. The conversation naturally turned to people they knew in common. "Then it took a turn for the worse," Philip said. "We heard in rapid succession about three people we all knew who had died in the past year, then about many others who were ill, and then we went on to our friends' various and sundry physical problems and concerns." Myrna quickly added, "Who are you to talk? You were the one who brought up the whole prostate thing and the ways you were dealing with your PSA." Philip confessed, "I did. I got totally caught up in the medical woes discussion and went off with my own worries and ills." Myrna added, "Once he brought up the whole cancer treatment thing, it opened the floodgates for the rest of the meal."

They agreed that it was one of the worst dinners they had ever been to. Myrna said, "It was like all of a sudden we became those old people who are always talking about their bowel movements and visits to specialists who can never figure out how to properly treat us." Philip added, "Yeah, it was like that Pogo cartoon—we became our own enemy." Then laughing with awareness of what he was about to relate, continued, "It was so bad that after the dinner I was up all night with acid reflux."

There is evidence that awareness of problems is healthy but dwelling on the negative aspects of health can also become a limiting factor in living more fully by encouraging a more dormant lifestyle.

# Sexuality

It's no surprise that for the generation of the sexual revolution, enjoying sex and feeling sexually competent remain important. Studies have indicated that sexual connection is related to both better health and longevity. However, as we age, keeping our sexual experiences alive and fresh requires accommodations.

As in previous life stages, the quality of sexuality is enhanced by emotional intimacy, a comfortable balance of togetherness and autonomy, stress management, some control over external distractions, and the development of a satisfying sexual equilibrium.

Beginning in midlife, both men and women often experience a decided change in sexual functioning. Because of a decrease in hormone levels, other physical conditions, beliefs about how older people should act, and a reduced biological imperative for propagation, sexual desire commonly drops with aging.

For most men, erections aren't as frequent, hard, or long lasting. Both men and women seemed surprised that direct and lengthier physical stimulation had become necessary for male sexual readiness. Correspondingly, as part of the menopausal transition, many women's natural lubrication lessens. During this shift, many feel a host of symptoms, such as sweats, hot flashes, and aches—none of which are very conducive to sexuality. On the other hand, postmenopausal women today don't fit well into the stereotype of the 50- or 60-year-old woman as a gray-haired, frail, asexual granny.

Reduced sexual capability often hits men in very sensitive places. Few have been able to talk without embarrassment about erectile dysfunction with doctors or therapists, let alone friends. Yet, those difficult conversations can go a long way to easing a sense of being unique or of finding ways to compensate.

## New Factors: Every Gift Has a Cost

Just as the birth control pill ushered in a period of more open sexuality beginning in the mid-1960s, another pill is providing both a solution and a challenge to post-midlife couples. By making it more possible for men to develop and maintain erections even as they age, erectile dysfunction treatments such as Viagra and its competitors have brought a new focus on aging sexuality.

Does this change women's sense of feeling desired? As Inge reported, "During the half hour while we are waiting for it to take effect, I can't help but wonder if he'd need the pill if I were younger looking." Does the pill-induced erection prevent men from exploring less phallic aspects of their sexuality? What will the psychological impact be for relationships? Will there be a counteracting impact of the lowered biological desire?

Some women also complained that their male partner's revived capability for sexual intercourse was contrary to their own physical comfort in doing so.

## Sex and Mental Health

When sexual competence is part of self-esteem, a flagging readiness and a drop in feeling desired may lead to emotional concerns. Feeling less desired can activate psychological concerns about rejection and abandonment. As several interviewees reported, the combination of seeing their bodies age, feeling less sexy, and observing their partner's decreasing desire creates a deteriorating cycle: The more we feel unlovable, the less we approach our partners, and that further reduces the chance of sexual connection, which makes us feel even more unlovable and isolated. The emotional intimacy we need to maintain the quality of our sexual relationship is crucial here to protect against this potential negative spiral.

Perhaps it seems like a joke, but it is important to note the significance of sexual connection for men for their general health and longevity. It has been noted humorously that for men sexual attraction may not diminish until a few years post mortem.

## Mental Health

Stress has been a frequent companion of competition and drive. In addition, members of both these generations have experienced more divorces, more transient lifestyles, more recreational drug use, and a greater discrepancy between what they expect of themselves and the reality of their lives. This discrepancy comes into vivid focus after midlife, when opportunities to win the old battles diminish.

## Depression

A recently published study by Dr. Catherine Ettman[2] and her colleagues exploring data from three Northeastern cities found that symptoms of depression were more than three times as prevalent during the pandemic than before, with an outsized toll exacted on lower-income populations. That is an alarming statistic, but it is not just COVID-19 and its sequelae. According to 2016 data from the National Center for Health Statistics, those currently aged 45 to 64 are more vulnerable to depression and have the second highest suicide rate of all age groups.[3] Clinical depression is noticeably higher among women.

Suicide may be the most extreme manifestation of depression, but it isn't the most common. Many mental health professionals consider depression to be second only to stroke in its debilitating impact. Depression goes way beyond sadness and is a major demotivator. The despondency and incapacity of someone afflicted can ruin lives and relationships.

---

2   Ettman, C. K., Abdalla, S. M., Cohen, G. H., Sampson, L., Vivier, P. M., & Galeaa, S. (2020). Prevalence of depression symptoms in US adults before and during the COVID-19 pandemic. *JAMA Network Open*, 3(9), e2019686. https://jamanetwork.com/journals/jamanetworkopen/fullarticle/2770146

3   https://www.cdc.gov/nchs/index.htm

## Process and Reactive Depression

There are essentially two causes of depression: organic and environmental. The former is usually caused by brain chemistry. It is frequently chronic and genetic. It may have occurred prior to the stretch years. The most effective treatments for this type of depression usually combine psychoactive medication and psychotherapy. Although the symptoms have a biochemical basis, it is important to treat it behaviorally as well as chemically. One example of this type of depression at this age for women is that caused by hormonal changes common in perimenopause and menopause.

Environmental depressions are reactions to life events that have gone awry. Major losses can instigate powerful feelings of despair, hopelessness, and helplessness. These may occur without a history of prior despondency. Unemployment and job failure in a down economy and relationship losses are two frequent precursors to reactive depression. People with these conditions usually respond best to psychotherapy, although if the symptoms are severe, medications can be prescribed to take the edge off sufficiently for therapy to be possible.

One reason psychotherapy is effective in overcoming depressive episodes may be the intense, intimate relationship with another person who isn't asking for reciprocity. The opportunity to explore one's self with another, caring person tends to instill hope in the future, an antidote to feelings of despair. Such intimate relationships are far more challenging on telehealth and video conferencing sessions.

## Anxiety

Although there is an increase in anxiety in the years following midlife, its nature shifts, reflecting more themes of mortality and helplessness in the face of unknown threats. Of course, some of this reflects changes in reality. Although the 45- to 65-year-old group cannot be considered frail by any means, they are more vulnerable as their bone density decreases and their physical capacities begin to wane.

As Arvin described it, "I've become a white-knuckle flier in my old age. I never used to give a second thought to jumping on a plane and going off somewhere for work or vacation. Now I worry almost endlessly about the safety of the flight, being exposed to the coronavirus, terrorism, and whether there will be an available bathroom when I need one." Later, he added, "When I'm on vacation, I can spend far too much time wondering whether I locked the front door or closed the garage door at home, brought my cell phone charger, stopped the mail and newspaper deliveries, and made sure my dogs are well cared for. It makes traveling an ordeal rather than an adventure."

Sandrine and Pierre claim that since they reached middle age, whenever they travel, they take separate flights: "So if anything happens, the kids will still have one parent." They laughed about a few of the mishaps that have occurred when one of them missed connections and they were separated for 2 days during a European vacation.

Some anxieties become more severe, dramatically reducing the range of life activities. Sasha reported, "I was always an anxious person and pretty much avoided new things." As an adult, she lived at home, caring for her aged mother, going few places besides work, shopping and taking her mother to doctors' appointments. Although she said that she had never been interested in moving out or finding an adult romantic relationship, she also confessed that it was far too threatening to do so.

When her mother passed away, Sasha was alone for the first time. Her anxiety increased to the point of being able to leave her home only to go to a local grocery store or pharmacy. When she came into therapy, she said that her brother had to drive her the three blocks to the therapist's office. She related, "I guess it came to a head when he and my nieces invited me to a movie and I couldn't go. That's when he brought me in to see you."

The challenges presented by the unknown were far beyond Sasha's ability to transcend. She clung tightly to the familiar, but as happens so often in life, the more we hold on to something, the more it slips away, and the higher emotional price we pay. Her mother's death was the catalyst for her fears to be magnified.

Fortunately, Sasha responded well to individual, and then group psychotherapy. Two years after her initial session, she took her nieces to a movie and dinner. She also had left her home for social events and was thinking about the possibility of developing a deeper relationship with a coworker at her new job.

Not only was Sasha's anxiety painful, but it also blocked the cure. Being a caretaker and keeping the status quo was truly a gift to her mother, but it also kept Sasha from facing her personal fears of independence and new relationships. Her brother and the therapy gently nudged her toward a healthier goal by offering opportunities to bridge her fears of the unknown and start in safe new endeavors. The answer was not to thrust herself into the teeth of the anxiety but to approach it experimentally and in small bites.

## Dealing with Anxiety

Anxieties can have several roots, and people who suffer from anxieties often either endure them, take medication, or stop doing whatever seems risky. As a result, they tend to live in an ever-decreasing circle of "safe" activity. Others turn to methods that can ameliorate the problem either at the roots or at the behavioral level. Psychotherapy and meditation are commonly employed when the anxiety becomes debilitating.

# Additional Stressors

Individual stressors can occur at different times and different intensities for all of us. Some folks are just luckier than others. For example, we can find stressors to be opportunities for new growth—adhering to the well-quoted aphorism that the Chinese symbol for crisis and opportunity are the same. By contrast, daily stressors can have a dominant impact on our lives and our satisfaction with life. Some of these liabilities are related to our lifestyle; others occur because of beliefs, values, commitments, expectations, and the discrepancy between these and our personal experiences.

# Round Up the Usual Suspects

Some general stressors related to these years of life require us to adapt both emotionally and behaviorally.

During these years, most of us have to deal with the loss of our parents through death or infirmity. Career transitions and declining opportunities force considerations of shifts in lifestyle. Financial pressures may increase during this period. With retirement looming, we may need to buttress our nest egg or shift our lifestyle and expectations. Often, there are important renegotiations in family roles and relationships (such as the empty nest or, conversely, being sandwiched between the needs of two other generations) that create significant pressure. For couples whose primary relationships fail during these years, the need to adapt to a different lifestyle can be substantive.

Respondents in the MIDMAC study reported that daily stressors occurred in almost 40% of the days studied. These stressors ranged from feelings of overload, interpersonal conflicts, and time demands. Most of the stress days were experienced as loss or threats of loss, danger to the status quo or person, or increasing frustration. Our interviewees reported that the anxiety about COVID-19, it's lethality in older individuals and its sequelae such as job loss and financial and even shelter and food insecurity had made 2020 a year of almost constant stress; a condition that plays havoc with physical systems.

## Loss of Psychological Well-Being

Victor's stress was based on his increasing perception that "I could lose everything at work, and I just don't have the time or capacity to recover." He described an employment situation in which the cut-backs were so severe during the recession that he was now actually occupying what were formerly three job lines. "I am so frustrated because there was no fat in the system before. Now things are falling down and I have the kind of boss who doesn't look at the causes, just the fumbles, and she's ruthless. Four times last week, there were people in tears in the unit after one of her 'meetings.'"

Victor related that when situations got bad like this in the past, he left, found a new position, and built up again from scratch. Now 59-years-old and with COVID-based unemployment at record levels, he believes that he has to remain in this adverse position. This is a cause of daily stress and subsequent guilt at being unavailable to his wife and children when he brings work home or broods about the job.

When I was called into his company as a consultant, I was instantly struck by the emotional toxicity of the workplace. Victor talked openly to me about going on disability, and a coworker reported that she was devastated by the loss of all her friends at work and was quite frightened of her boss's threats. A single mother and sole support of her family, she believed that she couldn't risk anything that would "upset the applecart," and as a result, she, like Victor, was doing the job of several former employees. This kind of stress at work is fertile ground for errors, impulsivity, anxiety, and depression.

## Self-Control

Related to well-being is the sense of being in control of one's own life. It's almost axiomatic that a sense of control is associated with both better mental health and better job performance. For more than 4 decades, psychologists have studied a phenomenon they call *locus of control*. A locus of control scale first developed by Dr. Julian Rotter of the University of Connecticut in 1966 measures how much individuals feel able to influence the events in their world by what they think, feel, or do. Hundreds of studies using variations of this scale indicate that better mental health relies on feeling that we have control over what happens to us.

In fact, people who expect fate, luck, or chance to guide their lives tend to be far more stressed and prone to depression. A feeling of self-control is a subjective state that at times is illusory. Nonetheless, as we pass midlife our belief in personal control over our lives helps us adjust to the changes and achieve better mental and physical health.

# Appearing Healthy, Getting Healthy

Many in the so-called, 'eternally young' boomer generation have responded to the vagaries of aging with an unprecedented use of exercise, diet, yoga, spa programs, and elective cosmetic surgery.

# You Look Mahvelous, Darling

There is an increasing interest in and use of products and techniques that make us look younger. Terms like "liposuction," "tanning salons," and "Botox injections" have become everyday jargon. No part of the boomers' bodies has failed to attract an antiaging product—all of which are designed for a more youthful appearance; not necessarily a healthier body. In fact, there has been a surge in requests for both surgical and non-surgical plastic surgery treatments worldwide during lockdown periods of the COVID-19 pandemic. This is based in part on what Dr. Jill Owen has called a "Zoom Boom;" perceptual distortions caused by screen-related self-images, and the pressure cooker of quarantine.[4]

When the appearance of health or youth supersedes being healthy many problems are exacerbated. As Rita, a veteran of several voluntary cosmetic surgeries, maintained, "I look so young; I shouldn't be having trouble with my knees."

Artificially creating a younger appearance can create a disconnect with aging naturally and facing issues in real time. As boomers try to look and act more like their 30-year-old selves, many simultaneously try to postpone some of the normal developmental transitions. This can create an illusion of youth that encourages ill-advised risk taking and a stagnation in emotional growth, creating a backlog of psychological conflict.

Stephen commented, "I'm still in good shape, basically a good-looking guy. I can hold my own and hang out with the younger, more attractive girls, and I like their energy and looks. What I don't like is that they're mostly wanting to start a family; I'm done with that."

## Healthy Living

Despite the craze to look younger than our years, this generation is hitting its mid-40s to mid-60s healthier and more energetic than any prior generations. From a life span perspective, we are actually aging slower than our ancestors.

How are we doing it?

Modern medicine, inoculations, better understanding of physiology, better diet, and more active lifestyles all play a role in our improved health. It's also a generation that has struggled with and been largely successful at reducing certain addictions that aged its parents. We are aware of the dangers of nicotine, and its use has been on the decline for decades—although the use of prescription and other recreational drugs, including alcohol, has not.

Many between the ages of 45 and 65 have been educated to pay attention to their medical histories and those of their families.

---

4   https://www.bbc.com/worklife/article/20200909-why-plastic-surgery-demand-is-booming-amid-lockdown

They are aware of prevention methods and are more likely to have frequent medical checkups.

## We Know More, but There Are Other Pressures

By contrast, while many of us have adopted more active recreation, socioeconomic changes have led to work that is far less physically demanding. This, in turn, has led to a greater incidence of obesity and many illnesses related to immobility. In addition, the competitive business environment has promoted longer hours at work and greater pressure to succeed. Because of these changes, we have to consciously add exercise to our lives.

## Promoting Health by Reducing Stress

There is no way to live fully and totally avoid stress, but there are numerous unnecessary stresses that we can minimize. What are some of the things we can do to reduce stress and increase health in daily life?

Of course, we know that regular exercise and good sleep promote better health. Moderate daily physical movement increases energy and reduces the potential for depression. Avoiding addictions and negative habits also promotes better health.

Alternative medicine proponent Dr. Andrew Weil strongly endorses touch and sex for a healthier life. He is among many who decry skin hunger as a potential serious stressor.

It's important for everyone to experience the healing and comfort of touch.[5]

---

5  It is curious that the importance of touch is often minimized in Western medicine. In addition, because of our collective fears of improper touch, we have established professional "ethical" standards that essentially make a hug impermissible. The only two professions that still encourage touch for healing are nursing and massage therapy.

## Mind-Body Techniques

Meditation and massage reduce stress and promote positive health. Some studies have shown that the stress reduction resulting from meditation has a significant effect on hypertension, cardiovascular disorders, pain, musculoskeletal diseases, respiratory problems, skin disorders, anxiety, depression, panic disorder, binge eating, emotional distress, substance abuse, and some cancers.

In addition to ameliorating health-related problems, these practices help us attain or maintain general wellness. For example, our interviewees specifically identified their use of these methods as preventing or minimizing asthma attacks, easing PMS and menopausal symptoms, and preventing ulcer flares and headaches. Meditation has also been credited with improving cognitive abilities and reducing some forms of memory loss with aging.

## Two-Way Street

It's evident that if the mind can affect the body in positive ways, the reverse is also true. Just as physical behavior such as exercise can improve our mental outlook, so can chronic pain and other physical symptoms create anxiety or depression. Similarly, emotional stress can be quite deleterious to physical health.

Stress and depression can cause psychosomatic illness—real physical symptoms produced by a psychological state. The most commonly reported psychosomatic illnesses include rashes, diarrhea, and vomiting.

One advantage of practices such as meditation, Tai Chi, Aikido, and similar practices that reduce stress, anxiety, and depression is that they work on both the mind—reducing psychosomatic illness—and body—reducing somatopsychic ones (psychological symptoms produced by physical conditions). Even if the symptoms aren't fully ameliorated, we can endure them better.

## Mechanisms

It's clear that stress is deleterious to body, mind, and spirit. Anything that increases general feelings of well-being and, specifically, concentration, creativity, and productiveness is likely to reduce feelings of stress and enhance other positive attributes such as intuition, compassion, and love, as well as spiritual pursuits.

Stress in our lives activates our defenses and protective systems naturally. To help mobilize us for action, our sympathetic nervous system's "fight-or-flight" activation increases heart rate and breathing, allowing more effective reactions to danger.

This biological emergency response system protects us, but if overused it can cause system breakdown and physical and mental symptoms. Health-promoting practices improve the mind's ability to minimize the experience of stress, increase awareness, and add a sense of well-being and personal control.

Popular mind-body expert Deepak Chopra adds the notion that attitude about aging is central to the experience and believing we get better as we grow older allows a far more graceful and beneficial experience of the physical, emotional, spiritual, and social aspects of aging.

# Positive Health Practices During the Stretch Years

We can do some simple daily activities to promote health and fight off stress during our stretch years.

1. Slow down. Less can be more.
2. Sleep well and rest. Short naps (siestas) can be a beneficial part of your daily routine.
3. Eat fresh, nutritious food. Avoid food that gives you digestive problems. Rich food and caffeine at night, for example, can cause acid reflex or interfere with sleep.
4. Move. Do something physical daily. Walking and swimming are particularly useful.
5. Practice a mind-body technique such as yoga or Tai Chi.
6. Avoid toxins. Don't smoke. Avoid excessive alcohol intake. Avoid negative relationships whenever possible.
7. Become far more flexible in dealing with normal hassles in daily life. Try to avoid getting too worked up because of stupidity, administrative snafus, endless phone trees and holds, and incompetence.
8. Try to find the opportunities in the face of problems.

9. Nurture loving relationships. Spend time with family and friends. Especially enjoy time with children.
10. Try to maintain an attitude of curiosity, learning, and wonder.
11. Question the externally generated "shoulds." Just because someone else wants something, doesn't mean you have to comply.
12. Get help when your ship of life seems to be listing. Experienced psychotherapists or elders can help foster your intrinsic healing attributes.

# chapter fourteen

# Spirituality

*If there is to be any peace it will come through being,
not having.*

—Henry Miller

More than half of the baby boomers and almost 70% of the Generation Xers that we interviewed believe that traditional Western religions provide but one of the many pathways to a spiritual quest. Those who take the teachings of their religion to heart are frequently involved in the search for meaning in life. However, many who believe in a greater power and spirit but don't belong to any religious group are spiritual at heart, as are many who ascribe to the New Age perspective that transcendence involves a vital, active connection to a force, power, or spirit or a deep self-awareness.

## Spiritual Paths

When her husband was hospitalized for 2 weeks with a life-threatening illness, Judith found herself drawn back for the first time in years to the comfort, community, and rituals of the religion of her childhood. Her husband recovered and had a very different reaction. He started to rid himself of a lot of stressful job responsibilities. He insisted on more time off from work and spent hours fishing with their youngest son. Both had glimpsed at mortality and, in response, were seeking new ways to approach the essence of their lives.

A Pew Research Center report that explored the relationship between regular religious worship and aging in America concluded that as people age, an increasing percentage of them discover an increasing value of religion in their lives. In this study, reported in the April 12, 2018, *AARP magazine*, the numbers grew from 44% of those in their 20s to 61% in the 50 to 64 post-midlife age group, and to 70% at age 75-plus. There is a fairly significant difference between the sexes. Women are far more likely to become more avid churchgoers.[1]

Religion is but one form that the seeking takes. The personal quest for spirituality intensifies and takes on increasing meaning as we pass the midlife years. Recognizing even slightly that we are on the "back nine" or beginning to descend the mountain we have climbed during the earlier years of life should give everyone pause. That recognition of the inevitability of mortality instigates poignant questions about life, transcendence, meaning, and spirituality. Of course, for many of us these questions are not occurring for the first time, but today they begin to seem far more vital in the scheme of our future years.

Adding to this recognition of the latter half of life is a strange subjective phenomenon: the personal experience of an accelerating passage of time. We are no longer the children asking every few (long) minutes, "Are we there yet?" No. Most of us are like Esther, who wondered aloud at her 50th birthday celebration, "How in the world did I get here so fast?"

More quietly, she was also asking herself, "What in the world is my life all about?" Like Judith, she initially sought answers in her church. Unlike Judith, she did not find what she was seeking there. Instead, Esther began a personal quest to find her meaning in life. She studied Eastern religions, practiced meditation, and studied with learned gurus. When we spoke, she was 54. After jokingly

---

1   https://www.aarp.org/home-family/friends-family/info-2018/boomers-religion-study.html

referring to her 50th birthday as having occurred "last month," she related that the quest was and continues to be "the best thing I ever did for myself … next to my son of course."

Characteristic of many on a spiritual pursuit, Esther spoke glowingly about the process of her search and little about finding her particular personal grail. Most of all, she described seeing the world from a "much wider perspective." Looking at life from a less parochial viewpoint offered Esther the opportunity and option to face new (and larger) unknowns. Her journey was her goal.

## Boomer Spirituality

Spiritual quests are not new for the generation who lived through or were influenced by the 1960s. This generation has encompassed both a revolutionary break with past conventions and strict adherence to those very traditions. The public search for spiritual answers has long been a part of the boomers' way of life.

In 1968, for example, the Beatles traveled to India in search of altered states of consciousness sans drugs. Many icons of the boomer generation have reportedly been seeking answers to the larger questions of life. The media has focused on the more high-profile boomer celebrities such as Madonna (mystical Jewish Kabbalah) and Tom Cruise (Scientology). Celebrities may be more public or extreme about it, but they are not alone.

Increasing numbers of both generations are seeking answers to divine questions during these years: Who am I? Why am I here? Who or what is God? How can I find my true self? Worldwide, fundamental religions are growing faster than ever and "religious correctness" has become a necessity in U.S. national politics. Many boomers, like Judith, have contributed to this trend by returning to the religions of their childhoods; others, like Esther, by pursuing new spiritual directions.

Wade Clark Roof, who has studied boomer spirituality extensively, reports that one third are "born-again" Christians. Of the remainder, 60% preferred to explore a variety of religious teachings. He also reported that 53% preferred to pray (or meditate) alone versus 29% who preferred to worship with others. In addition, 28%

of boomers believe in reincarnation and 26% in astrology. Only 28% felt it important to stick to one faith.[2]

As Tanya (aged 45) said, "I look for a religion where I feel a sense of community. They all preach the same love and belief in something greater than self. I just want my children to feel connected to a group with good values and lots of kinship."

## A Generation Molded by the Sixties

During the late 1960s and the 1970s, the media were far more interested in the sensational aspects of the boomer generation than in its earlier spiritual searches. Free love and disobedience to authority made for much more lurid headlines than did the generational search for self-actualization. Indeed, many of the iconic stories, such as those of draft card- and bra-burning demonstrations of those halcyon days were more apocryphal than actual. If such events occurred when the cameras weren't rolling, they must have been quite rare.

The excesses of the generation, such as hippie communes, sexual experimentation, recreational drug use, nude encounter groups, and Woodstock were far better documented than the underlying search for meaning that underscored many of these behaviors. Along with cross-generational conflict, social upheaval, and the questioning of authority was a powerful unifying trend: an intense orientation toward self-realization.

There is little doubt that some of the methods used to reach expanded consciousness were ultimately self-defeating. Harvard psychology lecturer Timothy Leary's dream of the wonderful insights possible through mind-altering chemicals such as LSD turned out to be unhelpful and often downright dangerous for users.

Leary's advocacy of a chemical approach to open the mind echoed somewhat Sigmund Freud's early promotion of cocaine as a panacea in the late 19th century. During the turn-on, tune-in, dropout period that marked the 1960s, heavy marijuana use, perhaps initially to gain insight paradoxically, turned into demotivation and stagnation for many.

---

2   Roof, W. C. (1993). *A generation of seekers: The spiritual journeys of the baby boom generation.* HarperCollins.

Some of the social experimentation with sexuality and relationship styles was also liberating for some and debilitating for others. Yet at the core of all the experimentation was a desire for new insights, new ways of expanding the personal universe, and novel perceptions unbounded by the rules and rigidity in the culture and traditional religions of the 1950s.

Although the experimentation sometimes became excessive with predictable deleterious consequences, it also had a positive effect, both on those who were engaged in new ways of thinking and behaving and on the culture as a whole. The process of exploration not only impacted for life those engaged in it but also entered the dominant social mores. We emerged from that era with a profoundly different level of openness to change. This can be seen in continuing advancement in civil and women's rights and in facing fears of the unknown in personal challenges.

The process of exploration also led to a greater sense of individual freedom and self-esteem. As boomers have aged they show a greater willingness to trust their own instincts and judgment and to be wary of "truths" that come from others. Generation Xers, the "last analog generation" have shown an expanded sense of self-determination and mistrust of institutions. Although many have rejected the mainstream religions of their parents, a significant number have long been involved in transpersonal issues. They turned to psychotherapy, meditation, Native American spirituality, Eastern religions and practices such as Buddhism, yoga, and popular psychology as pathways to self-growth and self-empowerment.

# New Age, New Paths

Neither the Orthodox–New Age split, nor the important focus on spirituality is unfamiliar to the boomer generation. When they were much younger, they rejected the common paternalistic orthodoxy of their parents that separated men and women. They challenged practices that excluded those with other beliefs. Nonbelievers in a particular religious denomination were no longer seen as apostate and doomed to hell. They rejected ideas such as limbo in the Catholic Church as unfair and took to task a subservient role of women and persons of color in other churches. It was the first generation to commonly recognize women rabbis and ministers.

Not all members of the cohort accept these changes. A significant group considers sexual orientation, same sex marriage, and abortion rights to be dividing issues between forces of good and evil, of biblical intention and admonishment.

Even as secular laws change in one direction or another, it is obvious that the answers to these big questions are profoundly personal and unique. There are no clear-cut, one-size-fits-all universal answers. However, there are two divergent approaches to understanding the mysteries of the universe. A close reading of the studies of post-midlife spirituality uncovers an apparent split in beliefs between fundamentalists and those who pursue less conventional paths. These differences mirror the contrasts in many of life's paths, reflecting differing beliefs about individualism, fate or destiny, theism versus mysticism, and the role of authority in spiritual pursuits as well as the familiar security ↔ freedom continuum.

# The Quest

Two forms of this pursuit continue to this day: (a) *decoding* the mysteries of the divine (such as finding and holding a personal savior sacred), and (b) creating or *encoding* a new form of personal faith. Sometimes the two are referred to respectively as "ultimate" or "cosmic" and "terrestrial" or "phenomenological."

When Amy, a 47-year-old mother of three, spoke she indicated her devotion to her beliefs with a constant reminder of her decoding approach: "As a Christian, I am always aware of my duties to my savior and to my faith. I teach Sunday school and try so hard to help the children look for answers to their life problems in scripture. My husband and I pray together most nights at bedtime and beg for an understanding of God's will. It's not always the easy path for us, but I know that if I keep my faith well enough and believe in the miracles the Lord can bring, the answers will be there." In describing heroes in her life, she listed her parents and "Jesus of Nazareth."

By contrast, Tony spoke of a very different search pattern. He believed that the great cosmic questions were not something fixed and to be revealed but rather something to create by giving them a personal meaning.

> I grew up in a crazy household, where there were no
> rules or standards when my mother drank. I had to

learn to figure it all out for myself. Her answer to everything was 'Do what I say.' When I went to college and studied philosophy, I realized that everyone had their own way of understanding the world and none was better than the others. So, after a while I figured that I had as good an answer as the priest.

For encoders like Tony, there is no shortage of ethical standards or consistent beliefs. He lives what most would consider an upright, moral life. Like Amy, he is generous, giving both time and money to his community and the less fortunate, albeit with a different rationale. He reversed the anxiety founded in the unsafe chaos of his upbringing by creating a world that better matched his inner truths. What's important to him is what happens between him and others and the meaning he attributes to his experience.

In *A Generation of Seekers: The Spiritual Journeys of the Baby Boom Generation*, Dr. Roof conceptualizes the differences in terms of inner authority versus outer authority or individualism versus uniformity, mystical versus theistic, letting go versus mastery and control, spiritual versus religious.[3]

Describing the boomers, he reports that most believe in God but not in a single true religion for all. Although their theistic view is similar to that of the U.S. founding fathers, boomers differ somewhat in that almost 25% visualize God as a mother.

Clearly, spirituality can emerge from either an encoding or decoding perspective. Yet regardless of method, spiritual growth can be seen to have a predictable pattern.

# Spiritual Development

In *The Five Stages of the Soul*,[4] Dr. Harry Moody and David Carroll provide a common spiritual sequence that encapsulates well what

---

3   Roof, W. C., Greer, B., Johnson, M., & Leibson, A. (1993). *A generation of seekers: The spiritual journeys of the baby boom generation.* Harper San Francisco.

4   Moody, H. R., & Carroll, D. L. (1997). *The five stages of the soul: Charting the spiritual patterns that shape our lives.* Anchor Books.

many of the interviewees in this study reported. The stages of the soul according to Moody and Carroll are as follows:

1. The call (loosely, a refocus on the inner voice)
2. The search (finding fellow travelers and seeking guidance)
3. The struggle (trials and difficulties)
4. The breakthrough (inner awakening)
5. The return (integrating the enhanced self into everyday life)

Their formulation, which draws from the writing of Carl Jung and Joseph Campbell as well as the field of gerontology, seems timeless and useful to those of all generations. The process of spiritual practice is profoundly individualistic, but the content is often culturally or generationally specific. For example, at one time in Western history the "retreat" or a solitary period in nature was the proper and recommended location for spiritual searching. In modern Western times, the paths seem more diverse on the surface, but the internal quest may be quite similar.

At age 58, Zach turned to the very orthodox Hassidic form of Judaism to find his answers. He described the path he was on:

> You know, I've been a secular Jew my whole life. By the time I was Bar Mitzvahed [at age 13], I had already stopped believing in God. I did it for my parents—my dad actually; my mother wasn't religious at all. So fast forward to last year and a friend asks me to go with him to a Chabad for a Sabbath service. So, on a whim, I went, and while I was there, I thought, "What are all these men doing? They look like idiots with the funny hair and the [sable] hats and those praying motions." And then this voice in me says, "So what makes them the idiots? They all seem to know what they're doing." Well, the voice is still going off, "What am I doing with my life? Isn't there something more?" You know, all those college freshman bull session questions. And now I'm going almost every Friday night to the Chabad, and now I'm even walking there and back (two miles) and I'm looking for answers to those questions. And, so to answer your inevitable question, no, I don't have any

answers yet, but it seems right to go. Check back in a year or so. Maybe I'll have something juicy for you.

An opposite experience is depicted in the 2020 TV mini-series *Unorthodox* where a young woman has to break away from the Hassidic tradition and community to find herself. In Moody and Carroll's formulation, Zach and "Esther Shapiro," the *Unorthodox* heroine, had heard the call and were well into the search.

Lydia (aged 55) talked about her struggle to keep in tune with her newfound spirituality. She described becoming a vegetarian and studying various meditation practices. She related that soon after she invested in a lengthy trip to study in India, she had to deal with a sudden opportunity and restriction on her trip. In May, 4 months before the proposed trip, she had arranged with her work to be gone for a 3-month period. "I had all the vacation time I needed and was able to train my assistant to cover the bulk of the work, and my boss had agreed on the best timeline for the company. I was still a little worried about my work and whether it'd still be there when I got back, but it was right for me to go."

In June, her company gave her 2-weeks notice, and let her go, along with her boss and the rest of her department. "So now," she continued, "I have all the time to go and no worries about that job, but I knew money would be tight." Approximately 3 weeks after she was fired, her husband was also laid off. Money now would be a more serious object, although time was far less structured. Although with her husband's support, she decided to continue with the plans, she discovered on the eve of leaving that the revered teacher she planned to study with in India would be traveling in the United States and Canada during her time in India.

> My dilemma was huge. Do I go for the teacher or for my own personal search? If I go and it doesn't work out because I am with the wrong teacher, we've blown all that money we can't replace or afford with both of us out of work. Do I wait and be practical as usual or do I plunge ahead with this one chance to feed my spiritual side?

Moody and Carroll might identify her as fluctuating between her search and her struggle.

## Complications With the Path

Several of those interviewed expressed being at a stage in this process that was far different from their partners'. Lydia's husband supported her quest despite the financial risk. By contrast, Christy's spiritual search was both threatening and aversive to her husband. In a couple's therapy session, when she began talking about joining a yoga group that had begun a series of studies into reincarnation, Zack quickly interposed a description of himself as "a scientist who has no reason to believe in all that mumbo jumbo." He was quite evidently disquieted by Christy's increasing belief in both a deeply meditative practice and reincarnation.

When they entered couple's therapy, this had become a wedge between them—one that threatened their 30-year marriage. Their children had also split their support, with their son endeavoring to join his mother's meditation-yoga group and the daughter, a veterinarian, firmly in her dad's camp. In addition to the spiritual issue, this couple was struggling with one person's need for more similarity and connectedness (and his fear of emotional abandonment) abutting the other's pressure for self-growth and separation (and her fear of emotional suffocation).

In their year in therapy, they were able to enlarge their perspectives. Zack was reassured that although Christy's path didn't make sense to him her pursuit of the path wasn't tantamount to a personal rejection. At the same time, Christy was able to accept the fact that his disinterest and nonbelief didn't mean she had to convince him he also needed to pursue that path. She also became more capable of fighting her personal ambivalence without making him the spokesperson for the negative side of her own thinking. They also had to come to grips with a previously unagreed to shift in how they would deal with family finances. Until Christy's immersion on her new path, they had always made large expenditures jointly. Suddenly, Zack felt that he was not allowed to question the cost of her new endeavor.

As with many couples who lock horns around a specific issue, they needed to address the unconscious value of the fight itself. When one person began to move away in the relationship, it generated a predictable fight that reaffirmed their connection. As part of the therapy, they were better able to discover and employ more direct means of communicating the need for intimacy and reassurance during new individual growth spurts without having to first engage in a conflict.

It doesn't always turn out for the better. Sometimes the divergent paths of spirituality can be as divisive as an extramarital affair. Indeed, one's enhanced internal focus may seem like the loss of primacy of the relationship to the other. When Melanie at age 50 threw herself back into the Evangelical Christian church of her childhood, her husband and three children felt deserted. Her personal studies with the minister took up several days during an average week, and she took special "faith trips" with him and a few others over weekends. Her increased donations of both time and money to the church led to major battles with her husband about both losses. Her response was to leave the family and move into a special faith group house on the church campus. To her husband, she was "under the influences of a cult." To her, she had finally found herself in the values and practices of her childhood and felt "connected for the first time in years."

Melanie and her husband were unable to bridge this gulf, and he instigated a divorce 2 years after her "call." Although her spiritual quest was successful for her personally, she was unable to reintegrate her new learning into her life (the return stage).

Daniela's early religious experience was far less compelling.

> I grew up in this really strict Catholic home, and by the time I was in fifth grade in Catholic school, I didn't believe in any of it. I just began hating the whole thing and all their crazy rules, but my parents sent me to parochial school until I graduated and my mother would only pay for Catholic college. She even sent me to Holy Names summer camp. I remember coming home one day and complaining that my college required that one quarter of all my classes be in religion and philosophy, and my mother literally dragged me to the priest to confess my "sin of complaining." When I got married, I left the church forever and won't step foot into it again unless it's a family wedding. I refused to go to my niece's baptism or first communion, but I'm happy to take her for summers and vacations to the farm.

After college, she moved to a commune in Oregon and married a man with quite similar views. Later, in the midst of a diatribe about the evils of organized religion, Daniela said, "My husband and I are two of the most generous people in our community; we are deeply spiritual—mostly Native American beliefs about treating the land well—and Alejandro is probably the kindest person I ever met."

To her delight, Daniela was able to find spirituality with her husband outside of the religious practices of her parents and despite her anger and aversion to dogma.

## Emergence of New Religions/ Spiritual Guidance

Ralph, a successful CEO of a mid-size company, described his own spiritual awakening in terms that might be surprising for anyone from prior generations. He had been in individual therapy for almost a year when he confessed,

> You know, there's something about me you don't know, and I don't want you to laugh at me. My religion ... it's not that weird, but I feel like I'm a Jedi. Ever since I heard Obi-Wan's voice say, "Use the force, Luke," I haven't been able to get it out of my mind over thirty years later. I really think there is a force and I need to tap into it, and when I trust it, I just seem more connected and whole. I was in the Sand Hill Road (Palo Alto) meeting with this group of tough VCs [venture capital principals], and it was going south. So, I took a bathroom break and just decided to let the force guide me. In no time, they were right there with me and on better terms than I had originally hoped.

It's interesting that Ralph was not alone. A 2002 BBC news story reported that according to 2000 Census reports, worldwide more than half a million people consider Jedi their religion.[5]

---

5   http://news.bbc.co.uk/2/hi/uk_news/1589133.stm

# Search for Meaning

Whether you approach the post-midlife spiritual quest from an orthodox (decoding) approach or a more personal (encoding) manner, the bottom line is a pursuit of meaning.

After we have followed the well-laid out developmental stages during the early phases of life, we feel a growing pressure from internal forces to figure out what this life is all about. Viktor Frankl, in *Man's Search for Meaning*,[6] maintained, "Between stimulus and response, there is a space. In that space is our power to choose our response. In our response lies our growth and our freedom."

The choice for Dr. Frankl was both the result of and path to finding life's meaning. The essence of meaning is not in what occurs to an individual, but in how they respond to the event. For Frankl it was how individuals responded to one another in the devastation and suffering of the Auschwitz Nazi concentration camp. Indeed, according to his perceptions, those who had an internally-based meaning in life were more likely to survive those horrors.

Philosopher Martin Buber[7] wrote of the differences between I-thou and I-it relationships. The former is a deep, intimate, and open connection that confirms the value of the other person. By contrast, an I-it relationship is functional; in it, others are used in utilitarian ways rather than for themselves as people. For Buber, the elusive, difficult, and all too rare I-thou connection was the essence of intimacy with others, with oneself, and with God.

For both of these significant writers and for philosopher Martin Heidegger and others, the spiritual moment of meaning is always current. Past and future are far less salient in finding meaning than the here and-now of life. How you respond now allows either an I-thou moment of intimacy and connection to that which is larger than our selves or an I-it interaction that represents "business as usual."

At this stage of our life's trajectory, mortality increasingly becomes a part of conscious awareness. The growing sense of life's limitations crystallizes questions such as,

1. Why am I here?
2. What is the purpose of my life?

---

6  Frankl, V. E. (2006). *Man's search for meaning*. (H.S. Kushner, Trans.). Beacon Press.
7  Buber, M. (1970). *I and thou*. (W. Kaufman, Trans.). Scribner.

3. Is there something after death?
4. Do I have a soul?
5. What is the nature of my soul?
6. Who or what is God, and what is my relationship to God?

In short, what is the meaning of my life?

As best as we can understand, we find the answers to these questions through an internal search. Indeed, according to most experts who study this phenomenon, it is the *questioning* and the *search* that is crucial, more than any specific answers found. These experts find the pursuit of answers to be a spiritual quest and in fact the arrival of spirituality itself.

Recent brain imaging studies support this conclusion, showing that the process of prayer and meditation are more salient than who we pray to. It's the act of faith that provides spiritual growth; the act is more dominant than the specific aspects of faith itself.

## Social and Spiritual Needs

In *Modern Man in Search of a Soul*, Carl Jung[8] underscored the conflict between the spiritual and the social needs at midlife. While at times these needs coincide, you may find times when the paths diverge. When is a richer life experience related to the transcendent and when to relationships, duty, and responsibility? How may you determine in Matthew's terms in Romans 13:1 when to "render to Caesar the things that are Caesar's; and to God the things that are God's."

The key to maximal personal growth is to be able to respond to both the inner, spiritual focus and the outer, relational intimacy. In *I and Thou*, Martin Buber argues that in an intimate relationship with another, one may truly experience the presence of God.

Whether love of the eternal or of another takes primacy, the whole package requires attention to both. Summarizing this, the Dalai Lama has said, "The salvation of man is through love and in love."

---

8   Jung, C. G. (1933/2001). *Modern man in search of a soul.* Routledge.

# Exercise: 18 Big Questions to Ponder

1. When and where do you feel most connected with aspects of life that are larger than yourself?
2. Do you believe in a god, a higher power, or a mystical force that transcends you? If so, how do you define this entity?
3. To what extent is it universal and to what extent personal?
4. What is your relationship to this force or being?
5. If you do not believe in a god or similar force, what is your belief about how the universe operates?
6. Is there life after death, and, if so, what aspects of your self will be transferred or transformed into this new or next life?
7. What are the religious practices of your childhood, adolescence, and young adulthood? What feelings do you have about those practices and beliefs?
8. Which of those beliefs work for you now and which are less important?
9. What aspects of your life meet your spiritual needs?
10. In what ways are you spiritual? In what ways do your spiritual beliefs affect your day-to-day life?
11. Would you like to explore the spiritual side of life more today or in the future? What forms or aspects of spirituality are most interesting?
12. What thoughts do you have about mortality and the reasons for your life on earth?
13. Do you prefer to explore these matters privately or in a group setting with like-minded individuals? Do you know of such a setting?
14. Are there beliefs you hold that you do not share with others for fear of being ridiculed or shunned?
15. How can your spiritual beliefs lead to more fulfilling and loving relationships?
16. Where do spirituality and intimacy merge?
17. Does your spiritual growth require surrender?
18. What is the role of gratitude and appreciation in a spiritual life?

chapter fifteen

# Our Heroes, Our Selves

*Old myths, old gods, old heroes have never died. They
are only sleeping at the bottom of our mind, waiting
for our call. We have need for them. They represent the
wisdom of our race.*

—Stanley Kunitz

My heroes have always been (a) astronauts, (b) teachers, (c) cowboys, (d) doctors, (e) artists, (f) athletes, (g) parents, (h) other—choose as many as apply.

Why in the world would we want to look at heroes during the stretch years? Aren't heroes for the young? What possible influence could they have after we are 45 years old? It turns out, as we age, that we continue to need models, measuring sticks, and examples of creativity. Personal heroes enhance our self-esteem and provide visions of what is possible. Ultimately, one of our roles during these years is to become an exemplar and aide to those who are younger as well.

# Now That I'm All Grown Up, What Do I Want to Be?

As we leave midlife and grow toward retirement, we continue to seek out positive role models. Historically, heroes have been pathfinders and archetypes, raising expectations of us all and permitting us to see ourselves succeeding beyond our norm. They show us how sacrifice promotes morality and the public good. The ancient Greek heroes were honored as demigods, owning a middle place between the gods and humans. Even now, doers of great deeds and celebrities are worshipped.

To the extent that we resemble or emulate our heroes, we approximate our personal fantasies of living the more courageous, more moral life. So, even as we age, heroes are models of what we could be—what we aspire to.

## Generational Heroes

Who are your personal heroes? Who serve as icons for the boomer and X'er generations?

We asked interviewees about important influences in their lives. The answers fell into four categories: family members, mentors and contemporaries, the well-known or famous, and fictional characters.

### Family Members

By far the highest number of interviewees called their parents, an older family member, or their partners the model for their lives. There were both heroes and antiheroes. "I'd like to think that I could be as gracious and generous as my mom," said 49-year-old Shanti, "She was my hero as a kid and is even more as an adult." By contrast, Ellen responded, "Well, the one thing I don't want to do is be like my mother—mean, selfish, bossy, and a real pain in the ..."

### Heroes

In his one-man show and book *700 Sundays*,[1] entertainer Billy Crystal provided an homage to both his father and his childhood

---

1   Crystal, B. (2005). *700 Sundays*. Warner Book Group.

heroes growing up in New York. From soulful blues singers to Mickey Mantle, Crystal described in exquisite prose how his own life path was formed and how those influences evolved as he matured. He related one of the great doubleheaders of his life—sitting on Billie Holiday's lap watching the Alan Ladd movie *Shane*.

Jaime (aged 60), a successful CPA, said that his father at age 86 was still practicing a little law in the firm that bore his name and was always available for grandchildren and great-grandchildren. "He was wounded in World War II and still has pain, but he keeps going and always has a smile for the family. I doubt I can live up to his example, but I hope to get as close as I can."

Liliana credits her upbringing and family with all of her successes in life. She claims to have grown up "just above the poverty line, but never at a loss for love and encouragement." An intensive care nurse, she maintains a positive attitude and love of family in all aspects of her life. She enjoys being with her aging parents and loves how they enjoy their grandkids.

R.J. replied, "My grandma and grandpa took me in when I was four and did everything to raise me and teach me proper. They worked hard their whole lives, took care of us kids, and always had a good thing to say. I owe everything to them. I know that's the way I want to be remembered also."

## Antiheroes

The opposite picture is seen in another household. Brother and sister principals in a family business, Wally and Candace decried the fact that both their mother and father meddled incessantly in the office and expected salaries years after they sold the business to their children.

Betsy revealed, "I'm sixty-one years old, and I'm still trying desperately to please my mother. I still inhibit what I do, say, and probably even think to avoid her scorn. What's worse, she can't give me her approval, even if she ever wanted to—she's been dead since 1996." Betsy's challenge is to learn to refocus on her personal standards rather than on the maternal attitudes she's internalized and embellished.

Otis (aged 48) suffered from childhood parental abandonment. When he was 6, his father deserted he and his mother. Her response was to take to her bed, and she was eventually hospitalized for major depression. Otis lived with relatives for a few years before she returned. He reports that he is still very influenced by his mother's dark mood. He claims that he also reacts like she does, worrying about any new experience and feeling "dread at the hint of happiness." Otis has married twice. His first wife left him and their two sons after 4 years of marriage, essentially replicating his experience with his father. His second wife is remarkably similar psychologically to his mother.

## Too Much the Heroes

Jackson (aged 58) has a different challenge. In his evaluation, he cannot live up to the standard of his perfect parents. His father was not only a renowned scientist but also an involved and supportive dad. He described his mom as the "classic earth mother. She could do anything and usually was doing three or four things at once." His parents were living in retirement in Southern California, were active in their community, and frequently took care of the grand-kids. Jake's problem was that despite having a successful career and healthy relationships, he felt inadequate by comparison. Even in his 50s, he is still trying to live up to his idealized parents and struggling to use a more Jake-oriented yardstick.

## Almost Family

Some of the heroes were parental figures rather than parents per se. Many of the people in this generation are like Andres, who fervently believed that his godfather "saved my life and turned me onto the right track. If it weren't for him, I'd have been like the other guys in the neighborhood." Andres' godfather provided a safe retreat, encouragement and funding to send Andres and his brother to college, and Andres to law school. Now a judge, Andres has presided over criminal trials of some of his peers. "I never actually judged those I had a relationship with, just guys who were on the same trajectory I was until my godfather stepped in and put me to work in his barbershop and used that as a way to keep me in high school and off the streets."

## Mentors

Several individuals indicated that mentors at work or in their community provided archetypes for their future. They spoke about former bosses who took them under a wing, showed them the ropes of the business, and encouraged them. Russ, a 59-year-old college professor, relayed a story about his dissertation supervisor, who "even today is available by phone when I need advice." Others identified a person with whom they had a meaningful interaction that "still is a part of me today."

Patty related how her piano teacher and his family took her in after her parents died. She was 12 when she went to live with this unofficial foster family.

> My mom was sick from as far back as I could remember, and my dad was killed in Korea. So, I guess, music was my way to cope. I used to spend hours playing the piano, which my mom loved and which I grew to love. When I moved in with them, piano was all I had. I loved Mr. G., but my [foster] mom taught me how to bake cookies and how to be a young woman. She was the one who went through my first period with me about a week after I moved in. I was sure they'd be disgusted and throw me out when that happened, but she just told me how normal I was and actually made me a "becoming a woman" cake.

During my own turbulent high school years, the one teacher who stood out was quite unlikely. My high school had mandatory military drill as one of our classes. It was the military drill instructor, Major Kelly, who "got me." He understood who I was far better than subject teachers and the guidance counselor. Although he was hardly a favorite among my classmates, I enjoyed just being around him. He was the teacher who encouraged me to reach for my goals despite my less than stellar grades and others' expectations. The relationship was close emotionally; but like one with a therapist, it was very much one way. I knew him as "Major" and later as "Colonel," but only discovered his first name (Edward) years after I had graduated and happened upon his obituary.

For years, while Sunil worked to become an engineer, Bill Hewlett and David Packard greatly influenced his early life. He worked for Hewlett-Packard "in the glory days, when the HP way meant everything." His most recent hero is Steve Wozniak, who walked away from the daily rigors at Apple Computer to serve his community and teach computer skills to fifth graders. Sunil was also very impressed with Woz's stint, as an emotional favorite, on *Dancing with the Stars.*

Carla returned to the workforce after almost 2 decades as a full-time mother and homemaker: "The very first day, my boss took me into his office and told me how glad he was to have a mature person in the company. He offered a very kind entry, 'I'll teach you the office ropes,' he said, 'if you'll use your experience and intuition with people to help the company.' It was amazing; he invited my husband and me over to his home, and by the time I had talked to his wife one evening and saw how they treated each other, I was convinced that he was sincere."

Carla was lucky. Not everyone is fortunate enough to find a mentor immediately, but most of us need that kind of help at some point in our careers or when we become parents. It's also important to assume the mentor role as we become the elders.

"Aunty Ruby" was a local cultural icon for many years and a significant guide for women reentering the workforce. A clinical psychologist by profession, she also was a community leader, providing both support and advice. One of her former clients revealed, "I'm still paying the fees for my therapy (three years after her last session), but I'll never be able to pay back what she gave me."

## Leaders

When I worked with the Pacific Air Force, the commander in chief was General Lewis Wilson, whose dedication to equal opportunities and race relations made him a hero to many under his command. I greatly respected and have tried to emulate his leadership style in my own positions of authority.

# Cultural Icons and Historical Figures

Many related to public figures and wanted to emulate their lead. One frequently mentioned cultural icon for boomers was former vice president Al Gore. A number of boomers talked with great admiration about how after losing the 2000 election, he went back to his personal roots, reinvented himself, and then emerged as a major figure in the worldwide battle for a better environment, ultimately winning a Nobel Prize in 2007.

Other cultural representatives who members of this generation mentioned were (the late) Justice Ruth Bader Ginsberg, Mother Theresa, Oprah Winfrey, Mohammed Ali, and Presidents Obama, Clinton, Reagan, and Truman. Several people identified heroes in their professional field such as Steven Hawking and writers from prior generations such as Jane Austen, Fyodor Dostoyevsky, Mark Twain, and George Bernard Shaw.

Several men in the interviews responded like Dale, "Well, if you want the 'official story,' it was a few great teachers, my dad and one uncle, and my first boss ... but if you want to know who really was influential in my life, then it's mostly baseball players—like Ted Williams. He loved kids and wouldn't take any guff from the press or most adults. Well, I was a kid, and he was my first hero." It was interesting to hear men talk emotionally about boyhood sports idols like Stan Musial, Willie Mays, Ernie Banks, Jackie Robinson, Jim Brown, Rafer Johnson, Arthur Ashe, Mickey Mantle, Bill Russell, Hank Aaron, and Sandy Koufax still influencing their lives today.

Women also mentioned how the exploits of athletes such as Billy Jean King, Venus and Serena Williams, Mia Hamm, Dara Torres, Sheryl Swopes, Brandi Chastain, Megan Rapinoe, and Nancy Lieberman were a continuing influence in their lives.

What does it take to be an icon of success for this generational group? It's no surprise that being rich or famous was a key, but chance meetings, events, and even fantasies and stories make some folks heroes to us.

Marcus very perceptively noted that as he aged, his heroes became more and more ancient. Laughing out loud, he said, "When I was younger, it was Willie Mays, McCovey, Nate Thurmond, and Bill Russell. I played basketball and baseball in college, probably because of them. And then there was Rosa Parks, Martin Luther King, Jr., and Gandhi. Nowadays, I am mostly impressed by the amazing exploits of Thurgood Marshall, Nelson Mandela, Booker T. Washington, Spike Lee, and John Lewis."

When asked how they influenced his life, he said that they all taught him to do what was right and to care first for others. Marcus has dedicated his life to doing for others and to teaching his children to do likewise. He was especially proud that he and his daughter were both members of Doctors Without Borders who were among the first to go to Thailand after the 2004 Indian Ocean tsunami, to Haiti in the wake of the 2010 earthquake, and to Puerto Rico after Hurricane Maria (2017). He voiced a general theme for this generation: Heroism involved giving to others, a kindness, a realistic sense of self, a capacity for honest self-reflection, and the ability to laugh at oneself.

Other interviewees concurred in their choices. For example, David's hero was Elie Wiesel. "Wiesel's great work inspired me to look beyond myself and find a deeper kind of truth in my life as a clergyman." One of the most commonly mentioned heroes for both women and men in both generations was Michelle Obama.

Two interviewees said that they were most impressed by Abigail Adams; two more by Mother Theresa; and several by Jesus of Nazareth and Christian saints; St. Francis in particular.

Sometimes it's harder to find a current hero. As Takeshi said, "When you're an adult, you don't have those kinds of heroes anymore. When you look closely, they all have feet of clay." Other times, the heroes we have early continue to inspire.

As a college freshman, I had the good fortune to meet Viktor Frankl, author of *Man's Search for Meaning*.[2] That chance meeting was influential in my choice of career and even my worldview. I had the opportunity to visit with him twice again as an adult professional. At each meeting, my admiration for him grew.

## Fictional Characters

It seemed whimsical to ask participants about fictional characters who influenced their lives, but the answers we received were quite telling. Many of them had childhood idols:

> "I've always tried to view the world like Alice in Wonderland. When I've been open to new and strange events and didn't try to control them, life has been more rewarding."

> "Any of Jane Austen's heroines. They had such a rich inner life, full of romance and sentiment. I'd like to be more charming and captivating (although I think I'd forego Darcy for more of a partner)."

---

2   Then titled, *From Death-Camp to Existentialism*.

"I think a little part of me always felt like the Lone Ranger. He overcame adversity, helped others, and didn't need a lot of praise for doing good deeds."

"The Little Engine That Could. That was always my motivation to succeed and still is. No matter how heavy your load, you've got to keep trying and persevere."

"Yoda. He's the top of the Jedi. He's smart and powerful and nobody can make fun of his looks or his fractured language."

"I think I always wanted to be Santa Claus. You know, what's better? He brings happiness to kids and teaches a rudimentary morality: that rewards come to those who are nice."

It's interesting that loners and underdogs were overrepresented in the group of fictional heroes. This could reflect a personal experience of feelings of isolation and being out of the mainstream, although it may seem a paradoxical theme for members of a generation that has been the most populous (and arguably most influential) in American history. Yet, the more contemporaries we have, the more talent, grit, hard work, or good fortune we need to stand out from them.

Erle Stanley Gardner's fictional attorney Perry Mason is an excellent example. His signal skill was his capacity to stand up for the victimized by always adopting an outlier's perspective. By opposing the prevailing perspective and defying authority in defense of his clients, he emerged a winner.

Another television character hero identified was Hawkeye Pierce of *M\*A\*S\*H*. He was the prototypical successful doctor who was irreverent and always at odds with military authority. Something about his combination of competence and irreverence is particularly appealing.

It's important for most that their heroes be slightly imperfect. Would Superman be as valued without his vulnerability to kryptonite? Would Columbo be as appealing if he were a snappy dresser and said what he meant directly instead of his "just one thing" as a tag line? Would we applaud Nero Wolfe's brilliance if he were in good physical shape? Would Achilles's name be a part of our vernacular if he had received a text from the River Styx Quality Assurance people and had gone in for a recall on the ankle his mother held when she dipped him in the river. There is something about being deceptively competent or being open about one's vulnerability that is particularly appealing.

## The Two Sides of the "Bat" Hero

Pedro reported that his childhood hero was Batman. "Even today, I read comics—now they're expensive and called graphic novels—and still like Batman." He reported, "Although Batman was good, there was this dark side to him. I don't know why, I always liked that he was also mean, vengeful, and just negative sometimes."

In describing his own life, Pedro related that he was always the good kid and adult. He was the oldest son of five children in a second-generation Mexican-American family. He "had to excel at school" and did so, winning National Merit scholarships and other awards to pay his way at one of the nation's top-tier small colleges. Later he went to graduate school, earned a doctorate in engineering, and went back to his community to support his aging parents. He also helped his younger siblings go to school and was generous to relatives who were struggling financially.

When I suggested that he was like Bruce Wayne and that Batman might be the part of him that never got a voice, he laughed and said, "Yeah, you nailed it. I always think of the darker thoughts and the bad things to do, but always do the best ones I can. So, in a way, I keep the bat in his cave. Ooh man, as a shrink, I bet you love that idea; here's Pedro with a light exterior and a cave in his unconscious."

I asked, "So if you could be Batman now, what would you do?" He replied, "You know, I don't think I'd do much differently, except maybe tell this guy in the next office to keep the noise down when he watches videos all day instead of working." He paused, got a grin on his face, and continued, "Well, if I was Batman, I'd secretly remove the sound card from his computer and not let him know why it didn't work anymore."

# Current Heroes

It's easy to see how fame and power influence who is seen as a hero. After all, this is the generation that once determined Henry

Kissinger to be America's "most eligible bachelor" because of his power and influence. However, many of our heroes are closer to home and far less known outside of their immediate community.

These heroes, who look a lot like us, have certain qualities in common. They have honed their skills over the years and developed new ones that are uniquely necessary to navigate this life stage. Much of their heroism may have emerged as they eschewed past successes, turning their attention to the public good.

What do some of these quiet heroes look like? Consider the heroism of the following eight:

- First-generation American Mai Lin opened a small nonprofit business in her neighborhood to provide a much-needed service.
- Former nurse Billie Jo has become an activist for the aged.
- Charles and Will, retiring from their Silicon Valley jobs, have helped fund an incubator for new entrepreneurs and are serving as angel investors in early start-up companies.
- Cherise has recaptured her love of photography and, armed with a new digital SLR (single-lens reflex) camera and her own electronic lab for processing, is dedicated to capturing seasonal views of buildings and people in her rural community. Profits from selling her prints support a local high school art and photo studio. She also takes on two interns a year to teach the intricacies of her art.
- Retired CEO Alfonso is spending his retirement being a member of nonprofit boards of directors and setting up a philanthropic organization.
- Eric at age 63 became the sole childcare provider for his three young grandchildren and is "being the dad I couldn't be for my daughters."
- Marika at age 50 decided to go back to school for her master's degree and license as a marriage and family therapist. Now 57, she is using these skills in an agency in her community that caters to low-income families.
- Glenn, having taken early retirement from his company, is parlaying his pension and skills into a brand-new endeavor—carving ebony toys for craft shows.

Each of these individuals is finding ways to give back to their world some portion of what they have received. Each is offering something to make their often quiet, little corner of the world better.

## We Are Our Heroes

Not only do we all need heroes to look up to, sometimes we also need to feel like heroes. This phenomenon that Erik Erikson called "generativity" includes productivity and creativity but is more encompassing than these traits.

Just as our heroes embody aspects of life to emulate, when we pursue those aspects of ourselves, we provide a model for the next generations of the value of personal growth throughout life and a meaningful reflection of the golden rule.

Important though our heroes have been in forming our identities, at this life stage they need to give way to the heroics of our own generation.

Not everyone gets to be famous, influential, or wealthy like Oprah Winfrey and Warren Buffett. Most of us find personal heroism in our families, in our communities, or on the job. Our capacity for heroics is not limited to celebrity or those who have many millions of dollars. It is likely that you have already served as a valuable model as a parent, businessperson, community member, or caregiver to those younger and older than yourself. These roles and influences are likely to expand as you move through this age period. If they have yet to begin, their time may be drawing nigh.

## Common Factors in Heroism

What makes any of us a hero? What qualities do heroes have that make them stand out from the crowd? In the most basic sense, a hero faces fear and overcomes adversity. They perform deeds that others agree are noble or outstanding or have special impact.

It could be a one-time event such as performing bravely during a crisis. Firefighters, EMTs, and people in law enforcement are in the position to do this, but so are those of us who think of ourselves as common citizens. Passing an accident on the highway, do we stop and help the injured and find a way to get additional help? Do we, like Sheila, jump into a cold stream to save a child who has fallen in or, like Darryl, a schoolteacher who noticed that a child in his class was failing, stay after school to help tutor him?

Perhaps we would consider Alice a hero when she called 9-1-1 to get help for a friend who was threatening suicide. Her friend was furious with her when he was taken to a hospital for an evaluation and refused to speak with her for some time. Yet 5 years later, Alice was certain that she had saved his life, a belief that was reified when he sent her a note after years of no contact, telling her that he would be dead if she hadn't acted.

Each of these people took a risk, faced their own fear, and did something for another. True heroism involves actions taken despite fear, not in its absence. In addition, the true hero typically has to rise again after suffering losses. One of the reasons we love athletics is because it offers so many opportunities for renewal in a new season. Those long-suffering baseball fans in cities like Chicago and Boston long lived by the mantra, "Wait till next year;" and in Cleveland, still are.

## Heroes After Midlife

How does heroism shift in focus after midlife? There is an inherent paradox here. Largely, the hero we have known prior to this is the person actively engaged in doing the deeds. Acting in the face of fear is not new, but the fears of the unknown at this age are different and so are the appropriate responses. For most of us during these stretch years, the new challenge is to face the fear of playing the supportive background roles while allowing others to take over and make their own mistakes, while we avoid jumping in and doing what needs to be done ourselves.

To be a true hero at this life stage, the best we can do is model and serve as a guide. In short, being a hero may well involve being far more passive than it did earlier. Our new anxiety is related to not acting and to trusting in the next generation. When Paolo asked his 20-year-old son to take the lead in a challenging, physical project that required dexterity, he admitted, "He can probably do it just as well—okay, better—but it's hard to step aside and take direction from someone when you used to change his diapers." It's akin to recognizing that our adult children have become better drivers than we are. Their reflexes are better, their vision and hearing more accurate. It's a truth that comes with dread but also a relief from the responsibility.

In short, we have to give up the role of obvious hero and adopt the role of wise elder. This involves being uncomfortable in our own shoes and finding some that fit us better at this stage of life.

# Exercise

On a piece of paper or on your computer create two columns. On the left-hand side answer the following questions. Include both living, dead, and fictional heroes.

- Who were the positive and negative influences in your family when you were growing up—in preschool, elementary school, high school, and in young adulthood?
- Were there cultural icons in the news, politics, sports, or movies that you tried to emulate? Who were they at various times in your life?
- How have these earlier heroes changed? Has Sandy Koufax given way to Warren Buffett?
- Who served as your heroes when you were in your 30s and early 40s?
- Who do you consider models today?
- To what extent are you a model for others?

Now go back, and on the right-hand side list characteristics for each hero that you admire or emulate.

- What does this tell you about your values?
- What is evolving in your sense of heroics?
- What do you imagine is your next step toward being heroic in your life?

chapter sixteen

# The "Autumn" Project

*Winter is an etching, spring a watercolor, summer an oil*
*painting and autumn a mosaic of them all.*

—Stanley Horowitz

I have been a clinical psychologist for 50 years. Throughout that time I have taught counseling and psychotherapy to graduate students and have worked in private practice in Hawaii and California. This project began in 2004, 16 years ago, when I was in my own stretch years. While working on the research and writing, I became eligible for Medicare and full Social Security benefits. In short, I am somewhat older than most of you who have been reading this book. Hopefully, those additional years have given me some perspective on what are now your life experiences.

In addition to my personal experience traversing those years, I have had the privilege of treating members of the boomer and Xer generations. In fact, because clients involved in insight-oriented psychotherapy typically seek a therapist who is their age or older, boomers have been my most frequent clients.

Through my psychotherapy practice with clients who are between 45 and 65 years old, I have been privy to their innermost and secret thoughts, their desires, and their concerns.

One of the challenges of working with people in this cohort is that because of both sheer size and a penchant for pushing against the status quo, boomers have changed the rules as they have traversed every developmental stage. Textbooks, professional guides, and supervision designed for my (silent) generation and my parents' "greatest generation" progressively became outdated and less useful when it came to the boomers. Building on these innovations, Gen Xers bridged the analog to digital gap and became more "natives" than "immigrants" to the digital world. My generation was the first to have television. My 5-year-old, Generation Z granddaughter is accustomed to streaming personalized videos on smartphones. Clinicians of my era had to be increasingly flexible in applying our theories and techniques. There were the early days of "the pill," "sex, drugs, and rock n' roll," and "Never trust anyone over 30"— at least until the late Jerry Rubin, the author of that last maxim, crossed that barrier himself.

It was a generation of civil rights, women's rights, and the rights of children. There was the era of involved and dedicated parenting, later overextended and distorted by "helicopter parents" and "tiger moms." The boomers have always wanted the best for themselves. Many boomers and a majority of Xers have been willing to extend that to others, sometimes at no small cost.

Psychological practice had to adjust to the boomers' shifting priorities. Our prior roadmaps were inadequate once boomers reached early adulthood. As they aged further, there simply were few guides to appropriate developmental mileposts. Methods to compare my clients' needs and concerns were being reconstituted regularly.

It is not surprising that there were no ongoing standards. For one thing, prior generations have not had the same life expectancy or time affluence. Until now, the adult stages of development were either relatively unplotted or simply lumped together in a 40- or 50-year period. Most of the former standards saw midlife as extending directly into old age, demise, and then death.

Detailed, more nuanced descriptions of older life stages became more salient, because we now needed them as we experienced greater longevity, socioeconomic shifts, changes in the nature of how we earn a living, and the evolution in retirement planning.

# Right Time and Place

As I was studying my clients' psychological development, I was personally traversing many of these years and experiencing personal struggles with aging, some of the same issues that boomers and Xers would face when they were between 45 and 65. Throughout my career, I have found it beneficial to study what was most relevant to me personally (in particular, fatherhood), and so I undertook another project, this time on what normal life is like for men and women after the midlife transition.

In 2004, as I was personally getting close to leaving the target years, I decided to put this age range under a new spotlight in an attempt to begin a rudimentary guide to the era. Since then, my research team at Santa Clara University and I have been engaged in the exploration of this stage of development through clinical observations from my practice and those of my colleagues, extensive interviews, web-based queries, and the existing literature.

With the literature that did exist, much of which is referenced in this book, I tried to tease apart from studies that covered far larger periods of life those indices that were relevant specifically for a 20-year post-midlife period. It is important to note that the 20-year period chosen (midlife to retirement) was a bit arbitrary. Many in their late 40s are still in the throes of midlife transitions. Similarly, it is becoming increasingly common for individuals, me included, to continue working well past the age of 65. In addition, chronological age is but one measure of life development. What is characteristic for one person at age 50 may not be so for another. Nonetheless, there are some compelling reasons for concentrated study of this segment of the population. Not the least of this is that it encompasses two generations today and their sheer numbers.

# The Data

Using interview methods that have guided my previous studies on fatherhood, we developed and administered 122 in-person, in-depth interviews of women and men in the age range. The interviewers were all experienced in techniques that allowed for follow-up questions in addition to the protocol prompts. The resultant data allowed a greater richness and depth in response, and for much more open personal replies.

One of the most surprising and gratifying aspect of the interviews was that the interviewees really wanted to talk about their personal experiences. In fact, although the interview protocol was designed for a 45-minute period, many of the actual interviews went almost twice that long. Even after the interviews were complete, some of those interviewed called or emailed additional, unsolicited information they thought of later and believed might be helpful.

Once those were complete, we conducted two rounds (2008, 2020) of 98 certified online interviews to more closely match our participants' cultural origins to the U.S. Census figures by including more African Americans and fewer from Latinx, East Asian, and Pacific Islander ethnicities.

Finally, additional material was culled from my experience as a psychotherapist over the past 50 years with an ethnically diverse group of adult clients. Of course, this sample was more selective—lending less to generalization to the population as a whole—and far more in-depth.

These data were then tabulated into a database and analyzed. Based on the results, it is likely that the material presented in previous chapters of this book offers a viable perspective on the current lives of the boomer and Xer generations as they traverse the life stage we have called "the stretch years."

## Describing This Stage

Autumn was the label used to describe this stage in the first edition of this book. Indeed, it was no easy task finding a way to describe these years of adult life that provided some solid sense of their social, psychological, emotional, and behavioral experiences between midlife and retirement.

Initially we began with sports-based analogies. The "third quarter" matched up with some prior work such as Daniel Levinson's (although his went from 50 through 75) and also conveyed that it was after halftime but not yet close to the final quarter, the 2-minute warning, or overtime, that ended with "sudden death."

## The Seventh-Inning Stretch

For the first 4 years, my working title for this project was "The Seventh-Inning Stretch." My hope is that this book will lead you to take a break in the action of developing your career and raising your family. Perhaps it provides a brief respite, a time for evaluation, a chance to focus on what's coming next, and, most important, an opportunity to stretch in your capabilities and vision. I have returned to this description in this edition, because it reflects the psychological and emotional realities, if not the chronological reality of life.

Hopefully, this is an occasion to find some relief from the pressures that dominated the previous years. This is a time when you can try new approaches that might serve you now and well after retirement. It's a time to recognize that what worked for the first six innings may not be as effective over the remaining ones.

The metaphor of this being a time to stop and stretch is predicated on the belief that at this stage of life, new problems, concerns, and challenges have arisen and different skills and a new orientation are necessary to traverse life well from now on.

I am sure that as other researchers turn their attention to this era of life, we will learn more about the stretch years. New insights will be achieved, new labels designed, and a far better awareness developed. The research explicated in this book is viewed as a step in that direction.

## Some Surprising Findings

When I began this project, I fully expected that people would be invested in finding more meaning in their lives, have increased interest in spiritual quests, and be worried about retirement finances. Indeed those predictions were confirmed. What was surprising was the number of individuals who were most concerned with sexuality and money in general, issues I would have assumed would be central for those in another new stage of development—the extended adolescence that is defining those now in their 20s and early 30s.

## Good News

Another surprising finding was how good most of the interviewees felt about their lives. Even in the throes of reactions to the disaster-laden pandemic year 2020, most reported that they liked looking back at what they had accomplished and forward to what they will accomplish in the future. When the interviewees described looking inward at what was in their "shadow"—the underexplored aspects of their lives—they often described it as both difficult and exhilarating.

# Finding Meaning, Facing Fears

The essence of these years is that personal times are a-changin' and that each change in routine or the existing life path evokes anxiety. During this time of life, you are, or will be, facing shifts in work, changes in relationships, a renewed need to focus on health, losses, and the financial issues of funding your own retirement. Each of these anxiety-provoking changes in life needs to be confronted, embraced and managed.

It is a time when sticking to the status quo and the illusion of security of doing what you have always done will likely lead you into feelings of guilt and stagnation. It is a time to refocus more on *doing the right thing* than on *doing things right*.

Primarily, it is a period during which new paths to growth and meaning can be developed and new directions set, and a more integrated sense of self can evolve by facing fears of the unknown and experimenting with the road less taken.

During the stretch years, we get a chance to revisit old passions, develop new ones, and rebalance our lives.

# What's Next?

The stage of development that follows is retirement and another significant adjustment. There are obviously changes in the look and feel of retirement today. Indeed, even the word seems somewhat inaccurate and outdated. "Rebalancing" may be a more apropos term. The best question about the next stage is "How would you like to spend your time when you no longer have to work for a living?" Although in truth, many will have to work well beyond age 65.

For me, the new equilibrium looks like a time for more writing; more time with my wife, adult children, and grandchildren; getting back into music and photography; mentoring younger professors and psychologists; and continuing to train marriage and family therapists part time. It looks like a progression to a less intense, rebalanced version of today.

My friend Lupe says she is interested in really expanding her photographic art and "working part time now, just to keep me in supplies and software."

A woman I recently met casually talked about how important it was for her to be involved politically as a retiree. She was dedicated to leaving her grandchildren a better world. Indeed, she was not alone. In the 2020 survey, a large number of interviewees were reportedly far more active politically.

One couple, both former professors, is busily writing: He is creating lovely short stories and a novel, and she is writing her memoirs. Able to trace her family back several generations, she is also absorbed in a comprehensive family genogram and an expanded life scrapbook.

Two close friends will continue working as psychotherapists, working fewer hours but not giving up the practices they love. Thankfully, this kind of work gets better as we age and doesn't require heavy physical lifting.

What about you? What would you like to do for the one third or so of your life that may come after retirement age? What dreams does retirement bring? Is it work as usual; new career or job; artistic pursuits; a hobby; or time with family, friends, and grandchildren?

For the next 20 years, more than three million of you will turn 65 each year. How will you deal with your financial, spiritual, psychological, physical, and relational challenges? What groundwork will you lay to support yourself after 65? Perhaps the better question for this generation is to alter somewhat the lyrics of the great Beatles' song and ask yourself, "How will I need me? How will I feed me when I'm 65?"

The obvious answer has to do with harvesting the fruits of your life to date, savoring past experiences and future opportunities. This is best accomplished by focusing on your legacy; fostering an experimental, open attitude; being increasingly aware of yourself; appreciating intimate relationships; recognizing the tension between the needs for security and freedom; and struggling to face those fears of the unknown that offer new growth. Remember, unlike the neurotic fears that keep us stagnant, those existential fears are the fertile ground for personal growth.

# Index